DICTATORSHIP ON TRIAL

DICTATORSHIP ON TRIAL

COUPS AND THE FUTURE OF JUSTICE IN THAILAND

TYRELL HABERKORN

STANFORD UNIVERSITY PRESS
Stanford, California

Stanford University Press
Stanford, California

Printed in the United States of America on acid-free, archival-quality paper

Library of Congress Cataloging-in-Publication Data

Names: Haberkorn, Tyrell, author.
Title: Dictatorship on trial : coups and the future of justice in Thailand
  / Tyrell Haberkorn.
Description: Stanford, California : Stanford University Press, 2024. |
  Includes bibliographical references and index.
Identifiers: LCCN 2023045894 (print) | LCCN 2023045895 (ebook) | ISBN
  9781503635463 (cloth) | ISBN 9781503639409 (paperback) | ISBN
  9781503639416 (ebook)
Subjects: LCSH: Khana Raksā Khwāmsangop hǣng Chāt (Thailand) |
  Political crimes and offenses—Law and legislation—Thailand. |
  Dissenters—Legal status, laws, etc.—Thailand. | Political
  persecution—Thailand. | Justice, Administration of—Political
  aspects—Thailand. | Human rights—Thailand. |
  Authoritarianism—Thailand. | Thailand—History—Coup d'état, 2014.
Classification: LCC KPT40.P64 H33 2024 (print) | LCC KPT40.P64 (ebook) |
  DDC 349.593—dc23/eng/20231005
LC record available at https://lccn.loc.gov/2023045894
LC ebook record available at https://lccn.loc.gov/2023045895

Cover design: Jason Anscomb
Cover photograph: Peter Treanor / Alamy Stock Anti-government protests following the
military coup. May 25, 2014. Victory Monument, Bangkok, Thailand

For all those who
fight against
dictatorship

CONTENTS

NOTE ON LANGUAGE, TRANSLATION, DATES, AND COURT DOCUMENTS

All translations in this book are mine unless stated otherwise. The Thai words in this book have been transliterated into roman characters with the exception of the bibliography. Both the original Thai and an English translation of the bibliographic information for Thai-language materials are included to aid readers in locating my sources.

For transliterated words, I have followed the guidelines of the Royal Institute outlined in "Principles of Romanization for Thai Script by Transcription Method," with one exception. With respect to individual names, if there is already a transliteration familiar through general use, I have used it rather than following the Royal Institute guidelines.

In Thailand, dates are calculated in terms of the Buddhist era (BE), which is the common era (CE) plus 543 years. This means, for example, that 1932 CE is 2475 BE and 2016 CE is 2559 BE. Although I use CE dates in the main body of my text, when citing Thai-language sources, I first specify the BE publication date and then include the CE date in brackets immediately following.

Finally, I draw extensively on court documents, particularly judgments, in this book. They occupy a semipublic, semiprivate space in Thailand. In the main text, I cite judgments by court, case number, and date. The appendix provides additional information on where readers can find these decisions.

ABBREVIATIONS

BACC   Bangkok Art and Culture Center
CDC   Constitution Drafting Committee
CDRM   Council for Democratic Reform under Monarchy
CSD   Crime Suppression Division
DoC   Department of Corrections
ICCPR   International Covenant on Civil and Political Rights
IESCR   International Covenant on Economic,
         Social, and Cultural Rights
iLaw   Internet Dialogue on Legal Reform
LRC   Law Reform Commission
MCB   Military Circle Base
NARC   National Administrative Reform Council
NCPO   National Council for Peace and Order
NPKC   National Peace Keeping Council
OIA   Official Information Act
TLHR   Thai Lawyers for Human Rights
UDHR   Universal Declaration of Human Rights

PROLOGUE

LAW FOR THE PEOPLE

Historians who treat legal decisions as a source of evidence about state violence, as I do, may read a case file and then offer an interpretation of the series of events or a conclusion different from the one reached by the judges. An alternative vision of justice may emerge from a rereading that lays bare the cover-up of perpetrators in cases of state violence carried out against the people or the injustice committed against the people either openly or by sleight of hand of the court itself. But what if the historian stepped out of scholarly narrative and wrote in the voice of a judge and in the format of a decision? The series of events that make up the past or evidence in a decision might be ordered, or even constituted, differently. The evidence needed to hold state perpetrators to account could be foregrounded rather than the evidence that must be elided for them to be exonerated. A different, and more just, decision becomes imaginable. Rather than remaining at the level of critique, the alternative vision of justice—as well as the gap between the law as practiced and the law as ideal—then becomes central to scholarship.

Inspired by feminist judgment projects, in this book I pick up a judge's pen to write a history of the five years of dictatorship under Thailand's most recent coup regime, the National Council for Peace and Order (NCPO). On 22 May 2014, led by General Prayuth Chan-ocha, the NCPO carried out a coup that ousted the elected government of Prime Minister Yingluck Shinawatra. The NCPO promised to restore the rule of law after ten years of political conflict, but the regime instead undermined its most fundamental principles.[1] The NCPO employed the arbitrary, disproportionate, and politicized use of the law to violate the rights of civilians, facilitate extrajudicial violence, and guarantee impunity for the coupmakers. Martial law provided authorities with broad powers and was in force for the first ten months of the regime; civilian cases of crimes against the crown and state were placed within the military court system for the first half of the regime. Existing criminal law was used to target dissidents, criminalize their beliefs and actions, and create a climate of fear. The most fearsome of these was Article 112, the measure of the Criminal Code that defines the crime of lèse-majesté—or defamation, insult, or threat to the monarch—and stipulates the punishment of three to fifteen years' imprisonment per count. Despite the end of absolute monarchy in 1932, the monarch remains in an ambiguously powerful, elevated, and unquestionable position in the polity. Once a person is accused of lèse-majesté, a guilty verdict is almost guaranteed.[2] The NCPO also promulgated 557 executive orders that were given the status of law and authorized detention, reeducation, and other violations. Torture, disappearance, and the threat of harm to oneself or one's family often took place during the processes of arrest and prosecution. During the NCPO's time in power, justice—the equal and fair quality of the law as written, interpreted, and applied—long tenuous in Thailand, disappeared entirely for those whom the junta identified as its enemies. The NCPO officially ceased to exist when a civilian cabinet was formed following a general election in March 2019, but the junta's influence remained in its policy legacies and in the figure of the prime minister, who won the election through unfree and unfair practices.[3]

When the coup took place, I was completing *In Plain Sight: Impunity and Human Rights in Thailand*, a book on the history of impunity—the inability and failure to secure accountability—for state violence.[4] Beginning with the end of the absolute monarchy on 24 June 1932 and ending with the NCPO's coup, I traced arbitrary detention, torture, disappearance, extrajudicial killing, and other human rights violations. As I wrote, I learned that impunity is the foundation of state formation rather than an aberration. Across the seeming political instability of frequent swings from dictatorship to democracy and back again, the people experience a constant lack of protection from violence and abuse of power by the state. In a twist on Max Weber's aphorism that the state is the entity that possesses a monopoly on the legitimate use of violence, the Thai state is characterized by holding a monopoly on the legitimized use of illegitimate violence.

After the coup, as for many people, my life turned toward contributing to raising the alarm about what was taking place under the NCPO, whose stark repression recalled the counterinsurgent regimes of the Cold War. Working with the lawyers and activists of Thai Lawyers for Human Rights (TLHR), an organization founded on the evening of the coup to document the junta's rights violations and defend those targeted by junta, I pilfered time from my day job as an academic to translate reports, write brief analyses and op-eds, submit written testimony to the court, and do court observation whenever I could. I did so because many of those being targeted by the junta were friends and colleagues, and also because remaining motionless was not an option. Writing a book about the history of impunity for state violence while it arose again in the present, with my freedom safeguarded by my position as an academic and my US passport, would have been a contradiction too heavy to bear.

When the NCPO regime officially ended but with no sign of an end to impunity, I decided to pick up chronologically where *In Plain Sight* concluded and write a history of injustice under the NCPO. Despite the fact that, or more accurately because, the law was their primary tool of repression, the generals of the NCPO, not those prosecuted by them, were the actual criminals. Looking toward a future transition to democracy and an accompanying accountability process, I planned to write in the form of a draft indictment categorizing the crimes of the junta in relation to

Thai domestic criminal, civil, administrative, and constitutional law. The NCPO repeatedly violated the very law it claimed to uphold. The NCPO's reliance on the law as a tool of direct repression or to frame extrajudicial violence means that a partial record of perpetrators and accounts of their actions exists in arrest records, interrogation transcripts, and court documents. TLHR archived these documents and allowed me to browse their files to gather evidence for the indictment. Delving into the files, I was reminded of the intensity of the five years of the NCPO's regime, in which nearly every day held an instance of arbitrary arrest and detention, prosecution for peaceful expression, or another rights violation. But the more I read, the more insufficient, and incorrect, a list of the junta's crimes came to seem as a history of the NCPO years. As I sifted through the files, another story of law shined as primary: one of unrelenting struggle against the junta. TLHR lawyers raced to accompany those arrested by phalanxes of soldiers in the middle of the night, repeatedly submitted requests for bail no matter how many previous requests had been denied, and recorded everything, including precise details of violence and intimidation conveyed by victim and families. On matters of both principle and procedure, TLHR held fast to an idea of the law as an instrument to protect people's rights and its application guided by an unshakable sense of equality. In so doing, TLHR followed in the footsteps of seventy years of Thai lawyers who brought cases against unjust governments and pushed the law to the limit to defend the rights of defendants unfairly prosecuted even when loss was all but guaranteed.[5]

But loss in the courtroom does not necessarily equate to failure in the struggle for justice. Unsuccessful legal battles—which bring people together around the aspiration of a new, different, and better society—are a key part of the long-term movement for justice by creating a community of solidarity and shared memory of struggle.[6] They also perform the work of describing and making such a society imaginable in legal terms. I decided to take a cue from this struggle and the TLHR files to work out whether, and how, the support of human rights and justice was possible within existing Thai law. What if the courts ruled arbitrary detention of dissidents to be illegal rather than permitted for the protection of national security? What if even one judge offered fulsome support for the exercise of the right to peaceful demonstration against the junta rather than casting it as sedition? What if the threat to human rights posed by detaining civilians on military bases was recognized as grave rather than dismissed as inconsequential? Instead of enumerating the junta's crimes within Thai law, I decided to reexamine political and rights cases decided under the NCPO and propose new decisions. Rewriting judgments is a mode of writing history that examines the injustice that has taken place under the law while outlining possible alternatives the dictatorship foreclosed. Sharing an orientation toward the future with drafting an indictment, the rewriting of judgments outlines what jurisprudence could look like in a future in which human rights cannot be swiftly pushed to the side each time a military junta launches a coup, and even a future in which coups are impossible.

To articulate what justice might look like and assess the depth of legal, social, and political transformation necessary to realize it, I revisit a series of cases in which the court adjudicated in favor of the junta and the abrogation of the people's rights, and I rewrite the decisions with a more just interpretation that approaches the junta, which the courts treated as the state, and people as equal parties. Chosen in consultation with TLHR, my selection of five cases was guided by the goal both to highlight opposition to the regime and to track the different ways that law was deployed by the junta to thwart it. I plot alternative legal logics, the interpretation of evidence, and conclusions that support justice rather than foreclosing it. The rewritten decisions join existing sharp analysis of the abuse of the law in cases under the NCPO.[7] But taking on the persona of judge creates a new position and perspective that unlocks the ability to imagine new interpretations of law through the very transgression of hierarchy, which is particularly sharp in Thailand.

In rewriting decisions, I build on the method developed by feminist judgment projects. In 2006, a group of feminist legal scholars in Canada observed that decisions that bolstered gender injustice persisted despite fulsome legal protections in Canadian law. They decided to form a new court—the Women's Court of Canada—to assess why it was so difficult for the courts to treat women as equal members of the polity and selected six Supreme Court of Canada decisions to rewrite. The judges of the Women's Court of Canada wrote in the language and structure of actual decisions and composed new rulings using the evidence available and the law in force at the time of the original decisions. They did so because "we wanted to explore the capacity and the limitations of the courts to further equality and social justice and to prove to ourselves as well as to others that our idealism could also be realistic."[8] They treated equality not as a gift from those with power but "as an organic, aspirational concept that needs to be developed and brought to life through its ongoing application to specific inequalities."[9] By working out new interpretations of the law and demonstrating that the existing decisions were only one possible interpretation, their work aimed to bring equality to life. They aimed "to go beyond critique to offer a fully articulated alternative. We wanted to see if within the limits of a judicial decision, we could say what we wanted to say and what we believe should be said. In this process, we are no longer offering a perspective or an argument or even an analysis; we are giving a judgment."[10] Rewriting judgements is a way to demonstrate the legal viability of another, more just interpretation of the law. Part of what makes this possible is the very act of daring to fantasize a new court into being, to use the Women's Court of Canada's words.[11] In a time of injustice, fantasy is needed to imagine justice anew.

Following the lead of the Women's Court of Canada, feminist judgment projects have proliferated in the United Kingdom, the United States, India, Australia, New Zealand, Northern Ireland, and Scotland, and with respect to international criminal and human rights courts.[12] They share a commitment to going beyond critique and stepping into the role of the judge and using the law at hand to explore context and tell a different story in the service of envisioning new outcomes.

Observing that the writing of judgments is largely treated as a matter of judicial education and ignored in academic work, they "challenge[s] the notion that judgment-writing is or ought to be an expertise confined to judges, and seek[s] to develop the practice of writing judgments as a form of critical scholarship."[13] The action of stepping into the judge's shoes is itself part of the dissident practice and those in the United Kingdom write that it is "a form of academic activism, an attempt to tackle power and authority not from the distance of critique but on their own terrain. By appropriating judgment-writing for feminist purposes, the judgment-writers engage in a form of parodic—and hence subversive—performance. . . . [T]hese feminist academics dressed up as judges powerfully denaturalize existing judicial and doctrinal norms, exposing them as contingent, and as themselves (the product of) performances."[14]

Scholars, like judges, are engaged in creating narratives and choosing which evidence to use to assemble their story and substantiate their decision. But judgments are not ordinary stories but those with the power to affect the lives of individuals and the polity. Feminist scholars who take on the role of judging focus on reshaping legal outcomes by both telling different stories and telling them differently. Judges are uniquely positioned "to shape—and reshape—the official 'story.'"[15] Self-appointed feminist judges found a persistent erasure of the context of women's lives and often of the very women themselves making claims for justice and equality. Rosemary Hunter, one of the coordinators of the UK Feminist Judgment Project, explains that writing a different story means "paying close attention to the persons involved, often giving voice to women who have been silenced, or at least sidelined, in other judgments in the case."[16] This also means paying attention to the "contextual materials, including legal, socio-legal, social science, historical, medical—and to a lesser extent feminist theoretical—literature and . . . feminist 'common knowledge' about the realities of women's lives."[17] Articulating a different set of evidence and placing it within often hidden social, political, and historical context foregrounds the experience of women and makes divergent, dissenting decisions possible.[18] Producing different decisions goes beyond critique because it "stimulates people to operate as if social structures were already transformed."[19] It is neither realist, in terms of accepting the limitations of the existing system, nor revolutionary, in terms of calling for the destruction or abandonment of the system—it is a third way that recognizes the limitations of the current system but treats them as changeable. Drawing on Margaret Davies, Hilary Charlesworth notes that feminist judgments are a form of prefigurative politics, "a way of moving between utopian imaginings and the material world in which we find ourselves, 're-creat[ing] present law in a manner that gestures towards a different and possibly more expansive future.'"[20] Judgment-rewriting projects are a form of activist scholarship that intervenes in existing injustice by treating the law and courts as what Davina Cooper calls an everyday utopia, in which "the utopian is not simply a depiction of another kind of place, but a process or challenge—a mode of striving toward something else that is better—in which questions of imagination, creativity, and processes of change are deeply entwined."[21] Writing from inside the decision-making process, rather than criticizing it from outside, they crafted new narratives about both individuals and society, relationships between the people and the law, and roles for the law in redressing injustice. New outcomes, or sometimes the same outcome but with a different logic, under the same law became imaginable and possible.

Yet all the existing feminist judgment projects have taken place in democracies with relatively equal and fair judicial processes in place. Gender equality and justice, the primary focus of the rewritten judgments, is accepted as a normative social good. Rewriting judgments made under a dictatorial junta when the transition to democracy remains incomplete, as it is in Thailand today, entails confronting history and reimagining the future in ways that differ from the judgments made in countries that already profess a commitment to gender equality in existing feminist judgment projects. Thinking and working through the differences of rewriting judgments in and against a repressive regime productively extends the feminist judgment methodology into a new, challenging context—one that could variously be called a democracy judgment, antidictatorship judgment, or people's judgment methodology. Coups rob all the people in the polity of justice. Although not all people in the Thai polity were actively targeted by the NCPO for opposing the coup, and some even supported the coup, this does not alter the fact that the junta violated their sovereignty by carrying it out.

When one rewrites judgments in the context of dictatorship, the problems and possibilities within the law are made particularly stark. The intertwined history of the law, state, and monarchy in Thailand means that despite other options available in the law as written, courts overwhelmingly rule in favor of the state and against the people. No state official involved in a coup that has succeeded in seizing power has faced prosecution or otherwise been held to account for either the coup itself or violations of human rights under the ensuing dictatorship. While not new, the range of rights abuses committed in the name of restoring the rule of law and the length of the NCPO's regime as the second-longest dictatorship, after the nearly ten-year Cold War regime of Field Marshal Thanom Kittikachorn (9 December 1963–14 October 1973), indicate a new level of impunity. This context makes rewriting judgments both more urgent and more challenging in Thailand than in the democratic contexts in which existing feminist judgment projects have been sited. Rewriting judgments rendered by judges under the NCPO makes it possible to at once write a history of the people's dispossession by the law and contribute to the imagination of justice after dictatorship.

The reasons to rewrite decisions under the NCPO are both scholarly and political. The NCPO was not merely enforcing the law but using the law as a tool to deprive citizens of their rights. As a historian, documenting how this took place illuminates unexpected continuities of legal support for coups and the persistence of citizen opposition to dictatorship in Thailand. As a person concerned with the eventual aftermath of dictatorship, understanding how judges and courts legitimated departures that may have adhered to the law as written but departed from the rule of law is a key part of understanding the transformations that will be necessary to build a democratic polity and the roles of the law and court in doing so.

In rewriting decisions issued during the regime of the NCPO, I have taken on the fundamental instructions and guidelines of the feminist judgment projects. The judgments in this book are not metaphorical but approach the real. The new decisions are not binding and are written by a non-Thai historian rather than a royally appointed judge. Yet they approach the real in the sense that I draft judgments in the narrative form used by judges in Thailand and by drawing on the same laws in place under the NCPO. I rewrite decisions using the same bodies of law used by Thai judges: Thai criminal, civil, administrative, and constitutional law, and Thailand's international human rights obligations, primarily the International Covenant on Civil and Political Rights (ICCPR). The five rewritten cases were originally decided by the civilian Criminal, Appeal, and Supreme Courts; the Military Court; the Administrative Court; and the Constitutional Court. I write using the same narrative form used by each of these courts. The civilian Criminal, Appeal, and Supreme Courts write in a prescribed form that generally follows a statement of the facts in the case as understood by the judges, then analysis of the defendant's action in relation to the laws they are accused of violating, and finally a reflection on intention.[22] Although I depart from some of the conventions, I aimed to craft believable decisions.[23] The rulings of the Constitutional Court and Administrative Court are far more varied in their form, and judges often draw on history and social context beyond the specific facts of the case—I have embraced that license as well.

Resonant with the elision of context and erasure of individual lives noted by the feminist judgment rewriting projects, I discovered that the people were conspicuously absent from most of the original decisions under the NCPO. By "the people," I mean both the individual defendants or plaintiffs in each case, as well as the people—citizens, civilians, and commoners—in the sense of all those not part of the NCPO, the monarchy, or the powerful institutions allied with them. The names of the sixteen plaintiffs who dared to bring a case against the junta, let alone the significant damages they suffered as a result of the coup, are left out. The reasons activists decided to protest were left out. The detention of a man's children on a military base until the authorities apprehended him and took him for reeducation was left out. The surveillance of dissidents by military intelligence so they could be prepared to arrest them before they even reached a demonstration site was left out. Alongside omission, judges routinely distorted the facts when adjudicating cases under the NCPO. Ominous intentions were attributed to defendants, the existence of torture was denied, and evidence manufactured when necessary. By rewriting the people into decisions and paying attention to the facts of both their lives and the NCPO's repression, different outcomes under the same law become imaginable. The new judgments form a history of the coup years that records dissent and repression rather than valorization of the junta.

But the rewritten decisions in this book differ from actual decisions in one crucial respect: there is no royal symbol of the garuda across the top, and they are not written in the name of the king. The court I fantasize into being is the Court for the People. To be clear: I am not Thai and do not presume to write in the name of the people. But I write *for* the people in that I place the protection of the people, rather than the elevation of the state, at the center of my analysis of cases and new jurisprudence. The garuda is replaced at the top with a symbol of the democracy movement, the three-finger salute, fashioned into a gavel.²⁴

Rewriting judgments under the banner of an imagined Court for the People is a utopian, and perhaps riskily republican, move. I aim both to counter the overarching and ambiguous presence of the monarch in the polity and to center the people, who were conspicuously absent from the five decisions I have rewritten.²⁵ The feminist poet and theorist Audre Lorde famously wrote, "The master's tools will never dismantle the master's house."²⁶ Although the law itself promises contingency and multiple interpretations, the court of the king does not. This is particularly the case when repression, including coups, in the name of the king, is an unquestioned, and unquestionable, part of governance. For a coup to be lawful, the order appointing the junta as the government must be signed by the king. Without this signature, a junta cannot take power.

The contest over law goes from being theoretical and hopeful to being real and present on the pages of this book. Rewriting unjust decisions made under dictatorships to be just and to foreground the people in a time when impunity still reigns is a form of what Saidiya Hartman calls critical fabulation, in which "playing with and rearranging the basic elements of the story, by re-presenting the sequence of events in divergent stories and from

Figure 1. Symbol of the Court
for the People. Designed by
Ben Winitchakul.

contested points of view . . . jeopardize[s] the status of the event, to displace the received or authorized account, and to imagine what might have happened or might have been said or might have been done."[27] Hartman does so in the context of the brutality of slavery in North America and its historical and historiographical erasure "both to tell an impossible story and to amplify the impossibility of its telling."[28] I rewrite judgments for the people to tell the impossible story of justice in Thailand more than ninety years after the transformation from absolute to constitutional monarchy. This impossible story begins with the history of the formation of jurisprudence that supports coups.

DICTATORSHIP ON TRIAL

INTRODUCTION

HISTORY AND JURISPRUDENCE

Every decision under the NCPO—whether seemingly about joining a political protest, not answering a summons to report, or opposing the draft constitution—was also a decision about the legitimacy of the 22 May 2014 coup specifically and coups as a mode of rule generally. Over the series of thirteen "successful" coups, meaning that power was seized, beginning with the transformation from absolute to constitutional monarchy on 24 June 1932, the grave crime of the coup has become the primary mode of the relationship between the people and the state. The foreclosure of justice builds on a series of amnesty laws and court decisions, beginning with the end of absolute monarchy, which cast the illegal seizure of power as legal and made coups a normal mode of transition from one government to another. Dissidents are not the only ones with a history: those who rely on the preservation of injustice for their power also accumulate lessons over time. A history of dispossession—for those who seize power and those who are subject to it—forms over time through the structure, promulgation, and adjudication of the law. This history is lived in the polity as a series of lessons that are communicated through institutions, laws, and daily life. Understanding this history and its lessons—and how it at once binds the military, the monarchy, and the judiciary and erases the people—is the first step to undoing its power.

THE LOCATION OF DISPOSSESSION

The first lesson of dispossession teaches the people that they have no standing in the law. The king—and those close to him—hold power. Although judges are commoners, they preside under gilt-framed portraits of both the king, Maha Vajiralongkorn, and his father, Bhumipol Adulyadej.[1] They receive their commissions directly from the king and write their judgments under the banner of the phrase "In the Name of His Majesty" and the royal symbol of the garuda.[2] The judges sit in plush chairs on a raised dais while the people crowd together on long wooden benches below the judges and the portraits of the kings in the courtroom.

The spatial layout of the courtroom reflects the hierarchy and apportionment of power within the law and its adjudication. Left largely unchanged by the transformation from absolute to constitutional monarchy, the Thai judiciary has long privileged the state over the people and the king over the constitution. In a March 2020 lecture honoring Puey Ungpakorn, an economics professor and university rector who fled for his life after the 6 October 1976 massacre and coup, Thongchai Winichakul laid bare the fiction of the existence of justice and the rule of law in Thailand and called for a new legal history.[3] He argued that two primary ideas constitute jurisprudence in Thailand: the legal privileged state (*nitirat aphisit*) and royalist rule of law (*rachanititham*). The legal privileged state is "a legal system that affords privilege to the state to violate private property and the rights and freedom of the people for public interest in law both applicable to ordinary times and states of exception. The most important Thai public good is national security, and therefore the military is the entity that overwhelmingly enjoys and exercises this privilege." The royalist rule of law is the principle "that holds that the king is above law and justice (not the constitution or parliament that are held to be universal norms)." Together, these are ingrained practice and uncontested history.[4]

To launch a coup—the violent upending of the existing regime—without being held to account, "is a privilege of bandits and murderers that is endorsed by the judiciary, it is the collusion to commit the gravest crime that can arise in a given state."[5] The legal privilege extended to the state reaches its apogee in the amnesty laws passed and judicial approval for coups, including that of the NCPO. This legality, and the ability of the military, monarchy, and other allied actors to overturn the existing regime when they choose to do so, is produced and guaranteed in the first instance by the series of amnesty laws that have followed after each coup.

Impunity has been secured in eight coups by stand-alone laws, in two coups by articles in postcoup constitutions, in one coup by both a constitutional article and a stand-alone law, and in only one case with no special legal measure promulgated. They protected the coupmakers from possible prosecution or other sanction and retroactively legalized the coup in question. Each amnesty has turned the illegal act of rebellion into a legal, administrative action. The Supreme Court then crafted the practice of judicial legitimation of coups beginning in 1949 through a series of four decisions about the 8 November 1947 coup. Together, the decisions and amnesty laws cemented what Somchai Preechasinlapakun calls "the rule of coups," in which the repeated failure to hold coup leaders to account functions as encouragement for future would-be juntas to upend the constitutional order.[6]

One way to encapsulate Thai history since 1932 is through the chronology of the repeated coups, what Thanapol Eawsakul and others call the vicious cycle of Thai politics: coup → new constitution → election.[7] Over time, this vicious cycle has come to seem inevitable or natural. Placing the evasion of accountability for coups at the center of the chronology demystifies this cycle by revealing how much effort has gone into creating it and the incremental expansion of the legal privilege of the state.

THE LEGISLATION OF DISPOSSESSION

The second lesson of dispossession, which is contained within amnesty laws, is that the history of law in the Thai polity is one of ever-increasing protection for juntas and their supporters. The amnesty laws are short: four total articles, with the third article the essential one. Since 1932, there has been a steady expansion of time, personnel, and actions covered in these brief laws and the court decisions that expand upon them. This is the essential context to understand the conditions of possibility for the NCPO's coup on 22 May 2014 and the urgency of developing a new jurisprudence.

The very beginning of the constitutional polity was inauspiciously sealed with an amnesty law. On the early morning of 24 June 1932, after years of planning, the civilian-military coalition of the People's Party seized and neutralized key figures of the absolutist regime.[8] Their manifesto deposing the king proclaimed: "The king maintains his power above the law as before. He appoints court relatives and toadies without merit or knowledge to important positions, without listening to the voice of the people."[9] They allowed the king to remain on the throne as long as he was willing to be placed under a constitution. He quickly assented, and no blood was shed. Pridi Banomyong, the civilian leader of the People's Party, explained that there was no word for *revolution* in the Thai language at that time, so they used the phrase "a change from the system of government in which the king is above the law to the system of government in which the king is under the law" to describe their actions.[10] But in an unfortunate turn, the People's Party placed the king under the law but themselves above it. Article 3 in the amnesty that they passed for themselves stipulated that "the entirety of the actions, regardless of whom within the People's Party [carried them out], are not to be considered a violation of any law, at all."[11] This provision made all of their actions not illegal. The amnesty that the People's Party passed to absolve themselves of the action of deposing the king became the point of departure for coup amnesty laws, including the royalist coup which deposed them less than a year later. The transformational impulse for the rule of law contained within the events of 24 June 1932 soon began to undergo a process of repression and erasure, and instead, the will to redefine illegal actions as legal become foundational through the series of subsequent amnesty laws.

The People's Party promulgated an interim charter authored by Pridi Banomyong, the civilian leader. The charter, which promoted people's participation and limited the role of the king, was immediately attacked by royalists.[12] On 20 June 1933, Phraya Phahon, the military leader of the People's Party, staged the country's second coup against the civilian government following the presentation to parliament of the Outline Economic Plan, drafted by Pridi and arguing for democratization of ownership and the economy. The Outline Economic Plan was cast as dangerously communist, and Pridi went into exile temporarily.[13] The amnesty law for the coup began by noting that, because the coup transpired smoothly and without violence, it was appropriate for those involved to receive royal grace; just as decisions are rendered in the name of the king, laws are as well. The text of Article 3 specified: "The entirety of the actions, no matter who within the army, navy and civilian factions [carried them out], if they were illegal, are not to at all be considered a violation of the law."[14] The amnesty delimited the specific categories of members of the junta as those covered by the amnesty. With the addition of the point that actions that might be illegal were not to be interpreted as such, the law implicitly acknowledged the illegality of the coup.

Fourteen years passed before the next coup. After serving as regent while King Ananda Mahidol (Rama 8) was outside the country during World War II, Pridi became prime minister on 24 March 1946. But then on 9 June 1946, the king died under mysterious circumstances, which remain unresolved today. Following accusations that he was involved in the death, Pridi resigned, and this time his flight into exile became permanent. Pridi's exile was both the removal of a jurist and politician who would have likely opposed the rule of coups and an attempt to drive out the idea of democracy. The formation of the rule of coups began in earnest after the third coup, on 8 November 1947, when a junta calling itself the Khana Thahan, or Military Group, seized power and began the turn away from democracy, the increase of the role of the military in governance, and the return of the political role of the monarchy. Article 3 in the amnesty prescribed: "The entirety of actions carried out . . . as a result of the coup . . . if they were illegal, the perpetrators who carried them out shall be absolved from guilt and all responsibility. Anything carried out under the various announcements and orders issued during the aforementioned coup are to be considered legal."[15] This amnesty went beyond delimiting illegal actions as not being illegal to making them legal and to protecting perpetrators from prosecution. Further, by making actions that follow from orders and announcements issued by the junta legal, the very meaning of law was transformed to include that which is issued from the barrel of a gun.

The Khana Thahan carried out two more coups. The only coup without an accompanying amnesty took place a year later during the 6 April 1948 coup, when the Khana Thahan replaced their civilian prime minister, Khuang Aphaiwong, with Field Marshal Phibun Songkhram. Three years later, the Khana Thahan carried out an autocoup against themselves to increase their power. Article 3 in the amnesty for the 29 November 1951 coup used identical language to that of the amnesty for the 1947 coup.[16] The use of *if* in various amnesties to delimit the actions covered by them functions as the opposite of the usual purpose of the conditional to signal the hypothetical or possible: the actions *were* illegal and that is the very reason the amnesty laws were passed by legislative assemblies appointed by the respective juntas.

A significant shift in the content of the amnesty law arrived when Field Marshal Sarit Thanarat launched his first coup on 16 September 1957 at the beginning of the intensification of the Cold War. Article 3 of the amnesty law stipulated:

> The entirety of actions carried out . . . whether by an instigator, supporter, a person acting for another, or a person who was used, in the course of seizing the administrative power of the country on 16 September 1957, and other related actions, no matter how they were done and no matter if they were carried out on the aforementioned day or before or after the

aforementioned day, if those actions were illegal, the perpetrators who carried them out shall be absolved from guilt and all responsibility. Anything carried out under the various announcements and orders issued, in whatever form, that are related to the aforementioned actions, whether directly or implicitly, are to be considered legal and in force.[17]

A wide range of actors was specified—many, not only the high-ranking officers in the junta, are covered by "instigator, supporter, a person acting for another, or a person who was used." It is difficult to imagine who would not fit into these categories. The time covered was also expanded: on, before, or after the date of the actual coup.

A year later, on 20 October 1958, Field Marshal Sarit launched an autocoup to consolidate his power. Article 3 prescribed that

the entirety of actions carried out . . . that resulted from the coup on 20 October 1958 and other related affairs, all of the actions of the head of the junta or people delegated by the head of the junta carried out for the order and happiness of the people, including punishment and other administrative actions, no matter how they were done and whether they were carried out by an instigator, supporter, a person acting for another or a person who was used, and no matter if they were carried out on the aforementioned day or before or after the aforementioned day, if those actions were illegal, the perpetrators who carried them out shall be absolved from guilt and all responsibility. All of the announcements and orders of the head of the junta, in whatever form, and whether they have administrative or legislative effect are to be considered legal and in force.[18]

The expansion of the terms that surfaced following Field Marshal Sarit's first coup remained in the amnesty for his second coup. The announcements and orders of the head of the junta were given the status of law, even though they passed no review, even by a body appointed by the junta. The vague, broad category of "punishment and other administrative actions" was also added, as long as they were carried out for the "order and happiness of the people." This is the first time that the concept of a coup as a generator of happiness surfaced. Similarly paradoxical, the fourth coup announcement stated that the junta would respect the Universal Declaration of Human Rights (UDHR).[19] But Sarit's dictatorship instead foreclosed happiness and human rights, particularly through Article 17 of the 1959 Interim Constitution, which gave him authority to take any action he deemed necessary and was used for summary detention and execution. The idea of a coup in the service of the happiness of the people has surfaced several times since then, most recently when General Prayuth Chan-ocha claimed that he and the NCPO would return happiness to the people.

Reference to the monarchy enters for the first time in the amnesty for the coup that Field Marshal Thanom Kittikachorn, who took over the dictatorship after Field Marshal Sarit's death in 1963, launched against himself to consolidate his power on 17 November 1971. Although the monarchy had receded from public life in the immediate years following the end of absolutism, its role in politics steadily grew and particularly intensified during Field Marshal Sarit's dictatorship, when the military and monarchy joined hands to fight communism. Article 3 of this amnesty noted:

> The entirety of actions before the law enters into force, that were carried out in relation to the coup on 17 November 1971 or related affairs, the entirety of actions of the head of the junta or people delegated by the head of the junta or people ordered by the person delegated by the head of the junta that were carried out for the security of the nation and the crown, and for the order and happiness of the people, including punishment and other administrative actions, no matter how they were done and whether they were carried out by an instigator, supporter, a person acting for another or a person who was used, and no matter if they were carried out on the aforementioned day or before or after the aforementioned day, if those actions were illegal, the perpetrators who carried them out shall be absolved from guilt and all responsibility.[20]

The people are positioned third here, after the nation and the crown. The institution of the monarchy has since remained a frequent feature of amnesty laws and an ever-increasing, and murky, presence in political and legal life.[21]

The dictatorship of Field Marshal Thanom Kittikachorn ended on 14 October 1973 after hundreds of thousands of students and citizens took to the streets and demanded a constitution. During the subsequent three years, the most vibrant democracy since 24 June 1932 emerged in Thailand, and a wide range of citizens participated in politics, including farmers, workers, teachers, artists, and many others.[22] But transitions to communism in Cambodia, Vietnam, and Laos in 1975 and the rising right wing in Thailand led to a backlash in the claimed service of protecting the monarchy as well as the nation and the Buddhist religion. This culminated in a massacre of university students at Thammasat University on the morning of 6 October 1976 and a coup that returned the country to dictatorship on the same afternoon.[23] In the amnesty soon promulgated, perpetrators of a wide range of violent actions in addition to the coup itself were absolved of their guilt. Article 3 of the amnesty passed for the 6 October 1976 coup carried out by the National Administrative Reform Council (NARC) stipulated:

> The entirety of actions taken along with the seizure of the administrative power of the country on 6 October 1976 and the actions of individuals connected with those aforementioned actions were undertaken with the intention of fostering the security of the kingdom, the crown and public peace. The entirety of actions of the NARC or the head of the NARC or those who were appointed by the NARC or the head of the NARC, or those who were ordered by someone appointed by the NARC or the head of the NARC that were carried out for the reasons noted above including punishment and the bureaucratic administration of the country, all of the aforementioned actions, irrespective of their legislative, administrative, or judicial validity, irrespective of whether they were carried out by someone in the position of a principal figure, a supporter, a person acting for another, or a person who was used, and irrespective of whether or not

they were carried out on the aforementioned day or before or after that day, if the actions were unlawful, the person is absolved from wrongdoing and all responsibility.[24]

During the drafting process and the debate in the appointed legislative assembly, the importance of tweaking the grammar designating actors in order to prevent prosecution of grave crimes for all involved, including soldiers at the rank of private and ordinary citizens, not only the officers in the junta, was highlighted.[25]

However, the far-right regime of Thanon Kraivichien put in place by the NARC did not last long, and a little over a year later, on 20 October 1977, General Kriangsak Chomanand launched another coup. Article 3 of this amnesty was identical to the amnesty for the prior coup, with only the date of the coup and the name of the junta changed.[26] Even though there was no need to apply the broad coverage used for the amnesty for the 6 October 1976 massacre and coup to this one, which resembled a more typical coup in which the existing government was illegally ousted, the drafters left it in place.

During the waning years of the Cold War, Thailand entered a period without coups, and almost fourteen years passed until the next one. On 21 February 1991, General Suchinda Krapayoon and a junta calling itself the National Peace Keeping Council (NPKC) ousted the elected government of Prime Minister Chatichai Choonhavan, which they claimed was corrupt. Article 3 of the amnesty passed for the coup was again identical to that of the 6 October 1976 and 20 October 1977 coups, with only the date and the name of the junta changed.[27]

The 1991 coup was the last for which a stand-alone amnesty law was passed. Dictatorships flourished in the 1970s and 1980s and finally began to ease following another uprising for democracy in 1992.[28] In 1997, Thailand's seventeenth constitution, known as the People's Constitution given the relatively participatory process behind its drafting, was promulgated, and coups seemed to be a phenomenon of the past.[29] But precisely in this context, military and monarchical elites grew anxious about the wide-ranging support for the populist prime minister, Thaksin Shinawatra, elected in the 2001 election, the first under the new constitution.[30] The 19 September 2006 coup by the Council for Democratic Reform under Monarchy (CDRM) that ousted his government was addressed by a constitutional article. Article 37 of the 2006 Interim Constitution stipulated:

> All acts done by the Chairman of the CDRM which were related to the seizure and control of the state administrative power on 19 September 2006 as well as any act done by persons involved in such seizure or of persons being assigned by the CDRM or of persons being commanded by the Chairman of the CDRM which done for such above act. All these acts, whether done for the enforcement in legislative, executive or judicial force as well as the punishment and other acts on administration of the State affairs whether done as principals, supporters, instigators or persons being commanded to do so and whether done on such date or prior to such date or after such date which if such acts may be unlawful, the actors shall be absolutely exempted from any wrongdoing, responsibility and liabilities.[31]

This constitutional provision dialed back impunity slightly and interrupted the trajectory of increasing protection for perpetrators in terms of both time and individuals covered.

But in a reversal of the minor limits placed on impunity after the 2006 coup, the two amnesty provisions in the 2014 Interim Constitution called on every expansion of impunity built into amnesty laws over the preceding ninety years. Resonant with Field Marshal Sarit Thanarat's second amnesty, Article 47 made all orders and announcements of the NCPO or the head of the NCPO legal, constitutional, and final.[32] Then, Article 48 stipulated:

> In regard to all acts which are performed on account of the seizure and control of state governing power on 22 May 2014 by the Head of the NCPO, including all acts of persons incidental to such performance or

of persons entrusted by the Head of the NCPO or persons ordered by persons entrusted by the Head of the NCPO, which have been done for the benefit of the abovementioned performances, irrespective of whether such acts were performed to have constitutional, legislative, executive, or judicial force, including punishments and other official administrative acts, and irrespective of whether the persons performed such acts as a principal, an accomplice, an instigator or an agent and whether those acts have been done on, before or after the aforesaid date, if those acts constitute offences under the laws, the persons who commit those acts shall be entirely discharged from such offences and liabilities.

The NCPO's two amnesty provisions signaled the kind of regime it planned to be: repressive and mired in law.

THE JUDGMENT OF DISPOSSESSION

The third and final lesson of dispossession is that when it comes to coups, the courts are not on the side of the people. The junta-appointed legislative assemblies provide the first layer of impunity for coups. Then, the civilian criminal courts, particularly the Supreme Court, the third and final level of the three-tier system, contribute to the rule of coups by choosing to affirm their legality and legitimacy. In a canonical article surveying postcolonial common-law cases about coups, beginning with the 1958 coup in Pakistan, Tayyab Mahmud argues that courts not dissolved as part of a coup must decide which stance they will take regarding the legitimacy of the new regime. Judges have four possible options, each of which entails deciding the extent to which the line between politics, meaning governance, and law, meaning the rules of the polity and the court as their arbiter, should be blurred. First, they may validate and legitimate the coup. Second, they may interpret the coup as contravening the constitution and therefore neither valid nor legitimate. Third, they may resign their position and refuse the question. Or fourth, the only option that Mahmud views as just, the courts, "being an agent and instrument of the state and the legal order," may conclude the matter of the coup to be outside their jurisdiction.[33]

Thailand has a civil-law system. The courts have never been dissolved as part of a coup and have always chosen the first option—validate and legitimate—when faced with the question. In doing so, the courts reveal the lack of separation between law and politics and themselves become part of the conflict present in the polity.[34] Further, although binding precedent is not a feature of Thailand's legal system, the rule of coups was cemented through an additive process in which a series of four key Supreme Court decisions built on one another between 1949 and 1954. The logic offered in each decision demonstrates the flexibility of the law and the Supreme Court's willingness to further extend the parameters of the amnesties rather than restrain them.

All four decisions deal with the 8 November 1947 coup by the Khana Thahan, the first coup in which the military began to tighten their grip but before the harsh Cold War dictatorships. The process began with fulsome confirmation of the validity of the amnesty law passed in the immediate aftermath of the coup. The strength of this law was put to the test in a case of subordination by two soldiers, Master Sergeant Pruay Nawarat and Sergeant Prathuang Intram. They refused to follow the orders of their commanding officer after the coup and demanded to know his position on it. Once they ascertained that their commanding officer supported the coup, as they did, the pair returned to following orders. They were prosecuted and punished in the military court system and appealed. In 1949, the Supreme Court interpreted their actions to be in support of the coup and therefore covered by the amnesty. Master Sergeant Pruay and Sergeant Prathuang were absolved. Without the amnesty, the Supreme Court noted, they would have been punished.[35] As long as it was in the service of the coup, even subordination was permissible.

Three years later, in a 1952 decision about an unsuccessful coup attempt in 1948, the Supreme Court outlined how and when the illegal action of a coup transforms into the foundation of a legal government. The defendants argued that their actions were not criminal because they acted against the regime that came to power in the 1947 coup, which they claimed was illegal.[36] The Supreme Court did not accept that claim and argued that, although the Khana Thahan's "toppling of the prior government and establishing a new government by force may not have been legal at first until the people accept and respect it . . . the government that the defendants were going to topple is a government that is correct according to reality, which means that the people accept and respect it."[37] The Supreme Court did not define what constituted either acceptance or respect but clearly did not recognize the various protests of the 1947 coup as significant.[38] The lack of clarity reflects legal thinking that was at once sloppy and precise. Similar to the expansive coverage for coup-related actions in the amnesty laws, by leaving acceptance and respect explicitly undefined, coupmakers and their courts may interpret them as they wish.[39]

In the following year, the Supreme Court rendered a third decision pertaining to the 1947 coup that consolidated the prototype for subsequent decisions about coups. Thongyen Leelamien, the permanent secretary of the Ministry of Commerce at the time of the coup and a close ally of Pridi Banomyong, was fired by the new minister of commerce appointed after the coup. Thongyen brought a case claiming that he was fired unjustly. The minister of commerce who fired him was appointed under the 1947 Interim Constitution, which was illegitimate because it was promulgated by the Khana Thahan, which had illegally abrogated the 1946 Constitution. Thongyen further alleged that the new minister of commerce had defamed him by announcing his dismissal on the radio, publishing information in the newspaper that he was an opium dealer, and instructing the police to hold him for seven days. The new minister of commerce responded by asserting that Thongyen's claim that the 1947 Interim Constitution was invalid was incorrect because the coup had been successful.[40] He claimed that he had neither given any information to the newspaper or radio nor instructed the police to arrest him.[41] The Court of First Instance and the Appeal Court found that the defendant was not involved in the newspaper, radio, or police matters and dismissed the case.[42] Thongyen then appealed to the Supreme Court. The Supreme

Court also dismissed the case and ordered Thongyen to pay the defendants' legal fees.[43]

Beyond ruling on the specific matters of Thongyen's claims of the damages he sustained, the Supreme Court commented on the legality and validity of the coup. The Supreme Court judges wrote: "The facts are that in 1947, the junta successfully seized the governing power of Thailand. The administration of the country in this manner means that the junta has the power to change, amend, abolish and promulgate laws according to the revolutionary system, in order to continue to govern the country. Otherwise, the country would be unable to establish peaceful order. Therefore, the 1947 Interim Constitution was completely legal," and the defendant was the legitimate minister of commerce.[44] The judges recognized the illegality of the coup but chose to privilege the maintenance of order above the law. Similar to the lack of a definition of what constituted acceptance and respect in the earlier decision, *success* in this decision was not defined. What it appears to mean is that as long as the junta that carries out a coup is able to take control of the state apparatus, even if this involves acts that are criminal, then the coup and the subsequent constitution are legal.[45]

The fourth relevant Supreme Court decision was handed down the following year in a case about another attempted coup against the Khana Thahan; it added a quality of timelessness to the acceptance and respect allegedly secured by the junta. Similar to the earlier case, the defendants argued that the government they attempted to topple was illegal because it was created by an illegitimate constitution.[46] The Supreme Court dismissed this argument and explained that even though the 1947 Interim Constitution was promulgated by a government that came from a coup, "the newly established government took control and governed the country successfully and absolutely, and it maintained the peace and order of the country-nation and has always been accepted and respected in general as a complete government for a long time until now."[47] The judges firmly noted that there was "no reason not to hold it to be a legal government according to the reality that clearly appears."[48] In this decision, the Supreme Court extended its assessment to existing reality and concluded that support for the governments put in place by the Khana Thahan had always existed. The Court offered no evidence for this timeless acceptance. With the decision, David Streckfuss argues, the court equated silencing the coup's critics with success, noting, "The more it established its authority and silenced its critics, the more legitimate it was. Who, exactly, had come to 'accept and respect' these governments? How was such acceptance or respect measured? The Supreme Court did not answer these troubling questions."[49] These questions remain unanswered in the present.

They remain unanswered because the truth would lay bare the fiction of the alleged total, seamless acceptance and respect for coup governments. Recognition of that fiction is the first step to undoing the rule of coups. Placing the protection of the people at the center of jurisprudence, rather than privileging the state, is the second step. This, in turn, requires approaching the analysis of law from a perspective as relentless in its commitment to the possibility of justice as that with which activists dissented and lawyers defended them under the NCPO. These are the conditions in which scholars and activists should, and must, dare to step into the shoes of judges.

TRANSFORMING JURISPRUDENCE

The rulings by the Supreme Court in the four cases related to the 1947 coup are not wrong in the sense of reflecting an erroneous interpretation of the law. But that does not make them right in the sense of being just interpretations that fostered equality under the law and the protection of rights. Instead, the interpretations legitimized and fomented violence, in the sense described by Robert Cover: "Legal interpretive acts signal and occasion the imposition of violence upon others: A judge articulates her understanding of a text, and as a result, somebody loses his freedom, his property, his children, even his life. . . . When interpreters have finished their work, they frequently leave behind victims whose lives have been torn apart by these organized, social practices of violence. Neither legal interpretation nor the violence it occasions may be properly understood apart from one another."⁵⁰ In the case of the rule of coups, the immediate object of the violence that follows from legal interpretation is the polity itself. The government is abruptly ejected and the existing constitution torn up as heavily armed soldiers occupy government buildings, media outlets, and the streets. This violence links the rule of coups to what I term the *jurisprudence of impunity*. The jurisprudence of impunity emerges across the indictments and judgments rendered during the NCPO years, characterized by the denial of the people's right to participate in the polity or at times even to think, a centering of the military and monarchy as unquestionable, and disproportionate punishment for dissent. In ruling against the people in the name of the law, judges under the NCPO both acted resonantly with judges under other authoritarian, rule-by-law regimes and built on existing legal practice in Thailand.⁵¹

But the jurisprudence of impunity is not the only possibility. As Noura Erakat writes in the context of Palestine: "The law is contingent and does not predetermine an outcome. It only promises the possibility of a contest over one."⁵² The interpretation of the law that the Thai civilian and military courts offered under the NCPO was not the only possible one, just as the earlier decisions in support of the coups by the Supreme Court were not the only possibilities. If one begins instead by privileging the people and recognizing dissent as protected under both Thai domestic law and Thailand's international human rights obligations, different narratives and divergent outcomes become possible. What I cast as a *jurisprudence of accountability*—one that values and centers, rather than erases, the participation of the people in the polity; holds state officials and institutions to account; and treats justice itself as an ideal to strive toward—can then be imagined and created. The jurisprudence of accountability calls on judges to interpret in the service of ending violence rather than furthering it.

In this book, I trace the formation of the jurisprudence of impunity and craft a jurisprudence of accountability through examining and then rewriting a series of decisions rendered by judges during the NCPO's regime. All the selected cases are those that are final, meaning that no more appeals are pending, and those in which the decisions are already in the

public domain. I chose not to take up some of the most devastating cases
to emerge under the NCPO, including extensive torture and intimidation
of defendants or victims and any others in which the parties have asked
activists and journalists not to report on their cases. They may be able to
be taken up and discussed openly in the future. The role of scholarship is
not to expose those who have experienced injustice who would rather not
be exposed. In reevaluating the cases and rewriting the judgments anew,
I draw on the records kept by TLHR, iLaw, *Prachatai*, and other human
rights and independent media organizations; court, police, and military
documents; and my own court observation and interviews.

One way to understand the five decisions, four of which were decided
in favor of the junta, is as part of the history of the NCPO's repression.
But they are also a record of how citizens held the line against dictatorship,
despite the sacrifices this entailed. Sombat Boonngamanong, a longtime
activist who is one of those whose case I take up, suggested: "All of these
cases are a record of the system of the judicial process. I hope that one day
they become small case studies, or the decisions are debated with respect
to the politics of law in the future. I hope that's how it will be. Let them be
recorded in history. Because they have the troops, they have the guns. All
we have are our voices."[53] Ordered chronologically, the first case rewritten
is one people brought against the junta for launching the coup; three are
cases in which people were prosecuted for noncompliance with the junta,
including those prosecuted for peaceful protest, and for not reporting
when summoned for detention and reeducation; and the final case is one
brought against the junta in the Administrative Court with regard to the
detention of civilians on military bases. Across all the cases, which were examined in courts around the country, the judges emphasize that the coup
and all subsequent actions by the junta were legitimate and lawful.

HOW TO READ THIS BOOK

The impossible story of justice—in which the overarching history of injustice both creates the urgency for and threatens to overwhelm attempts to imagine and create justice in Thailand—unfolds across five substantive chapters in this book. Proceeding chronologically across the NCPO's regime, each chapter takes up a particular kind of case from the coup years. The chapters pair the genealogy of similar cases and rights violations under earlier coup regimes with analysis of the judicial process and judgment for those rewritten. The chapters trace both how the NCPO went beyond enforcing the law to use the law as a tool to dispossess citizens of their rights and the persistence of citizen opposition to dictatorship in Thailand.

The rewritten judgments rendered by the Court for the People then follow each chapter. Powerfully freed of the need to legitimate the coup, the new decisions by the Court for the People first interrogate the lawfulness of the coup within the history of pro-coup jurisprudence. The Court for the People operates as an additional layer of adjudication and incorporates critique of the existing decisions in each case in order to offer new ones. Second, the decisions carefully consider the meaning of sovereignty. Although the original decisions tend to identify the NCPO as the sovereign on the basis that the junta was able to capture state power, the Court for the People decisions reflect on how to make real, in the exercise and interpretation of the law, the promise in many of Thailand's constitutions since the end of absolute monarchy in 1932 that sovereignty belongs to the people. Third, the rewritten decisions demonstrate a range of ways that the judicial process and judgments themselves can aid in the protection of rights and freedom rather than facilitating their violation. Fourth, each chapter takes up the status, meaning and form of law as experienced under the NCPO and contributes to the contest over the law and its outcomes that Noura Erakat so eloquently foregrounds.

This book is designed to be read in multiple ways. Readers may choose to read the entire book or only the decisions, which are separated from the chapters. A synopsis of each chapter and the rewritten judgments follows to provide a sketch of the entire book for readers who may choose to selectively read.

On the first anniversary of the coup in May 2015, Resistant Citizen, a coalition of fifteen activists, lawyers, artists, and survivors of state violence filed charges of treason and rebellion against the NCPO. Chapter 1, "The Impossibility of the People," places Resistant Citizen's struggle in the seventy-year history of attempts to hold coupmakers to account. Despite amnesty laws passed with each coup to foreclose accountability, Resistant Citizen and others who have brought cases advance an idea of the people's sovereignty that refuses its destruction by an illegal seizure of power by a handful of military generals. The protection of state officials from being impugned, never the protection or even recognition of the people as equal members of the polity, remains constant across the decisions. In this case, too, the Supreme Court adhered to historical precedent and dismissed Resistant Citizen's charges against the NCPO. In contrast, a jurisprudence of accountability would center the people and accord weight to the damage sustained by individuals and the polity by coups. The new judgment by the Court for the People reverses precedent and writes toward a different future in which sovereignty is not reduced to brute force but is a shared project between the rulers and the ruled.

One day after the coup, on 23 May 2014, Apichat Pongsawat, a recent law graduate, joined a protest against the coup. Carrying an A4 sheet of paper with the phrase [I] Do Not Accept Illegitimate Power printed on it, he joined several hundred people peacefully massed in front of the Bangkok Art and Culture Center. Upon seeing his sign, heavily armed officers swiftly arrested him and detained him incommunicado on a military base. Chapter 2, "Coups and Coupocracy," traces his four-and-a-half-year fight against what began as six criminal charges across the Court of First Instance, Appeal Court, and Supreme Court. Apichat's protest of the coup—and persistent refusal to cede that it was a crime—reflects the clarity of one citizen's commitment to the constitution. The court's steadfast judgment of Apichat as guilty, even when the junta order under which his protest was criminalized had been revoked, reflects the judiciary's unwillingness to protect the constitution or the rights of a citizen willing to sacrifice his freedom to do so. The new decision by the Court for the People instead finds Apichat innocent, develops a logic for how his actions were protected by both domestic and international law, and clarifies the role of the judiciary in protecting the constitution.

Within a day of the coup, the NCPO began issuing orders summoning citizens to report themselves to the military. Under martial law, anyone could be detained for up to seven days without a formal accusation being brought or a judge consulted. Lists of names of those summoned interrupted television programming and scrolled down the screen at uneven intervals each day. Others were summoned by a telephone call or the appearance of soldiers at their door. Those summoned were told nothing about what would happen upon being reported or even where they would be detained. When criticized by domestic and international human rights groups for institutionalizing a policy of arbitrary detention, an NCPO spokesperson gave the practice the even more Orwellian name of *attitude adjustment*. Those who harbored a negative attitude toward the coup would be held until they changed their views. A total of at least 1,320 people were summoned, and at least 14 were prosecuted for refusing to report. Chapter 3, "Refusal to Report," is about what happened to three who resisted attitude adjustment: Sombat Boonngamanong, a nongovernmental organization activist; Siraphop Kornarut, a poet and Red Shirt activist, and Worachet Pakeerut, a law professor at Thammasat University and leader of the Khana Nitirat, a central force for progressive legal reform before the coup. Across cases in the Supreme Court, Military Court, and Constitutional Court, the three defendants challenged the authority of the NCPO and the legitimacy of the orders it unilaterally issued. In response, the courts composed ideas of the polity in which the junta and the coup were automatically legitimate and lawful. Even the Constitutional Court, which found in 2020 that both the order for Worachet Pakeerut to report and the order criminalizing refusal were unconstitutional, left the argument for the necessity of the coup intact. The new Constitutional Court for the People decision instead offers a counterhistory of the coup that challenges the NCPO's claim to having restored order and charts a counterlegitimacy of reasons to dissent grounded in the specificity of the lives of the three defendants.

As part of the coup, the NCPO abrogated the 2007 Constitution, Thailand's nineteenth since the end of absolute monarchy in 1932. Two months after the coup, the NCPO promulgated an abbreviated, forty-eight-article interim constitution and immediately began drafting a new permanent constitution. General Prayuth knew that the days of the people's acceptance of outright dictatorship were numbered and ensured that the draft charter preserved the power of the military by cloaking it in the disguise of a constitutional, if not quite democratic, regime. The new constitution had to be approved by securing a majority of votes in a public referendum on 7 August 2016, but the NCPO promulgated the Draft Referendum Act to severely restrict discussion about the draft ahead of the vote. Only the NCPO and those authorized by it were allowed to disseminate information about the draft: any seminars, publications, or organizing by civilians was criminal. Chapter 4, "A Constitution without the People," takes up 2 of the 212 cases brought against the people under the Draft Referendum Act. Samart Kwanchai was an elderly man who made small flyers that read Down with Dictatorship, Long Live the People, 7 August Vote No and placed them under windshield wipers in a parking garage in the northern province of Chiang Mai. Samart was unexpectedly found innocent, but because of a fluke in the plaintiff testimony lacking requisite expertise, not because the court affirmed his right to dissent. Toto Piyarat Chongthep, who went into a booth on the day of the referendum, tore up his ballot, and yelled the same phrase printed on Samart's flyer was found guilty. In both cases, the civilian courts weighed the right of the defendants to express their views peacefully, yet decided in favor of the maintenance of order. The new decision delivered by the Court for the People in Toto's case instead argues for robust protection for rights and freedom of expression, which are particularly urgent in a time of transition from a dictatorship to a constitutional regime.

In September 2015, the NCPO-appointed minister of justice issued Ministry of Justice Order No. 314/2558 designating a section of the Eleventh Military Circle Base in Bangkok as a prison for defendants in national security cases. Less than two months later, there were two suspicious deaths of those held in custody in cases against the crown. Chapter 5, "Disavowing Responsibility," takes up a case brought in the Administrative Court regarding the order by Pansak Srithep, one of the members of Resistant Citizen who brought the case against the NCPO in chapter 1, and a defendant in a sedition case for staging a solo peaceful walk against dictatorship. The Administrative Court was established in 2001 for the people to bring cases against state officials or agencies that have caused harm or otherwise not carried out their duties appropriately.[54] Although Pansak had been granted bail in his sedition case, he worried that if bail were revoked, he could be detained at the prison. He argued in his Administrative Court case that the definition of "national security cases" in which defendants were subject to detention at the prison was vague, there were reports of torture, and the facilities were generally poor. The Administrative Court did not dispute the existence of problems at the temporary prison but ruled that they did not merit revoking the order or closing the prison. The new ruling by the Administrative Court for the People places the protection of civilians, rather than state officials or agencies, at the center of its action. Instead of dispensing with the reports of torture and the unresolved deaths in custody merely by stating that they were not caused by the order establishing the prison, the Administrative Court for the People proposes an investigation to discern which individuals or agencies were responsible. In other words, rather than looking for a legal loophole to protect the state from responsibility, the Administrative Court for the People takes the mandate of protecting the people and securing accountability for violence against them as paramount.

The book closes with an epilogue on judgments that cannot be rewritten. There were 162 prosecutions for lèse-majesté under Article 112 during the regime of the NCPO, which included those prosecuted for performing plays, writing graffiti in bathrooms, and making posts on social media, with sentences reaching up to forty-three years imprisonment. Despite the prominence of these cases under the NCPO, I do not rewrite Article 112 cases in the book. The reason is that the law is one law that I, along with many Thai activists, think must be revoked. The law has no place in a future democracy, whether realist or aspirational. The epilogue concludes by reflecting on Article 112 cases as those that cannot be rewritten by returning to the comparative questions of both feminist judgment methodology and utopia that frame this book.

ONE

THE IMPOSSIBILITY OF THE PEOPLE

Sixteen members of an anticoup network called Resistant Citizen walked from the Lad Phrao underground train station up Ratchada Road to the Criminal Court in Bangkok and filed charges of rebellion and treason against the National Council for Peace and Order (NCPO) on the afternoon of 22 May 2015, the first anniversary of the coup. They acted both as individuals directly injured and on behalf of all Thai people, whom they identified as the owners of sovereignty who were collectively dispossessed by the coup. If found guilty of the charges, General Prayuth Chan-ocha and the other four members of the junta faced maximum punishment of life imprisonment or execution for rebellion and up to fifteen years imprisonment for treason. But neither General Prayuth nor any other members of the NCPO have seen the inside of a courtroom, let alone the inside of a prison. On 22 June 2018, the Supreme Court affirmed two earlier decisions by the Court of First Instance and the Appeal Court and dismissed the case brought by Resistant Citizen.

The Supreme Court did not rule on whether the junta was guilty of rebellion or treason, only on whether there were sufficient grounds for the case to be examined. Had the Supreme Court reversed the decision of the two lower courts, the case would have returned to the Court of First In-stance and witness hearings commenced. By denying that Resistant Citi-zen had grounds to bring a case, and therefore affirming the legality of the coup, the Supreme Court adhered to the rule of coups and the practice of judicial legitimation of coups crafted through the series of decisions begin-ning in 1949 discussed in the introduction.

Under the rule of coups, the abrupt ejection of the prime minister and the tearing up of the constitution becomes an ordinary feature of rule rather than an exception that interrupts it. But the violent destruction of the existing order also entails another displacement that is both less appar-ent and more fundamental. In the 22 May 2014 coup, and in every prior Thai coup, the constitution abrogated by the coup explicitly stipulated that sovereignty belonged to the people. Even though the people's sovereignty remains aspirational and incomplete within constitutional regimes, the possibility—and therefore a defined role for the people to participate in the governing of the polity—is present. The action of the coup eliminates that possibility. It is that orientation toward the people that creates a strong al-legiance between the rule of coups and the jurisprudence of impunity. The jurisprudence of impunity both requires and perpetuates the condition in which the people are lesser than the state, which should be understood as necessary for perpetuating the status quo of Thongchai's "legal privileged state," in which the state is always privileged within the law.[1] To be lesser can variously include being wrong, being the enemy, or simply being invis-ible. Coups render the people inconsequential within the polity, and the rule of coups treats them as invisible within the law. The courts legitimize coups by crafting decisions that privilege the maintenance of order over law, equate the absence of dissent under dictatorship with support for coups, and make the monopoly on force the primary requisite for sovereignty.

Over time, court decisions define a "successful" coup as one by a junta able to take control of the state apparatus and suppress resistance. But an-other way to understand the meaning of a "successful" coup is one in which the perpetrators are not punished and may even be rewarded.[2] This is a vis-ible, national instantiation of the impunity that citizens who are victims of state violence routinely experience. The rule of coups is pedagogical for the people as well as for would-be coup plotters. If the prime minister can be tossed out and the constitution torn up whenever the soldiers decide their power is waning, without any concern that they may be held to account for their grave, public violations of the law, then what hope do the people have in holding state perpetrators to account for violence?

When considering the sheer number of coups since 1932 (thirteen) and the legal successes in challenging them (zero), it is tempting to focus on what appears as a seamless history of repression of the people by a military-monarchy-capital alliance.[3] But this is neither accurate nor aids in creating a different possible future. The history of the rule of coups, like the history of state violence of which it is a part, is a history of opposition as well as one of domination. To imagine a decision that can break the cycle of the rule of coups, as the new Court for the People decision rewriting the Supreme Court decision in the Resistant Citizen case aims to do, emphasizing the crimes of the junta is not enough. Resonant with the insight of feminist judgment-rewriting projects that telling a new story and foregrounding different figures in a case makes an alternative outcome visible, writing a new history is a necessary first step to imagining a future in which coups are impossible. Over time, coups have been presented as an inevitable, necessary and efficient solution to political conflict, unrest, or disorder. Instead, highlighting the incomplete and sloppy logic offered in support of coups and the courage of the people in standing up to dictatorship reveals the precarity of the seemingly strong justification for coups. Such an account challenges the rule of coups and sets the stage to reverse seventy years of precedent and protect the people's sovereignty.

Resistant Citizen brought its criminal complaint against the NCPO with the knowledge of the failure of prior attempts to thwart the persistence of the rule of coups. The complaint is significant because it builds an argument about the illegality of the coup on an idea of the people as defenders of democracy. Resistant Citizen writes: "Even the civil servants, whose salary comes from the taxes of the people, were not courageous enough to stand up to the power that emerged from the barrel of a gun.

It was only the people, the citizens, who dared to courageously rise up to oppose the dictatorial power of the junta, as has been seen from the past until the present."[4] By articulating a history of people's struggles against coups—and joining the struggle—Resistant Citizen refused the erasure of the people both necessitated and produced by coups. The new Court for the People decision sketches how a court might respond to the upending of the constitutional order in a manner that honors the history of people's opposition to coups and accounts for how they are affected by them. Fostering, rather than foreclosing, accountability begins with seeing the people.

WRITING A NEW HISTORY

The privileging of the state in the four Supreme Court decisions around the 8 November 1947 coup belies more heterogeneous struggles between the state and the people beyond their pages. The ten years following the November 1947 coup were what Craig Reynolds characterized as "semi-free, semi-unfree."[5] Socialist, communist, and other radical ideas circulated and were debated in a range of newspapers. Radical bookstores sold emerging leftist Thai books and imported those from overseas, including Beijing and Moscow. Many organized against Thailand's alliance with the United States and involvement in the Korean War.[6] But beginning in November 1952, more than two hundred journalists, writers, lawyers and others were arrested and accused of communist activities, revolt, and lèse-majesté. Many were released without being charged after several years; those who were convicted and imprisoned were pardoned in 1957. The combination of the flourishing of dissident ideas and the arrests for daring to think them illustrate the political heterogeneity at the time.

The remaining space for dissent disappeared with the 16 September 1957 coup by Field Marshal Sarit Thanarat and his reintegration of the monarchy in politics as the Cold War expanded in Southeast Asia. Field Marshal Sarit carried out an autocoup on 20 October 1958 to expand his power and then promulgated a new, interim charter of only twenty articles in January 1959. One of these, Article 17, provided him with the authority to take any action he deemed necessary to safeguard the security of the nation; Field Marshal Sarit ordered eleven summary executions of arsonists, drug producers, and communists.[7] When Field Marshal Sarit died in December 1963, his deputy, Field Marshal Thanom Kittikachorn, took over. Field Marshal Thanom's regime continued the authoritarianism put in place by Sarit, including the use of Article 17 and the promulgation of the expansive Anti-Communist Activities Act in 1969, which provided the state with extensive powers to curtail rights.[8]

But in the context of domestic and international demands for democracy, Field Marshal Thanom relented. In 1968, a new constitution was promulgated, and elections for parliament the following year allowed a modicum of representation of the people in politics. This was short-lived. On 17 November 1971, Field Marshal Thanom abrogated the constitution and launched an autocoup against his own government. In Revolutionary Council Announcement No. 6, one of the many announcements on the first day of the coup, the junta claimed that its action was necessary because of the internal and external threats to the country and crown. Some people were using their constitutionally protected rights for nefarious reasons, and resolution by constitutional means would be too slow to preserve the survival of the country.[9] In the amnesty law the junta passed for itself the next month, it defined the coup as "carried out for the security of the nation and crown, and for the order and happiness of the people."[10]

But not everyone was happy. Three members of parliament—Uthai Pimchaichon, Anan Phakpraphai, and Boonkerd Hirankham—whose roles as representatives of the people were cut short by the coup submitted a criminal case against Field Marshal Thanom and the other fourteen members of the junta on 9 March 1972. The three MPs described themselves as "representatives of the people" whose status as injured parties sufficient to bring a case derived from being MPs whose position and benefits were eliminated.[11] In sharp contrast to the logic of the necessary coup offered by the junta, they charged that Field Marshall Thanom and the others "dared to together commit a crime against the law by rebellion. They came together and used injurious force and threatened people throughout Thailand with the use of injurious force to overthrow the constitution, overthrow the legislative power, overthrow the executive power, overthrow the judicial power of the constitution."¹² The very choice of the three MPs to use the law and the courts—which had supported juntas and their coups up until that point—was a brave and dissident act. The power of their vision to unsettle the ruling dictatorship and the carefully built rule of coups was evident in the harsh punishment visited upon them.

The Criminal Court dismissed their case on 13 March 1972, only four days after they submitted it. The Criminal Court's dismissal contributed to the intertwined rule of coups and jurisprudence of impunity by explicitly excluding the three MPs, or any of the people, from being injured parties affected by the coup. If the three MPs were allowed to bring a case against the junta, people all over the country could bring cases and say that they were affected by the coup. The Criminal Court explained:

The meaning and required characteristics of the word "injured person" are not stipulated directly in law, and whether one must be injured directly or indirectly. If it is interpreted broadly, the plaintiffs, who are members of parliament, lost their position as MPs, cannot go to parliament meetings, do not receive their salaries and benefits, or anticipated benefits, it could be considered that all three are injured parties. And simultaneously, there are likely other individuals who are injured parties who could sue the junta on the same charge, or even other civil and criminal charges. For instance, the people in the provinces in which each of the plaintiffs are representatives, or people in other provinces, will charge that the coup of the Revolutionary Council caused them to be injured because they became people who did not have representatives. If it went on and on like this, one could say that there could be lawsuits brought all over the country. If this happened, instead of peace and order arising in the country, there would instead be chaos and many kinds of turmoil would follow. There would be examination [of cases], withdrawal of cases, including appeals and further appeals to the Supreme Court, because the actions of the Revolutionary Council may not only be charged as rebel-

lion, but they might be accused of other crimes, which cannot be. Therefore, the meaning of an injured party that has the authority to bring a
case according to the law refers to injured parties who were directly and
particularly injured.[13]

The reason the three MPs, or anyone else, could not bring a case against the
junta as injured parties affected by the coup was not because they were not
injured. They could not bring cases against the junta because it would lead
to disorder. By acknowledging the proliferation of civil and criminal cases
that would disrupt the junta's rule, the Criminal Court acknowledged the
illegality of the coup but chose not to act. The court concluded that the
state was the only party that could bring a case.[14] But given that the junta
had become the state through the coup, it seems unlikely that this would
have happened. Although every state, including the Thai state, is heterogeneous and less unified that the singular word *state* suggests, the dictatorship's response to the three MPs case suggests that internal dissent would
not have been tolerated.[15]

The Criminal Court's swift dismissal of the case was not enough for
Field Marshal Thanom. On 22 June 1972, three months after the dismissal,
the rule of coups reached its apogee when he used his expanded powers to
issue Head of the Revolutionary Council Order No. 36/2515 to summarily
sentence Uthai Pimchaichon to ten years in prison and Anan Phakpraphai
and Boonkerd Hirankham to seven years in prison. The plaintiffs became
the defendants, but they had no opportunity to defend themselves. In the
lengthy order, Field Marshal Thanom went beyond the Criminal Court's
willingness to acknowledge and then ignore illegal actions to define the
defense of law as its violation. Despite being an explicitly extrajudicial process aiming for impunity rather than justice, the order used the language of
the law and mirrored the format of a court decision. Rather than providing
legitimacy, this highlighted the departures from the very judicial process
it mimicked. Because the three MPs were punished via a summary order
issued by the head of the junta, specifying the laws they allegedly violated
was unnecessary. Field Marshal Thanom claimed that they conspired to

bring the case against him and the other members of the junta. The key matter for examination was "if the actions of the defendants were a sincere exercise of rights or with the intention to create turbulence and insubordination among the people, to the degree that it would create unrest in the country and be opposition, obstruction, and overthrow of the Revolutionary Council or not."[16] He claimed that the complaint distorted the truth because the MPs aimed to cause the people to be suspicious of the junta and create turmoil.[17] Field Marshal Thanom was accuser, investigator, prosecutor, and judge—all at once.

Field Marshal Thanom then explained that the coup was necessary

> as a result of the incidents both inside and outside the country that are shifting in a bad direction and are a danger to the nation and the crown. There are attacks in neighboring countries with increasing levels of violence. There is the provocation to support terrorists to create unrest among the people in various areas of the country, with the intention to change the form of rule to another type that is not democracy with the king as head of state. Inside the country, it has arisen that there are some individuals who rely on their constitutional rights, and some individuals, some groups, who refer to the constitution to act to agitate to subvert and use influence to stir up obstruction of the administration by the government. For example, instigating for people and various institutions to be the enemies of and insubordinate to the government, instigating university students to march in protest, instigating workers to strike, etc.[18]

What seemed to irk Field Marshal Thanom most was that the three MPs, and particularly Uthai, who was a lawyer, failed to understand both the necessity of the coup and the law. They should have known that once a junta was able to take government power, it became legal. Field Marshal Thanom wrote:

> All three defendants are former members of the National Legislative Assembly. They are people who know about the law, especially Defendant

No. 1 [Uthai], who is a law graduate and a barrister. The defendants must know well that a revolution or a coup, when a Revolutionary Council or a junta has successfully seized power, the greatest authority in governing the country, or sovereignty, belongs to the Revolutionary Council. The Revolutionary Council or Head of the Revolutionary Council can exercise sovereign power in every way. When the government, central, regional, or local, and the people accept and respect the exercise of authority by the Revolutionary Council or the Head of the Revolutionary Council, the Revolutionary Council is held to be the government that is correct in terms of both political science and law. . . . All this, in addition to being principles of political science and law that many nations have accepted and respected for a long time, is also a principle that the Supreme Court has ruled on to be a standard in many instances.[19]

Field Marshal Thanom then cited the series of decisions related to the 1947 coup forming the rule of coups discussed in the introduction. He consolidated the permutations of law and ideas of the role of the people in the polity that had formed into the rule of coups and used that as the basis to attack those who refused to comply with it.[20] Uthai, Boonkerd, and Anan were punished for believing in the law as an instrument of democracy.

The only correct expression would have been in support of the Revolutionary Council and its coup. The three MPs were guilty of ill intentions: "The view of the Revolutionary Council is that the lawsuit of the three defendants was not the sincere exercise of the right to expression of opinion, but was an action that intended to persuade the people to be misled to think that the actions of the Revolutionary Council were the actions of a group of rebels who should be criminally punished under the law. The actions of the three defendants are opposition to and overthrow of the Revolutionary Council that intends to create suspicion of the governance of the Revolutionary Council."[21] Field Marshal Thanom's statement reflected the key tenets of the rule of coups developed since 1949 but also unexpected recognition of its fragility. Would imprisoning the MPs be necessary if coups were as legal and legitimate as the courts claimed? Field Marshal Thanom's swift actions intended to impart a clear lesson that dissent, even or perhaps especially within the frame of the law, would be met with repression.

Uthai, Anan, and Boonkerd were not the only citizens unwilling to tolerate dictatorship and Field Marshall Thanom's government was ousted by a people's uprising for democracy on 14 October 1973. Sanya Thammasak, the rector of Thammasat University, was appointed prime minister, and an amnesty was a possibility for the quick release of the three MPs. But they refused on the basis that it would necessitate an acceptance of guilt.[22] They instead waited for a new legislative assembly, which passed a law on 25 January 1974 that nullified Field Marshal Thanom's order. They were immediately released. A note appended to the nullification explained that bringing a legal case cannot be considered a crime.[23] The note was not-so-subtle confirmation that the act of using the law was the gravest crime of the three MPs. In response to that act, the junta used the mechanism of the law to create and exercise power in excess of the law.[24]

Reflecting on their actions four decades later, Uthai recalled that the three demonstrated that they were not afraid of coups, and their actions led to increased dissent by others.[25] They brought the case because, he said: "We had the aspirational determination to do political work for the people. When we realized that the coup would harm the people in the long term, we used a lawful method to struggle since we were unable to pick up arms to fight in any way. Those of us who brought the charges used to work in law previously and used the method of the court in bringing a case against the junta because we saw that they were clear rebels in light of the Criminal Code."[26] Their political work for the people continued in prison, and Uthai succeeded in securing the removal of shackles and chains for all prisoners except those awaiting death sentences.[27] Uthai wrote: "I did not bring charges against them because I wanted to be famous, not because I wanted votes, but I brought charges because I could not bear a dictatorial government. This should not occur in a country that is governed as a democracy. What they did was clearly against the law, but no one dared to resist it."[28] They were the first politicians, and remain the only ones, to attempt to bring criminal charges against a military junta for carrying out a coup.

RESISTANT CITIZEN ON BEHALF OF THE PEOPLE

There were no legal challenges brought against the 1976, 1977, or 1991 coups. After 1991, there was a slow return to democracy and fifteen years without coups. But a pair of coups—the 19 September 2006 coup and the 22 May 2014 coup—changed everything. They took place as King Bhumipol Adulyadej's (Rama 9) life was winding down. The two coups appear at first to be completely different. After the 19 September 2006 coup by the Council for Democratic Reform under Monarchy (CDRM) ousted Prime Minister Thaksin Shinawatra, there were few restrictions on rights and freedoms and a swift return to a civilian, if not democratically elected, prime minister. The 22 May 2014 coup was instead the start of a full-blown dictatorship that recalled Field Marshal Thanom's rule and reshaped the political system so significantly that the junta remained the majority force in governance even after a general election in 2019. Despite their seeming dissimilarities, the two coups aimed to transform the Thai polity by reducing the avenues for people to participate and reinstituting the coup as both a threat and a mechanism of rule.

In this context of the attack on people's participation, Chalad Worachak, a former air force officer and democracy activist, brought the first case against a junta for launching a coup in more than thirty years since Uthai, Anan, and Boonkerd's case. He viewed the coup as equivalent to the plunder of the entire country, and he could not abide power secured in such a manner.[29] On 29 June 2007, he filed a case against General Sondhi Boonyaratklin, the head of the CDRM, and 308 people who supported the coup for violation of Article 112 and Article 113. He charged that they violated Article 112, or committed lèse-majesté, because after they illegally seized power and created a dictatorship, they asked the king to sign in endorsement. That constituted defamation of the king.[30] They violated Article 113 by overthrowing the constitution and government, interfering with the press and both government and private organizations, and not respecting the people's rights, as well as for many other reasons.[31] The Court of First Instance ruled that the case was without grounds. Chalad appealed, and the Appeal Court upheld the initial decision and cited Article 37 of the 2006 Interim Constitution that provided amnesty to the junta.[32] Not dissuaded by this defeat, on 10 June 2014, he brought charges of violation of Articles 112, 113, and 114 against the NCPO and its supporters.[33] This time he added Article 114, which criminalizes inaction by those who are aware of a rebellion being planned.[34] He brought the case against a total of twenty-eight people: Prayuth and seven other generals, twenty permanent secretaries of various ministries and departments, and one person from the Judge Advocate General's Department. The 2014 Interim Constitution that provided the NCPO with amnesty for the coup had not been issued yet, and so the court could not rely on it to generate impunity. Instead, the Criminal Court dismissed the case on the basis that Chalad was not an injured party. The loss of his rights and freedoms was an insufficient reason to be an injured party in a rebellion case. Echoing the dismissal of Uthai, Anan, and Boonkerd, the Criminal Court asserted that the state was the only party that could bring a case against a junta for carrying out a coup.[35]

In response, Chalad commenced a hunger strike in front of Parliament. Then at the age of seventy-one, he maintained that he would fight for democracy as long as he remained alive. For him, the very act of holding the line against the coup and demonstrating his willingness to sacrifice for democracy was a significant and essential political action.[36] The police asked Chalad what he would do if the soldiers summoned him. As I discuss in chapters 2 and 3, the criminalization of dissent began immediately after the coup, and the NCPO arrested many activists and summoned others for so-called attitude adjustment, which was actually arbitrary detention and reeducation. Chalad told the police that he would not go voluntarily and they would have to arrest him.[37] The soldiers never summoned Chalad, but he stopped his hunger strike after forty-five days because of the danger to his health.

On 22 May 2015, the one-year anniversary of the coup by the NCPO, Resistant Citizen, a loose collective of dissidents who engage in cultural-political and street protests, brought the fourth case ever against a junta for carrying out a coup. Fifteen members of the group charged that General Prayuth and the other four generals (army, navy, air force, police) who acted in the name of the NCPO carried out a rebellion and in so doing violated Articles 113 and 114 of the Criminal Code. They argued that the NCPO violated numerous laws during and after the coup. Over a period of three years, their case was dismissed successively by the Court of First Instance, the Appeal Court, and the Supreme Court. The only court to offer a substantive analysis was the Supreme Court, which upheld the rule of coups with a very slight hint of opposition.

Resistant Citizen's assumption of the possibility of justice—and its articulation in the initial criminal complaint and then petitions to the Appeal and Supreme Courts—contributes a new anticoup history and a different articulation of the people and their role in the polity that is in stark contrast to the rule of coups. The Resistant Citizen case against the NCPO resonates with Davina Cooper's idea of an everyday utopia, which "capture[s] a sense of hope and potential in that they anticipate something more, something beyond and other to what they can currently realize."[38] Their refusal to accept the rule of coups as unchangeable is the first step in changing it.

The Resistant Citizen criminal complaint began with the explanation that at the time of the coup, Thailand was a democracy with a constitutional monarchy in which sovereignty belonged to the people. The plaintiffs described themselves as "Thai people and owners of sovereignty [who] possess liberty and human dignity, [who] have a duty to protect the nation, religion, king, and democratic regime with a constitutional king as the head of state."[39] The elected Parliament exercised that sovereignty on the people's behalf to draft laws and monitor and audit the administration of the country. The courts functioned to judge cases and make other rulings in line with the constitution. The people were able to exercise their rights and liberties to participate in politics, including to peacefully protest as stipulated in the 2007 Constitution.[40]

The plaintiffs detailed General Prayuth's crimes. They began with his participation in the 19 September 2006 coup, during which time he was the commander of Army Region 1. He accepted an appointment from the junta to the National Legislative Assembly. Thereafter, General Prayuth participated in the April–May 2010 crackdown on Red Shirt protesters as the deputy commander in chief of the army and deputy director of the Center for the Resolution of the Emergency Situation.[41]

The criminal complaint then addressed the declaration of martial law on 20 May 2014, which set the stage for the coup by placing broad restrictions on rights and liberties. The plaintiffs argued that the declaration of martial law was illegal because the situation did not meet the condition stipulated in Article 2 of the Martial Law Act of 1914, which was that it could be declared "whenever there is necessity to preserve good order so as to be free from external or internal danger."[42] General Prayuth and the NCPO sent armed soldiers to occupy radio, television, and other media outlets to control broadcast media during the coup.[43] Then, on 22 May 2014, they summoned government, political party, and major protest leaders to a meeting in an army barracks on Vibhavadhi Road in Bangkok. The defendants claimed that they met to discuss a way out of the political impasse created by the preceding months of protests. Instead, the plaintiffs argued that this meeting was part of the defendants' plan to carry out a coup. During this time, the defendants sent armed soldiers to surround key government buildings.[44] The defendants would not allow those who attended the meeting to leave and used force to detain them. They next announced the abrogation of the 2007 Constitution; the dissolution of the Cabinet, Parliament and Senate; and the seizure of power from the current government.[45] The plaintiffs alleged that this series of actions constituted conspiracy to topple parliamentary democracy, the use of injurious force, and the destruction of constitutionally protected legislative, executive, and judicial authority—or, in sum, rebellion.[46]

The plaintiffs next explained that they sustained harm from these actions. The primary reason was that when the coup and its related series of events took place, the 2007 Constitution was in force; therefore, they were "Thai people according to the aforementioned constitution, who had constitutionally protected rights and liberties. In other words, we had liberty of life and person in movement and the freedom to select a place of dwelling, freedom of expression of opinion, publication, dissemination, association, and (to participate in) political demonstrations."[47] The defendants were dispossessed of those rights and liberties by the coup via three primary actions: the abrogation of the constitution, the provision of jurisdiction in civilian cases against the crown and state to the military court system, and the NCPO's promulgation of announcements and orders that structured many aspects of life.

Aware of the earlier dismissals of rebellion cases against juntas based on findings that the plaintiffs were not injured parties, Resistant Citizen then carefully elaborated the specific damages sustained by the plaintiffs.[48] Plaintiff No. 1, Pansak Srithep, a taxi driver and the father of a young man killed during the April–May 2010 crackdown on Red Shirt protesters, "had his existing freedoms curtailed and was unable to live normally due to the limitations placed on his rights and liberties by the junta led by the five defendants and their associates." He also faced military court prosecution for violation of NCPO Announcement Nos. 7, 37, and 38; Article 116; and the 2007 Computer Crimes Act.[49] Plaintiff No. 2, Wannakiat Chusuwan, a taxi driver, was also unable to live life normally and was being prosecuted in the Bangkok Military Court for violation of NCPO Announcement Nos. 7, 37, and 38.[50] Plaintiff No. 3, Siriwith Seritiwat, a Thammasat University student, was "dispossessed of his freedom of political expression by the junta led by the five defendants, who forbade him from carrying out sandwich-eating activities, using the three-finger salute symbol and holding academic seminars and other forms of political expression."[51] He was also being prosecuted in the Bangkok Military Court for violation of NCPO Announcement Nos. 7, 37, 38, and 39.[52] Since the coup, Plaintiff No. 4, Sriprai Nonsee, a labor leader in the Rangsit area of Bangkok, was deprived of her freedom to hold protests and call for justice from the bosses. She therefore could not exercise her freedom of political expression, academic freedom, or political assembly in line with her civil rights.[53] Plaintiff No. 5, Baramee Chairat, was a nongovernmental organization worker whose job was to provide villagers with knowledge and assistance in natural resource management. After the coup, he was no longer able to hold meetings with villagers or organize demonstrations with them to call for justice; as was the case with Plaintiff No. 4, he was unable to exercise his freedom of political expression, academic freedom, and political assembly in line with his civil rights.[54]

Plaintiff No. 6, Nattaphat Akkhad, was the younger brother of a person killed during the April–May 2010 protests. He was arrested during a demonstration that took place after the declaration of martial law and detained in a military camp. He was deprived of his rights of communication, assembly and political expression.[55] Plaintiff No. 7, Siraphop Kornarut, was summoned by the authorities, arbitrarily detained, and being prosecuted in the Bangkok Military Court for opposing the NCPO.[56] Plaintiff No. 8, Sansern Sri-unruan, was arrested following the illegal announcement of martial law. Following his arrest, he was administered electric shocks on his legs and abdomen. He was being prosecuted in the Bangkok Military Court and was denied bail and temporary release.[57]

Plaintiffs Nos. 9–14—Chonticha Jangrew, Natcha Kong-udom, Apiwat Suthararak, Phayu Bunsophon, Jatupat Boonpattararaksa, and Krit Saengsurin—were university students who were threatened by the defendants and those to whom they had given power. These plaintiffs, following their participation in protest activities expressing opposition to the coup, were forced to sign memorandums of understanding promising not to protest further, under threat of criminal prosecution.[58] Plaintiff No. 15, Arnon Nampha, was a human rights lawyer whose freedom was curtailed and who was unable to live his life normally due to the restrictions placed on his rights and liberties by the NCPO. Like many of the plaintiffs, he was being prosecuted in the Bangkok Military Court, for violating NCPO Announcement Nos. 7, 37, and 38 and the 2007 Computer Crimes Act.[59] The harm sustained by the plaintiffs covered a wide range, from arbitrary detention and torture to constriction of speech. Some of these were rights that were explicitly protected by the 2007 Constitution, and others were violations for which the 2007 Constitution provided mechanisms of redress or complaint. All the protections and mechanisms were erased by the 22 May 2014 coup.

After detailing the ways in which the fifteen plaintiffs were individually harmed as a direct result of the coup, the complaint then developed an argument for expanding the category of presumed plaintiffs. The plaintiffs note that Articles 113 and 114 of the Criminal Code are "intended to protect the interest of the state as well as to protect the individuals who directly sustain injury from the crimes as well."[60] In the case of the 22 May 2014 coup, this means that when the defendants staged the coup and abrogated the 2007 Constitution, they dispossessed the plaintiffs of their constitutionally afforded sovereignty, which made them injured parties.[61] The indictment then expanded the category of injured parties by arguing that the actions of the defendants injured all citizens in the country. If the state was viewed as the sole injured party, then the actions of the defendants did not constitute revolt. The reason was that when the defendants carried out their revolt, the Cabinet and the Parliament, which exercised the sovereignty of the people, were "all only scared of the [junta's] authority and yielded entirely to the junta. Even the civil servants, whose salary comes from the taxes of the people, were not courageous enough to stand up and oppose the power that emerged from the barrel of a gun."[62] Instead, it was the people who stood up: "It was only the people, the citizens, who dared to courageously rise up to oppose the dictatorial power of the junta, as has been seen from the past until the present."[63] The plaintiffs further noted that they chose to bring a criminal complaint against the defendants because the judicial system remained "the sole sovereign power that is steadfastly impartial at this time when the country is dark and bereft of hope."[64] By addressing its audience, the court, as an impartial and just body, Resistant Citizen called on the court to respond in such a fashion.

In addition to the rights violations, the complaint further noted that the coup and the junta's subsequent actions included corruption, financial mismanagement, and inept ruling of the country. There were no indications that the defendants were aware of their criminal behavior or intended to curtail it, as Article 44 of the 2014 Interim Constitution provided them with absolute executive power.[65] Their aim was to run the country as a totalitarian dictatorship.[66] Even though the junta members provided themselves with an amnesty for the coup and the orders and announcements issued in Articles 47 and 48 of the 2014 Interim Constitution, the plaintiffs argued that this was not in line with the fundamental principles of law and justice. If the court accepted the authority of the junta, then it would be as though the judges did not serve the people and were indifferent to the threats to democracy posed by military dictatorship.[67] The plaintiffs offered an elaboration of what would happen if the court chose Mahmud's first option of validating and legitimating the coup. The court would cease to be an arbiter of conflict in the polity, entering it fully by aligning itself with the junta and bolstering its power. In other words, the judges would contribute to the jurisprudence of impunity, as all their predecessors did.

The courts chose not to heed this warning and aligned themselves with the NCPO and against the principles of rights and justice outlined by Resistant Citizen. Only one week after Resistant Citizen submitted its complaint, the Court of First Instance dismissed the case for the reason that Articles 47 and 48 of the 2014 Interim Constitution provided immunity for the NCPO. Resistant Citizen appealed on the basis of the measures being illegal and in conflict with democratic principles. They also appealed on a procedural point: by dismissing the case on the basis of the amnesty provisions rather than holding a preliminary hearing, the Court of First Instance violated criminal procedure and denied the plaintiffs' legal right to use the courts to seek redress.[68] The Appeal Court threw out the case, again citing the amnesty provision.[69] Despite the two consecutive lower court dismissals, Resistant Citizen appealed further to the Supreme Court, on the basis that the case was socially significant and should therefore be examined by the highest court, which had never ruled on a direct challenge to a junta.[70]

Resistant Citizen's petition to the Supreme Court takes on the shape of an everyday utopia by adhering to the formal structures of legal argumentation and procedure, yet calling for an outcome that diverges sharply from the existing rule of coups. By showing that the existing rule of coups is not the only option, the members of Resistant Citizen "defamiliarize the world they know and inhabit; in the process they enable taken-for-granted aspects to be questioned and rethought."[71] The core of the petition was an explanation of the crisis faced by the country and the potential role of the Supreme Court in its resolution:

> Amidst the situation in the country in which the junta is destroying the rule of law, expansively violating the rights of the people who are the owners of the country, like a fire that is spreading through a field until it causes hardship and conflict for every blade of grass, only the power of the Supreme Court, as an organ that exercises the sovereignty of the people, can help to support justice and check the exercise of power and counter-balance the power of the junta. If the mechanism of the judicial process proceeds with justice and can bring perpetrators to be punished, society will realize that the judicial process and the judiciary remain pillars that can facilitate true justice for every side without bias.[72]

In short, the coup—an illegal seizure of the governing power of the country by force—was a crime. If the perpetrators were not held to account, the coup would be another pedagogical example encouraging future coupmakers.[73]

The Supreme Court upheld the ruling of the two lower courts.[74] Yet it did so in a way that hinted at Mahmud's fourth option: distancing itself from the very question of the coup. The Supreme Court framed its ruling by defining the meaning of a state:

> To fulfill the conditions of being a state, a given state must be comprised of a clearly demarcated territory, a population must reside in this territory, a government must rule this population, and the state must be sovereign. An important point of legal interpretation is that law must be interpreted in such a way that it can be enforced. Even though it may as well be as the fifteen plaintiffs have claimed that the 2014 Interim Constitution is an il-legitimate form of law, the interpretation of law must lead to enforcement according to what is written in the service of the maintenance of the state or country. Otherwise, the status of being a state or country will be dam-

aged and its sovereignty will not be intact. The facts indicate that on 22 May 2014, the NCPO seized the administrative power of the country in its entirety from the caretaker government. The NCPO declared that the 2007 Constitution, the cabinet and the senate were void. At that time, Thailand was without any unit that performed legislative duties.[75]

The Court's hands were tied because the law as written indicated that the NCPO was the state, and the law protects the state. If the law were not adhered to, the sovereignty of the state would not be intact. The Court was clear that it was acting in the service of the enforcement of the law as written.

Yet the Court was aware that the law might have an unjust basis. It continued: "The NCPO instead entered to exercise the authority of the sovereign, even though, as the fifteen plaintiffs have claimed, that authority was secured in a manner not in accordance with democracy. Whether or not that power was legitimately obtained is another issue to be discussed elsewhere. But the NCPO still retains power in the sense that it is a group of individuals that exercises the administrative and legislative power by controlling the mechanisms and agencies of the state." The message bears repeating for emphasis. At the very moment that the court affirmed amnesty for the 22 May 2014 coup, it noted, "Whether or not that power was legitimately obtained is another issue to be discussed elsewhere." The details of this discussion, including who would take part in it and when it would be held, were left unspecified. With one sentence, the Supreme Court signaled a question about the legitimacy of the coup and yet distanced itself from it. The decision left the door open for further debate, both by and beyond the court.

One interpretation is that the Supreme Court ruling was a victory for the NCPO: the legality of its actions, and so the evasion of accountability, was ruled to be correct. Arnon Nampha, Resistant Citizen's lawyer as well as one of the plaintiffs, explained that, regardless of the court's decision, the case was "the creation of a historical record of what comprises the various steps of the people's struggle, and the leaving of a scar upon the judicial process that once, in 2014, the Thai people accepted principles" of democracy and justice.[76] The text of the Resistant Citizen indictment, and the group's daring to file it during a military dictatorship, is significant both as part of the history of the people's action it cites and as part of laying the legal and jurisprudential groundwork for an eventual indictment in the future. By bringing a case against the NCPO, Resistant Citizen accounted for and challenged how the rule of coups has shaped both the law and history. Rather than treating the rule of coups as unchanging, Resistant Citizen wrote itself into history as opposition to the status quo and imagined a different future.

THE POSSIBILITY OF THE PEOPLE

The long-term impact of not questioning coups—as a form of rule, as a crime—is that "once the gun rings out, the law becomes silent."[77] The series of court decisions traced in the introduction and this chapter, culminating in the Supreme Court's dismissal of Resistant Citizen's case against the NCPO, illustrates the depth of this silence. This history makes it seem as though the law cannot speak in the face of a gun.[78] And yet to transform the existing jurisprudence of impunity, which protects coupmakers from being held responsible for their crimes and even the compilation of a full accounting of their crimes, into a jurisprudence of accountability, which would hold dictators to account and treat the people as equal participants in the polity, the law *must* speak.

Resistant Citizen assumed from the very beginning of its case against the NCPO that the law could, and would, speak for the people. This assertion, at once necessary and utopian, informs the jurisprudence of accountability crafted in the new decision offered by the Court for the People. Such a jurisprudence must see, recognize, and honor the role of the people in the polity to interrupt and counter the rule of coups. To treat the people as equal members of the polity means that they can be injured by coups, in contrast to the denial of injury, or at least status of injured party, in the earlier cases of the three MPs and Chalad Worachak. Once the people can be injured by the coup, it becomes possible, and necessary, to challenge the privilege afforded to the state. The creation of order is no longer automatically privileged over the maintenance of law, and how a government comes to power becomes as important as the exercise of that power. The conditions are created for the principles of law to speak in the face of the violence of the gun. In practical terms, the law talks back through pairing the will to prosecute juntas with the recognition that the people can be injured by coups. This forms the method by which a jurisprudence of accountability can be crafted and the people become the owners of sovereignty.

THE COURT FOR THE PEOPLE

**Pansak Srithep, Plaintiff No. 1 and fourteen
co-plaintiffs (Plaintiffs Nos. 2–15)**
versus
**General Prayuth Chan-ocha, Defendant No. 1 and
four co-defendants (Defendants Nos. 2–5)**
**Charge: Violation of Article 113 (rebellion) and
Article 114 (treason) of the Criminal Code**

Pansak Srithep and the fourteen co-plaintiffs charged that when General Prayuth Chan-ocha and the four co-defendants, known as the National Council for Peace and Order, or NCPO, abrogated the 2007 Constitution and carried out a coup to take over the governing power of the country on 22 May 2014, this was a rebellion. The rebellion began when General Prayuth proclaimed martial law on 20 May 2014 and remains ongoing due to permanent changes to the executive and legislative branches made by the 2017 Constitution and the lingering cultural, social, and political effects wrought by the coup. The plaintiffs charged that they were individually injured and that all Thai people were collectively injured by the actions of the defendants. The plaintiffs asked the court to find the defendants guilty of violation of Articles 113 and 114 of the Criminal Code.

The Court of First Instance, Appeal Court, and Supreme Court all dismissed the case without holding a preliminary examination. They ruled that the case had no grounds due to Articles 47 and 48 of the 2014 Interim Constitution providing amnesty and legalizing all of the actions of the defendants.

The Court for the People is to rule on whether or not the case has grounds and should therefore be returned to the Court of First Instance for preliminary examination. The Court for the People is aware that this is the first case in which a criminal complaint brought by citizens against a junta reached the Supreme Court, which noted with regard to the state power exercised by the NCPO that, "that authority was secured in a manner not in accordance with democracy. Whether or not that power was legitimately obtained is another issue to be discussed elsewhere." The Court for the People begins with appreciation for the Supreme Court's assessment that the NCPO did not come to power democratically, but disagrees that the discussion of the legitimacy of the power should be discussed elsewhere. By dismissing the plaintiff's case against the defendants on the basis of the amnesty provisions in the 2014 Interim Constitution, the Supreme Court treated the NCPO's power to govern and the laws it promulgated as legitimate. This question is at the heart of this case and cannot be deferred.

The first matter taken up by the Court for the People is whether or not the fifteen plaintiffs, as citizens of a range of ages and in a variety of professions, constitute those injured by the coup carried out by the NCPO. The Criminal Procedure Code's definition of injured party is vague; Section 2(4) stipulates that "'Injured Person' means a person who has received injury through the commission of any offence." Previous court decisions have diverged on whether or not citizens may be injured parties. In the case brought by Uthai Pimchaichon, Anan Phakpraphai, and Boonkerd Hirankham, the three MPs, against Field Marshal Thanom and other members of the Revolutionary Council that carried out the 1971 coup, the three MPs asserted that they were injured parties because of the loss of their position. But the Court of First Instance ruled that they could not be treated as such under the law because it would allow other citizens to be treated as injured parties. This would lead to disorder rather than the order that the coup aimed to create. Therefore, the case brought by the three MPs was dismissed. The Court for the People finds this to be a concerning and contradictory outcome. A plaintiff either is or is not an injured party entitled to bring a case. The decision to privilege order over the protection of the right to bring a legal case against those who caused injury is incorrect.

In the complaint submitted in this case, the fifteen plaintiffs explicitly described the injuries that they sustained as a result of the actions of the NCPO. In sum, the plaintiffs were unable to live their lives normally, be physically safe, or make a living as usual following the coup. All the plaintiffs had their liberty, freedom, and rights constrained and violated. These injuries correspond to the violation of a range of rights that Thailand is obligated to protect under the 2007, 2014 Interim, or 2017 Constitutions, and the International Covenant on Civil and Political Rights (ICCPR) and the International Covenant on Economic, Social and

Cultural Rights (IESCR), to which Thailand is a state party and which remain valid even when there is no constitution in force.

Six of the plaintiffs—Pansak Srithep (Plaintiff No. 1), Wannakiat Chusuwan (Plaintiff No. 2), Siriwith Seritiwat (Plaintiff No. 3), Siraphop Kornarut (Plaintiff No. 7), Sansern Sri-unruan (Plaintiff No. 8), and Arnon Nampha (Plaintiff No. 15)—were all prosecuted in the Bangkok Military Court as a result of their peaceful protest of the NCPO. Prosecution in the military court system led them to be deprived of their right to access justice, face limitations on appeal, and experience additional derogations of rights that followed from being civilians processed in the military court system. Three plaintiffs—Nattaphat Akkhad (Plaintiff No. 6), Siraphop Kornarut (Plaintiff No. 7), and Sansern Sri-unruan (Plaintiff No. 8)—were arbitrarily detained under the provisions of martial law, which permitted detention of up to seven days in a nonstandard place of detention and without presentation of evidence. One of these plaintiffs, Sansern Sri-unruan, was tortured by electric shock while he was in custody. Two plaintiffs were unable to perform their occupation and work as usual. Sriprai Nonsee (Plaintiff No. 4), a labor leader, could not organize protests and aid her colleagues in calling for justice due to the NCPO's prohibitions on protest. Baramee Chairat (Plaintiff No. 5) worked for a nongovernmental organization advising villagers on natural resource management. The NCPO's restrictions on meetings and surveillance made it impossible for him to meet with villagers or organize the demonstrations when needed. The five university students who were plaintiffs—Chonticha Jangrew (Plaintiff No. 9), Natcha Kong-udom (Plaintiff No. 10), Apiwat Suthararak (Plaintiff No. 11), Phayu Bunsophon (Plaintiff No. 12), Jatupat Boonpattararaksa (Plaintiff No. 13), and Krit Saengsurin (Plaintiff No. 14)—faced harassment and intimidation for expressing their views and protesting the coup both on and off campus. The Court for the People is also aware that the impact from the coup experienced and described by the fifteen plaintiffs does not comprise the entirety of those injured by the coup. This is only a small sample.

The Court for the People also wishes to note that in contrast to the ruling in the 1971 case brought by the three MPs that rather than causing disorder, when citizens injured by a coup bring a case against a junta, they are acting with courage to defend democracy. The role of the court is to meet this courage by examining and holding the coupmakers to account, if they have broken the law.

The second matter taken up by the Court for the People concerns the amnesty provisions cited by previous courts as the reason why the plaintiffs' complaint cannot move forward. Article 47 of the 2014 Interim Constitution stipulates:

> All announcements and orders of the National Council for Peace and Order or orders of the Head of the National Council for Peace and Order which had been announced or made between 22nd May 2014 and until the date the Council of Ministers takes office under this Constitution, irrespective of their constitutional, legislative, executive or judicial force, including the performance in compliance therewith, irrespective of whether those acts have been performed before or after the date of entry into force of this Constitution, shall be considered lawful, constitutional and final. Those announcements and orders applicable on the date before the promulgation date of this Constitution shall continue to be in force until there are laws, rules, regulations, resolutions of the Council of Ministers, or orders, as the case may be, issued to amend or repeal them. In the case where the National Council for Peace and Order issues an order appointing any person to assume office or removing from office of any position mentioned in Article 24 before the date this Constitution comes into force, the Prime Minister shall respectfully present to the King for appointing such person to assume office or removing such person from office.

Article 48 stipulates:

> In regard to all acts which are performed on account of the seizure and control of State governing power on 22 May 2014 by the Head and the National Council for Peace and Order, including all acts of persons incidental to such performance or of persons entrusted by the Head or the National Council for Peace and Order or of persons ordered by persons entrusted by the Head or the National Council for Peace and Order, which have been done for the benefit of the abovementioned performances, irrespective of whether such acts were performed to have constitutional, legislative, executive, or judicial force, including punishments and other official administrative acts, and irrespective of whether the persons performed such acts as a principal, an accomplice, an instigator or an agent and whether those acts have been done on, before or after the aforesaid date, if those acts constitute offences under the laws, the persons who commit those acts shall be entirely discharged from such offences and liabilities.

In all previous cases, amnesty measures have been treated as automatically releasing those who foment coups from even being considered to be possibly responsible for any violations of the law before, during, or after the seizure of power. In the case of the coup by the NCPO, one interpretation of Articles 47 and 48 is that the five defendants in this case are exempt in perpetuity for all of the planning prior to the coup, the actual coup on 22 May 2014, and all impacts and injuries caused, both immediate and delayed.

But two other provisions of the 2014 Interim Constitution raise questions about the potential limits to the applications of Articles 47 and 48. Article 3 stipulates: "Sovereign power belongs to the Thai people. The King as Head of State shall exercise such power through the National Legislative Assembly, the Council of Ministers and the Courts in accordance with the provisions of this Constitution." Article 4 stipulates: "Subject to the provisions of this Constitution, human dignity, rights, liberties and equality previously enjoyed by the Thai people with the protection under Thailand's constitutional convention of the democratic regime of government with the King as Head of State and Thailand's existing international obligations shall be protected under this Constitution." At a minimum, these two articles raise doubts for the Court for the People about the blanket coverage of Articles 47 and 48. Why should these two articles providing amnesty to the junta be automatically privileged over the two articles protecting the people's sovereignty and their human dignity, rights, liberties, and equality? In particular, Article 3 prescribes that the courts are one of the institutions through which the people's sovereignty should be exercised. The court must therefore speak up for the people. The view of the Court for the People is that the tension between these two sets of provisions with respect to this case can be resolved only through a full examination of the plaintiff's complaint, including submission of additional evidence and witness testimony by both the plaintiffs and the defendants.

The third matter the Court for the People takes up is the legal status of a coup. A coup is the forcible toppling of the existing government and the seizure of governing power by a junta. A coup, therefore, is within the scope of the actions defined as a crime in Article 113 of the Criminal Code, which stipulates: "Whoever commits an act of violence or threatens to commit an act of violence in order to: (1) Overthrow or change the Constitution; (2) Overthrow the legislative power, the executive power or the judicial power of the Constitution, or nullify such power; or (3) Separate the Kingdom or seize the power of administration in any part of the Kingdom, is said to commit insurrection, and shall be punished with death or imprisonment for life." The NCPO committed all three of these actions by its own admission. The gravity of these actions, and the NCPO's awareness of their status as crimes, was reflected in the inclusion of Articles 47 and 48 in the 2014 Interim Constitution.

The Supreme Court asserted that

> to fulfill the conditions of being a state, a given state must be comprised of a clearly demarcated territory, a population must reside in this territory, a government must rule this population, and the state must be sovereign. An important point of legal interpretation is that law must be interpreted in such a way that it can be enforced. Even though it may as well be as the fifteen plaintiffs have claimed that the 2014 Interim Constitution is an illegitimate form of law, the interpretation of law must lead to enforcement according to what is written in the service of the maintenance of the state or country. Otherwise, the status of being a state or country will be damaged and its sovereignty will not be intact. The facts indicate that on 22 May 2014, the NCPO seized the administrative power of the country in its entirety from the caretaker government. The NCPO declared that the 2007 Constitution, the cabinet and the senate were void.

If the 2014 Interim Constitution is illegitimate because the organ that promulgated it came to power through illegal means, does the enforcement of this illegal law contribute to the maintenance of the country and the preservation of sovereignty? Or does it damage both? This question is at the heart of the complaint brought by Pansak Srithep and his fourteen co-plaintiffs against Prayuth Chan-ocha and his four co-defendants. This question is also primary in the dilemma of what kind of polity Thailand wants to be and what the role of the people, the owners of sovereignty, is going to be in this polity.

The Court for the People rules to remand this case to the Court of First Instance for a preliminary hearing to determine whether or not the plaintiffs' complaint has grounds.

TWO

COUPS AND COUPOCRACY

On the afternoon of Friday, 23 May 2014, Apichat Pongsawat finished work at the Law Reform Commission (LRC) and went to protest the coup that had taken place the day before. Before leaving work, he printed out an A4 sheet of paper with the message [I] Do Not Accept Illegitimate Power.[1] He and a work colleague rode a van to the closest Skytrain station and then took the train to a demonstration in front of the Bangkok Art and Culture Center (BACC). When they arrived at around five o'clock, armed soldiers and military vehicles already filled the area. Apichat held up his sign as one of the hundreds of protestors facing off with the soldiers. Upon seeing his message, the soldiers surrounded Apichat and dragged him to a waiting Humvee. The first protest against the coup lasted only a little over an hour. That night was the first of thirty-two nights that Apichat spent in state custody before being released with a raft of charges against him.

For the following five and a half years, he fought the case against him all the way to the Supreme Court. On 8 November 2019, the final decision was read in the Pathumwan District Court: Apichat Pongsawat was found guilty of violating Head of the NCPO Order No. 3/2558, a junta order that criminalized the unauthorized assembly of five or more persons, and fined six thousand baht. Apichat was the first to be arrested and prosecuted for peaceful dissent against the National Council for Peace and Order (NCPO), and his case was the first and only one to reach the Supreme Court. How and why Apichat came out to protest the coup bears witness to the strength of one citizen's commitment to upholding the constitution, and the series of court decisions reflects how little the judiciary was willing to do to protect either the constitution or the rights of a citizen willing to sacrifice his freedom to safeguard it.

At the time of his protest and arrest, Apichat was a twenty-five-year-old law school graduate from the southern province of Nakhon Si Thammarat who was combining work at the LRC with postgraduate study at Thammasat University, the historical center of student protest.[2] The LRC was an independent organization envisioned in the 2007 Constitution and established in 2010 to offer advice to various branches of government on developing the law in support of the ideals outlined in the constitution, with a particular aim to promote people's participation in governance. On 20 May 2014, General Prayuth Chan-ocha, then commander in chief of the Royal Thai Army, announced martial law and summoned the heads of various government agencies, including the LRC, to a meeting at the Army Club. Apichat attended as an assistant to the LRC representative and recalled that everyone had to surrender their cell phone to the soldiers for the duration of the meeting.[3] General Prayuth was the only one who spoke, and no questions were permitted. Many senior officials present were confident that the combination of the meeting and the announcement of martial law foretold a coup.

Two days later, the expected coup took place, and the NCPO, with General Prayuth at its helm, proclaimed itself the government. The junta abrogated the 2007 Constitution and summarily issued the first 20 of 557 announcements and orders with the immediate status of law that would shape public life for the following five years. The seventh of these, NCPO Announcement No. 7/2557, criminalized "unlawful or political assembly, in any location, of five or more persons" and set the punishment for doing so as imprisonment of up to one year and/or a fine of up to twenty thousand baht.[4] Despite this prohibition, a group of activists called for a candlelight vigil at the BACC on the first night after the coup.[5] A similar order had accompanied the previous coup, but arrests were rare. There was no reason to think this time would be any different.[6]

Noppon Archamas, a legal scholar based at Thai Lawyers for Human Rights (TLHR), traced the genealogy of NCPO Announcement No. 7/2557 and found that it was the eighth time that a junta had issued an order banning protest after a coup.[7] Yet after the two most recent coups, 23 February 1991 and 19 September 2006, the orders were in place for only a short period of time.[8] But the prohibition on protest after the 22 May 2014 coup—first under NCPO Announcement No. 7/2557 and then under Head of the NCPO Order No. 3/2558 after the revocation of martial law on 1 April 2015—remained in force until 11 December 2018.[9] In other terms, this prohibition on political assembly—which was interpreted by the authorities under the NCPO to include street demonstrations, academic seminars, press conferences, and more—was in force for a total of four years, six months, and nineteen days.[10] At least 428 people were charged with violation of one of these orders, including 55 who were arrested across the country during the first month after the coup.[11]

Apichat's arrest signaled a break with the past and the genesis of a new kind of dictatorship in Thailand. As the soldiers led him away, he held up his sign, now torn, and yelled: "It is not possible to express one's opinion in this country. We have a democracy here. Here, I'll go [with you]. Do you see [this]? All I did was express my opinion and the soldiers arrested me."[12] Journalists asked for his name and phone number, and echoing the message on the paper that prompted his arrest, he yelled out in response: "My name is Apichat Pongsawat. I am a citizen who does not accept the illegitimate authority of the junta."[13] The soldiers did not inform him of either the crime of which he was accused or his rights.[14] Thanapol Eawsakul, a progressive publisher and one of the organizers of the protest, worried about what was going to happen to Apichat and asked the soldiers if he could come with them as a witness.[15] Within a day, Thanapol's own status changed to detainee.

The May night was sweltering, and the Humvee the two were shoved into was airless. In a recollection of that night written on the first anniversary of the coup, Thanapol asked the soldiers sitting in the vehicle with them, "Can you please crack the windows a little? I cannot breathe." None of the soldiers responded, and they opened the windows only after Thanapol attracted the attention of a superior who walked by. When the Humvee began to move, the soldiers did not tell Apichat and Thanapol where they were being taken. They arrived at the base of the Second Cavalry Division King's Guard in Bangkok and were soon joined by two others arrested during the protest.[16] The grumblings of a captain urgently called in and forced to forgo a planned weekend golfing outing in Kanchanaburi to deal with them illustrated how unexpected their presence, and the protests, were for the new regime.[17]

The four were then separated and interrogated. Thanapol recalled that as midnight approached, they were led into "a room with a barred door like in a prison. We were taken into the area where they held soldiers in detention. But perhaps you could say we got lucky. On the left was a cell with bars and a soldier being punished lay shackled on the cement floor. The four of us were fortunate to be taken into a much larger room on the right. The room was air-conditioned and had bedding. I suspect that this room was not a cell for prisoners, but it was behind the same door. Or, in other words, we were in an air-conditioned prison."[18] The next morning, he wrote: "The officer in charge bought chicken rice, soymilk, and crullers and gave them to us. He said that they were from the most delicious vendors in the neighborhood and that he had bought them himself. He said that he had to pay for it because no prior thought had been given to our detention."[19] In pointing to his own generosity, the soldier revealed how confident the NCPO was of its success. The junta presumed that simply issuing an order prohibiting protest would be enough to secure assent from the people.

After the four finished eating, the family of one of the protestors came to pick him up. The soldiers returned the mobile phones of the three who remained and told them to call their families to pick them up at the Crime

Suppression Division (CSD), the central criminal investigation bureau of the Thai police. But the soldiers' instructions were premature. The previous evening, Thanapol's name had been one of those included in a list of politicians, activists, journalists, writers, and academics who were to report themselves to the Army Club. The announcements were broadcast on television, with the names scrolling down the screen. Martial law permitted seven days of detention without charge, and no information was provided about what would happen to one after reporting. After arriving at the CSD, Thanapol was taken to the Army Club and then transferred to an army base in Ratchaburi, where he was held until 30 May 2014.[20] Apichat and the other protestor were both held at the CSD for six nights. On 30 May 2014, the other protestor was granted bail, with a pending charge of violation of NCPO Announcement No. 7/2557. Apichat was instead accused of violation of NCPO Announcement No. 7/2557 and five additional laws: Article 215 (unlawful assembly), Article 216 (refusing to cease unlawful assembly after being ordered to do so), Article 368 (refusing to follow an order by a state official), and Article 112 (lèse-majesté) of the Criminal Code, and the Computer Crimes Act. The two latter accusations, which stemmed from a Facebook post about an academic seminar critical of Article 112 itself, signaled the wave of Article 112 and Computer Crimes Act accusations soon to come under the NCPO. Apichat was sent for continued detention at the Bangkok Remand Prison. While in custody, he was not physically harmed but was verbally abused.[21] Bail is very rarely granted in Article 112 cases, but after two more appeals, Apichat was released on 24 June 2014.[22]

His release was the beginning, not the end, of his struggle. After being released, he had to report himself to the prosecutor every month.[23] He was finally formally indicted on 24 April 2015 with having violated all four charges related to the protest.[24] On 19 May 2015, almost a year after the coup, Apichat filed a plea of not guilty to the charges against him. The two other protestors who were arrested with Apichat chose to confess to the crime shortly after being accused at the end of May 2014. They were sentenced to suspended prison terms of one month and a fine of three thousand baht.[25] Apichat chose to fight the case against him even though it was inconvenient and time-consuming, with court hearings spread out over many months.[26] He did so with the knowledge that the choice to fight could itself garner a harsher punishment for the same crime.[27] Apichat explained: "The entirety of this is the path of struggle I have chosen. Just as I chose to come out to oppose the coup, I choose not to turn away from entering the judicial process. This is a challenge to [our] lives and the principles of law, and to the true democratic ideal to which we should aim. I think it is what one should do for our society."[28] Confession offered an ease that Apichat could not bear.

Accompanying his commitment to democracy was a belief that the judiciary would act and judge in line with the rule of law. Apichat defined what this meant for him by distinguishing between the junta and the court:

> If the judicial process used to determine my innocence or guilt is one that uses a standard that is based in the rule of law, listens to every side, gives me the opportunity to fully fight the case without intervention by any kinds of power, and respects the rights of the people following the universal principles of democratic rule, I will accept the judgment no matter how it comes out. But I maintain that I will not accept any orders that come from the coup junta or any entity that uses force to seize the sovereignty of the people and then severely violates the rights of the people.[29]

NCPO Announcement No. 7/2557 was one such order: a measure treated as a law that was unilaterally and summarily drafted, promulgated, and enforced by the junta. As the case progressed, the distance between the junta and the court quickly collapsed. What unfolded over the following four years of judicial proceedings and decisions was that the court did not see a difference between the law and the orders of the NCPO and placed itself firmly on the side of defending the coup, not democracy.

Apichat's legal struggle was a continuation of the protest he began on 23 May 2014 when he joined with others in front of the BACC to oppose the coup. In maintaining the possibility of the court to act justly and in the service of the people, he worked to make it real by living as if it were so. Apichat's recognition of the political importance and potential of his fight was a direct challenge to the court's defense of the junta. This stance, which can be understood as a defense of and for the people, accompanied by his insistence that to protest the coup was a duty, not a crime, recalls the potential of an everyday utopia which "anticipate[s] something more, something beyond, and other to what they can currently realize."[30] A different judiciary—and a different relationship between the rulers and the ruled—was imagined and envisioned through the labor of his struggle. The new Court for the People takes Apichat's struggle as inspirational and outlines the just outcome impossible when he fought his case.

A STRUGGLE OVER THE LAW

Another signal of the NCPO's break with more recent coup regimes was to place all civilian cases of violation of NCPO orders and announcements and crimes against the crown and state within the jurisdiction of the military court system beginning on 25 May 2014.[31] The was the first time that civilian cases were processed in the military court system since the 6 October 1976 massacre and coup.[32] This led to a range of rights violations, which I take up elsewhere in this book. But because Apichat committed his crime of protest on 23 May 2014, he was tried in the civilian court system, and his case was assigned to the Southern Bangkok Criminal Court. A total of six decisions were made in his case: two Court of First Instance decisions, two Appeal Court decisions, and two Supreme Court decisions. On the surface, the decisions are about whether Apichat protested the coup by the NCPO and, in so doing, violated the law. But the judges ruled on far more than Apichat's individual innocence or guilt. They advanced ideas about the sovereignty of the NCPO and the role of coups in the Thai polity. Across the six decisions, only three of which were substantive, the court privileged the NCPO. The near erasure of Apichat individually and the people generally, which left no space for the defense of the constitution or the principles of human rights contained within it, formed the foundation for the jurisprudence of impunity. This near erasure went beyond the abrogation of the people's human rights to render their actions in defense of democracy as inconsequential and criminal.

Before commencement of witness hearings, the defense requested that the Constitutional Court examine whether NCPO Announcement No. 7/2557 contravened Article 4 of the 2014 Interim Constitution. This article stipulated that, "subject to the provisions of this Constitution, all human dignity, rights, liberties and equality of the people protected by the constitutional convention under a democratic regime of government with the King as the Head of State, and by international obligations bound by Thailand, shall be protected and upheld by this Constitution." Even though Article 47 of the same constitution gave all orders and announcements of the NCPO the status of law immediately upon promulgation, the defense argued that the protection of rights and freedom form the core of the rule of law, which the court was bound to safeguard.[33] But the court refused to forward the petition.

The jurisprudence of impunity began to be crafted during the witness hearings that began on 11 September 2015. From the first day, the presiding judge served as arbiter of politics as well as law. There were two witnesses for the prosecution and four for the defense. The first witness for the prosecution, Lieutenant Piraphan Sansern, was presented as an eyewitness who had led the arrest. He described the protest, the arrest of Apichat, and the genesis of the Article 112 charge. After the prosecutor concluded his questions, the judge asked the prosecutor and witness to leave the room and recommended that Apichat confess. The NCPO was the sovereign, NCPO Announcement No. 7/2557 carried the status of law, and the penalty was minimal.[34] But Apichat declined to take the judge's advice. To confess to a crime he did not commit would, he said, make him feel eternally guilty.[35]

Upon the hearing's resumption and in response to cross-examination by the defense, Lieutenant Piraphan offered a critical view on the coup by asserting that it was the toppling of a constitutional democracy with the king as head of state. But then he seemed to remember his role. When asked if the defendant had the constitutional right and duty to protect the constitution, he grew flustered and asked, "And where is the duty to oppose Article 112 specified?"[36]

The judge did not allow the next line of defense questioning to be recorded. The transcript of witness hearings in Thai courts is not a verbatim record but rather a record of questions and testimony as interpreted by the presiding judge and dictated to a court reporter. At the end of each day of hearings, the transcript is read out so that all parties have an opportunity to correct omissions and elisions. These transcripts acquire another layer of significance because the Appeal Court and the Supreme Court do not hold their own hearings but rely on the transcripts from the Court of First Instance to make their rulings. What is absent can shape the possible outcome as much as what is present.

The defense lawyer asked Lieutenant Piraphan when the coup became successful, but the judge asked the lawyer to limit questions to those pertinent for an eyewitness of the protest to answer. Existing jurisprudence about coups provides that a junta becomes sovereign once the coup is "successful," which is described as when the junta is able to control the machinery of the state and there is no opposition from the people. The judge's prohibition on answering this question underlined its significance to the case. If the coup was not successful at the time of the protest, then Apichat's protest was not illegal but his arrest and detention by the witness was. Further questions that the judge did not enter into the record concerned whether the announcement of martial law had to have the king's signature to be valid, and whether the protest was an exercise of the rights protected by Article 4 of the 2007 Constitution. Also asked was whether the International Covenant on Civil and Political Rights (ICCPR), to which Thailand is a state party, was relevant during the two months after the 2007 Constitution was abrogated on 22 May and before the 2014 Interim Constitution was promulgated on 22 July.[37] The judge declared these questions irrelevant, but they were central to deciding whether Apichat's protest was a crime or the soldiers' actions were obstruction of a citizen exercising his constitutionally protected right to oppose a coup. Under the 1914 Martial Law Act, the commander in chief of the Royal Thai Army has the authority to issue an order of martial law for a specific area under his command, but its application to the entire country requires a royal proclamation. There was no royal proclamation on 20 May 2014: the announcement was from the Royal Thai Army. The issuance of a royal proclamation to revoke martial law on 1 April 2015 confirmed the role of the king in the mechanism. But had the court allowed this line of questioning, the witness might have either impugned the monarchy, by stating that the signature was unnecessary, or cast the declaration of the martial law and the coup as illegal, by stating that it was necessary. If peaceful protest were protected by Article 4 of the 2007 Constitution, or if the ICCPR had been applicable, then Apichat's dissent would no longer be a crime. The unanswered questions revealed what was at stake in the case and the judge's keen awareness of his role in not allowing this to be made audible or entered into the record.

On redirect, the prosecutor asked Lieutenant Piraphan whether Apichat was acting to incite the people. His response was that Apichat spoke about "the right to demonstrate, illegitimacy and the seizure of power by the soldiers" while being arrested. The judge did not strike this from the record, even though it was not an answer to the question.[38] At the end of the first day of witness hearings, the defense submitted a petition to request a change of judge. The judge seemed to have capitulated to the power of the NCPO, which could impact the provision of justice in the case. The petition was overturned at the start of the second day of witness hearings.[39]

The second prosecution witness was Police Lieutenant Chalit Maneephrao, the inquiry official at the CSD. His testimony was largely unremarkable and focused on his processing of Apichat and video footage of the protest. During cross-examination by the defense, he was asked whether a coup was the toppling of a government in a democracy. The judge instructed him not to answer.[40] If Apichat—not General Prayuth or other members of the NCPO—was the one on trial, why was this question unanswerable? Absence again signaled significance.

Police Lieutenant Chalit's view was that Apichat's actions were the peaceful expression of opinion. On the video clip, he heard Apichat say, "They arrested me simply for a piece of paper," but he did not hear him give a speech to the demonstrators. He also did not hear any order given to disperse the protestors, in contrast to allegations by Lieutenant Piraphan during the police inquiry.[41] He further testified that there was no evidence of violence or instigation of state officials in the video clips of the protest, also in contrast to Lieutenant Piraphan's allegations during the police investigation.[42]

All that was certain by the conclusion of the testimony for the prosecution was that Apichat was present and carried a sign at the protest in front of the BACC on 23 May 2014. The meaning of these actions remained unclear. Whether or not his actions constituted a crime or the defense of democracy as required of citizens by the constitution depended on the meaning assigned to the coup itself, which was the very line of questioning shut down by the judge. The defense witnesses returned to the question of meaning by elaborating on the purpose and necessity of protest.

The first witness for the defense was Jaran Kosanan, a law professor at Ramkhamhaeng University and expert in human rights law. Jaran testified that martial law applicable to the entire country required both a royal proclamation and for this proclamation to be published in the *Ratchakitchanubeksa* (Royal Gazette), neither of which occurred for the 20 May 2014 declaration. In response to the question of when a coup was successful, he replied that beginning with Supreme Court Judgment No. 1153–1154/2495, a junta gained the status of being the sovereign state when the people assented to the coup, which was interpreted as when there was no opposition.[43] This time, the question that perturbed the judge and was not recorded related to protest: could citizens resist state power under the NCPO? Jaran responded that this was affirmed in Article 4 of the 2014 Interim Constitution.[44] He further noted that opposing the NCPO could be interpreted as protecting one's right to personal liberty and the right to an election. The judge classified this response as opinion and did not record it. What is fact and what is opinion? What the judge labeled as opinion or irrelevant to the case was testimony that would have exonerated Apichat Pongsawat of the crimes against him and also called into question the very legality of his arrest and prosecution.

On cross-examination by the prosecution, Jaran testified that the coup was not successful on the evening when Apichat protested, but it was by the time he gave testimony.[45] In other words, a coup is successful once one can be prosecuted for opposing it.

Apichat himself was the next witness. He testified about how and why he protested on 23 May 2014. He learned about the demonstration from Facebook and joined because he believed that the coup by General Prayuth was an illegitimate action and was not yet successful. When asked by the prosecutor if his protest was unlawful political assembly, he said no. His protest was peaceful. He held up a sign against the coup and did not invite people to join the protest.[46]

The third witness for the defense was Samchai Srisant, a lecturer in the Puey Ungphakorn School of Development Studies at Thammasat University, where Apichat was then a graduate student. He testified to Apichat's diligence and offered the view that Apichat's actions were not a crime because it is the people's duty to oppose coups.[47] The only question from the prosecution was whether NCPO Announcement No. 7/2557 had been issued before the protest.[48]

The final defense witness was Woralak Sriyai, Apichat's colleague at the LRC who also joined the protest against the coup on 23 May 2014. She testified that she and Apichat met in front of the lift at the LRC, traveled together to the BACC, and then separated upon arrival. She did not hear the police and soldiers call for the demonstration to end and left the protest before Apichat was arrested.[49] In her view, Apichat's actions were not criminal because there was no disorder. The protest did not constitute unlawful assembly because people came individually to the protest.[50] During cross-examination, the prosecutor asked if she went to protest in order to oppose the NCPO. She said no, she went to express her disagreement with the coup. Her answer illustrated the line between opposition to the state and opposition to illegal modes of state building, and she reinforced Samchai's assertion that it was the people's duty to oppose coups. Woralak and Apichat both worked for an organization established under the 2007 Constitution to encourage citizen participation in political and legal reform. How could they not protest the coup?

When Apichat was indicted, he wrote a statement about his decision to fight his case and highlighted the significance of action in defense of the law: "To struggle in law and knowledge is a method to assert and support the principle that the 'coup d'état' itself is illegal, illegitimate, and in conflict with the rule of law and the legitimacy of the law. The court does not have the authority to prosecute or exercise power following the orders of the junta."[51] The night before the first judgment was rendered, Apichat wrote a declaration and disseminated it via social media. He said the outcome of the decision would have "no effect at all on my mental state, ideals, or path of struggle, even if the result of the decision is the worst possible and the court accepts the authority of dictatorship and imprisons me. . . . I will appeal and fight the case to the end, under the original principle that I maintain that the coup is not in line with democratic means. And I, as a citizen, have the right and duty to come out to oppose (the coup) and protect sovereignty."[52] Apichat further called on the courts to demonstrate their independence and the integrity of the judicial process. He aimed to create a norm and noted:

> I have no hope that the court will easily rule in my victory. Because my defense is no small matter. It is a defense to topple the power of dictatorship and to destroy the legal principles that emanate from the barrel of a gun. I intend to have the defense in this case create a norm for society in the present and the future. If the court upholds justice sufficiently so that the common people like the court can understand it is not difficult. And if the court has moral courage, it will be able to build credibility and faith among the people.[53]

He was uninterested in material compensation for the disruption to his life and liberty, but he wanted the court to affirm that the people have a constitutionally guaranteed right to oppose coups.[54] After the series of witness hearings in which the judge repeatedly displayed his support of the coup as a mechanism of rule, Apichat's faith in the court to rule justly and to side with the people rather than the junta may seem impossible or naive. But

what if instead of viewing it as such, it is understood as part of the necessary work of creating such a just judicial process? The gulf between what he
envisioned and the actions of the court the following day and over the next
few years revealed the work needed to make the utopia he envisioned real.

The court was heavily monitored from the early morning on 11 February 2016, the day the first decision was read. Journalists, diplomats, and
all other observers were questioned and had to leave their phones and
other electronic devices outside the courtroom.[55] The Court of First Instance dismissed the case on procedural grounds, finding that the CSD
did not have jurisdiction to investigate the case.[56] In so doing, it avoided
ruling on Apichat's guilt or innocence, as well as the more fundamental
question of the place of the coup in the Thai polity. None of the parties to
the case viewed this as a victory. Apichat felt the court had failed society
by not ruling on the case.[57] May Poonsukcharoen, the lead defense lawyer,
commented, "It is a shame that the court did not have the opportunity to
set norms . . . on the matter of the exercise of power of the junta to promulgate laws and the exercise of the rights and freedoms in an abnormal
situation."[58] The Office of the Attorney General appealed and argued that
the dismissal on procedural grounds was incorrect. On 6 June 2016, the
Appeal Court ruled in agreement and sent the case back to the Court of
First Instance to rule again.[59] On 19 December 2016, the Court of First
Instance judged Apichat to be guilty of violation of Head of the NCPO
Order No. 3/2558, which replaced NCPO Announcement No. 7/2557 on 1
April 2015, and Article 215 (unlawful assembly) of the Criminal Code. He
was sentenced to a fine of six thousand baht and a two-month prison term,
which was suspended for one year.[60] This time, Apichat appealed, and the
Appeal Court ruled for a second time on 31 May 2018. The reading of the
decision was postponed three times, allegedly because of its complexity and
its interest to the public.[61]

The Appeal Court ruled that Apichat was guilty of violating Head
of the NCPO Order No. 3/2558 but not guilty of unlawful assembly; the
punishment was reduced to a fine only.[62] Both the defense and the prosecution submitted appeals to the Supreme Court. While awaiting the deci-

sion, Head of the NCPO Order No. 3/2558 was revoked in December 2018, ahead of elections planned for 2019.[63] The legalization of political assembly was necessary for political parties, including the junta's own party, Palang Pracharath, to campaign. In all other cases of violations of Head of the NCPO Order No. 3/2558, witness hearings were either ongoing or complete but awaiting judgment by the Court of First Instance. They were all dismissed.[64]

The defense submitted a petition to the Supreme Court to dismiss the case given the revocation of the order. The law under which Apichat was charged and prosecuted was no longer law. On 14 August 2019, Apichat, his lawyer, and two observers, including me, went to the Pathumwan District Court to hear the decision. But the Supreme Court decision, despite carrying a date of March 2019, made no mention of the order's revocation.[65] Apichat was once again found guilty of violating Head of the NCPO Order No. 3/2558. The judge reading the decision was herself perplexed. She put the decision back into the envelope in which it had been sent from the Supreme Court, paper clipped a short note to it, and announced that she would send it back to the Supreme Court to reconsider. She would not allow the defense to copy the decision and asked for there to be no media dissemination of the decision or its return. A new decision came less than three months later on 8 November 2019. The guilty verdict held. Although Head of the NCPO Order No. 3/2558 was no longer in force, it was law when the defendant violated it. The Supreme Court fined Apichat six thousand baht, a fine he had long since paid.[66]

If one considers only the penalty, the decision may seem to be a positive outcome for the defendant. When Apichat was released on bail in the early aftermath of the coup, he faced an Article 112 charge, which carries a penalty of imprisonment of up to fifteen years. The Article 112 charge fell away. Articles 215 and 216, for which he was indicted and prosecuted, carry a potential punishment of up to nine years behind bars. But an outcome that did not land him behind bars was not his goal. Apichat fought the case against him because he wanted the court to rule on whether a citizen could protest a coup to protect the constitution. But instead of setting a legal standard affirming the right to protest, the Supreme Court set a standard of it being a crime to protest. The six decisions across all three levels of the court reflected and contributed to the jurisprudence of impunity. The court left unquestioned the success—and legitimacy—of the coup. The court affirmed the sovereignty of the NCPO, and therefore the validity of the order which Apichat was charged under was also affirmed. The Appeal Court went the farthest in consolidating impunity by normalizing the coup through the creation of a new word: *coupocracy*. A coup was defined as the first action of a new kind of government rather than the interruption of a government. Protection of the rights and freedom of the people, whether under the constitution or international human rights provisions, was ruled irrelevant.

Looking more closely at the series of decisions, and in particular at the method by which the coup was legitimized and the words used to describe it, reveals the formation of the jurisprudence of impunity. The fine Apichat faced may seem a minor sanction, but the ideas about the coups, the state, and the people were anything but minor for the polity. The affirmation of the validity and legitimacy of the coup over and over again began with the words and phrases used to describe it. In the first Court of First Instance decision, the court notes that the fundamental admissible facts were that "on 22 May 2014, General Prayuth Chan-ocha announced the seizure of the governing power from the government, of which at that time Ms. Yingluck Shinawatra was the prime minister, after seizing the governing power."[67] The same phrasing was also repeated in the first Appeal Court decision.[68] The court unquestioningly legitimized the coup by using the phrase "seized power" rather than, for example, "toppled the elected government" to describe the coup. The second Court of First Instance decision went even further, explaining that once the seizure of power was accomplished, General Prayuth possessed governing power and so had the status of being sovereign. He therefore was able to summarily issue orders and announcements that became law.[69]

The second Appeal Court decision built on these decisions to describe a new regime type with the coup as its center and savior: the coupocracy.

The Appeal Court developed a logic for its emergence by painting a grave picture of the "facts of the situation of Thailand" prior to the coup as one characterized by unprecedented crisis.[70] The court described this period as one well known as constituted by political conflict in which "the people were divided into various sides without unity and having an attitude of unfriendliness to one another." Violence had erupted and the well-being and lives of the people were in decline. The functioning of the legislative and judicial branches of power were affected, as was the economy. The Appeal Court explained: "The enforcement of law was without effect. . . . Even though the government solved problems with mechanisms and standards of law . . . it was not successful and created new political and legal conflicts. There was a continuous, unending loop of problems. The National Council for Peace and Order therefore had to seize and control the governing power of the country on 22 May 2014."[71] The Appeal Court created a narrative in which the coup was the only option and the NCPO was the hero in a dangerous time. The Appeal Court notes that, although the NCPO's methods were not in line with the constitution in force at the time, as the defendant had appealed, the coup generated positive change. As soon as the NCPO issued its first announcement, "the situation of Thailand at that time improved and became peaceful and orderly. There was no opposition or disobedience from the majority of the people in the country."[72] This statement did not acknowledge the significant military and legal apparatus behind the NCPO. Given that heavily armed soldiers immediately arrested those who protested, such as Apichat, and summoned a range of dissidents, including former political prisoners, former MPs, and many cultural activists like Thanapol, how could there be opposition from the majority of the population? The Appeal Court judges summarized how this new regime type came into existence and operated: "The use of force to seize power and change the government according to the meaning of a coupocracy has succeeded. The NCPO has the authority to issue any announcements and orders that are held to be law according to the coupocracy to use to administer the country."[73] Simply put, law comes from the barrel of a gun within a coupocracy.

Worachet Pakeerut, a progressive legal scholar at Thammasat University and one of those summoned to report by the NCPO during the first weeks after the coup, queried the precise meaning and function of the word coupocracy.[74] In an interview given after the Appeal Court decision came out, he commented that the word remains ambiguous, and the Appeal Court did not provide clarity at any point. Although the word was new, the legitimation of coups by the courts developed over time and has an entrenched legal genealogy.[75] Most significant, coupocracy is primarily a political rather than legal term, whose purpose is to make the abnormal appear normal: "When a regime like this operates, the junta has many ways to exercise power. From a political perspective, I hold it to be a fascinating thing to have been created. [They] were able to create and insert a legal mechanism inside the normal system and attempted to use it to give the appearance of normality. Put simply, it is the attempt to make the abnormal normal, and to make the majority of people feel that it is normal. If we talk about the coupocracy, then it is the further construction of another layer of normality, even though it is abnormal."[76] The Appeal Court's matter-of-fact coining of the word *coupocracy* and presentation of a narrative in which a coup is both inevitable and desirable is reminiscent of the Orwellian equation $2 + 2 = 5$. Apichat's opposition to the coup—in front of the BACC on 23 May 2014 and in the courtroom over the subsequent years—was dangerous to the state because it exposed the fiction of the coup as inevitable, desirable, or even legal. $2 + 2 = 4$.

There is no place for rights within a coupocracy. The Court of First Instance left the ICCPR unaddressed in its decision, but the Appeal Court ruled that neither the protection of the right to expression offered by the ICCPR nor the 2007 Constitution was relevant. The 2007 Constitution had been abrogated by the time of the protest, and so Apichat could not cite his right and duty to protect it as an excuse for criminal activity. Articles 19 and 21 of the ICCPR provide for rights protection to be derogated for reasons of national security and other crises.[77] Citing the description of the political, social, and cultural crisis during the period before the coup with which they began the decision, the Appeal Court judges explained that the limitation of rights was necessary "for the situation of the country to swiftly return to normalcy."[78] The Appeal Court made its decision halfway through the regime of the NCPO, and therefore the normalcy it recognized and called for was dictatorship. This was not a return to a prior state but the creation of a new one.

The Supreme Court left the outcome unchanged from the Appeal Court's decision. The defense's petition to the Supreme Court argued that NCPO Announcement No. 7/2557 was not law, as the junta had come to power unconstitutionally without the consent of the people. Further, martial law was not countersigned by the king, nor was the announcement printed in the *Ratchakitchanubeksa* until 26 May 2014, three days after the protest and Apichat's arrest. The Supreme Court refused to rule on these questions on the basis that they were questions of fact and that, in cases with punishments as minimal as Apichat's, the Court can rule only on matters of law.[79] What constitutes fact and what constitutes law? What the Supreme Court labeled as fact were precisely those matters that might lead to questions about the legality and legitimacy of the coup. The ability of the Supreme Court to sidestep these questions given the relatively minimal punishment meted out to Apichat belies the maximal punishments risked by those who launched the coup. Although not named as defendants in this case, General Prayuth and the other members of the NCPO were on trial in this and every other political case prosecuted during their regime.

The word *coupocracy* is not present in the Supreme Court decision, but the decision does leave unquestioned the normalcy of the coup. The Supreme Court acknowledged that the law under which Apichat had been prosecuted and convicted was no longer in force but dismissed that fact as irrelevant. Coupocracy creates a time in which laws favoring the coup are privileged over those which protect citizen's rights, such as Article 2 of the Criminal Code, which stipulates that a person cannot be punished under a law that has ceased to exist. The Supreme Court described the period leading up to the March 2019 elections and the political role of the people as follows: "This was held to be a transitional period that was important for the future of the country and therefore there should be participation from the people freely and independently selecting the political parties to govern the country. The political parties should be able to campaign for votes and present policies to the people that they will use in governing the country. This is a way of governing in a democracy according to the spirit of the constitution."[80] In such a time, it was appropriate for the people to gather and engage in political assembly. But the conditions were different when Apichat protested in the immediate aftermath of the coup, and political assembly was inappropriate. One of the primary goals of the coup, backed up by guns and laws, was to stop people from participating in politics.

Apichat's case reached its completion five and a half years after the night he spent in a military base with three others who were arrested for daring to protest the coup. He fought his case with the goal of the court ruling to create a norm that it was legal to protest the coup. Instead, the court set a norm that protesting a coup is always illegal, even on the very first day after a coup, when it is not clear that the coup has succeeded, and even years later when the law criminalizing protest has been revoked. Neither domestic nor international law can protect a citizen who dares to protest.

In contrast to this jurisprudence of impunity, a jurisprudence of accountability would recognize that the criminals in this case were General Prayuth, the other members of the junta, and all those, including Lieutenant Piraphan, who arrested Apichat, not Apichat. The role of the court is to examine the coup and protect the rights of the people, not to foreclose questions about the coup and legitimize the illegal toppling of a democratic government, however imperfect. A jurisprudence of accountability would refuse the success of a coup and reject the creation and normality of a coupocracy. The Court for the People begins to craft such a jurisprudence by telling a different story about the coup.

THE COURT FOR THE PEOPLE

The Office of the Attorney General, Plaintiff
versus
Apichat Pongsawat, Defendant
Charge: Violation of Head of the NCPO Order No. 3/2558
**   (prohibition of assembly of five or more persons)**

The facts that are admissible are that on 20 May 2014, General Prayuth Chan-ocha, then commander in chief of the Royal Thai Army, issued an army order declaring martial law immediately applicable throughout the country. Two days later, on 22 May 2014, led by General Prayuth Chan-ocha, a junta, the National Council for Peace and Order (NCPO), launched a coup against the democratically elected government of Prime Minister Yingluck Shinawatra. The NCPO immediately abrogated the 2007 Constitution and issued a series of announcements and orders to supplement martial law, including NCPO Announcement No. 7/2557, making it a crime for five or more persons to publicly assemble. One day later, Apichat Pongsawat, then a graduate student at Thammasat University and a civil servant at the Law Reform Commission (LRC), left work and traveled to a protest in the area of the Bangkok Art and Culture Center (BACC) with a colleague. They joined approximately five hundred citizens who were also protesting the coup. Apichat peacefully carried an A4 sheet of paper with the text [I] Do Not Accept Illegitimate Power printed on it. Soldiers in the area quickly took Apichat into custody as soon as they saw his sign. They tore his paper and forcibly took him to a Humvee vehicle. He was confined in the car, along with Thanapol Eawsakul, another citizen at the protest, who was concerned about the defendant's safety and asked the soldiers for permission to accompany Apichat. The soldiers did not

tell them where they were going. They were taken to the Second Cavalry King's Guard base in Bangkok, where they were interrogated and
detained for one night without being permitted to contact their families or lawyers. After one night in military custody, Apichat Pongsawat
was transferred to police custody, where he was held for six more
nights before being accused of six violations of the law: NCPO Announcement No. 7/2557; Articles 215, 216, 368, and 112 of the Criminal
Code; and the Computer Crimes Act. He was then sent to the Bangkok
Remand Prison for continued detention. Apichat was held for more
than a month before finally being released on bail. He was indicted on
24 April 2015 for violation of the first four laws above.

The Court for the People is supposed to rule on whether or not the
defendant is guilty as charged. Before doing so, the Court for the
People must comment on the role of the judiciary with respect to the
coup by the NCPO. The Court for the People notes with concern that
the Court of First Instance, the Appeal Court, and the Supreme Court
all framed the coup as immediately successful, and the latter court
deemed it inevitable. In so doing, the only option for the court was
to find the defendant guilty. Defense witness Jaran Kosanan testified
that the court is the institution best placed to examine the junta's
exercise of power.[81] The court takes this assessment as a mandate to
consider the success and inevitability of the coup, on which the guilt
or innocence of the defendant rests.

In previous decisions, the Supreme Court has acknowledged that
a coup may be illegal but becomes successful when a junta is able to
control the organs of the state and the people have given their assent
(for example, Supreme Court Judgment No. 1153–1154/2495). But the
definition of assent remains vague in existing jurisprudence. Defense
witness Jaran Kosanan testified that within the terms established by
previous Supreme Court decisions, the coup was not yet successful at
the time of Apichat's protest but was successful by the time he was
indicted eleven months after the coup and his protest.[82] The Appeal
Court noted the timing of the defendant's protest as being only one
day after the coup by the NCPO and so "in a period in which some
people such as the defendant expressed disagreement with the coup."[83]
The Court for the People holds that the coup was partially successful.
The state apparatus was controlled by the NCPO, as evidenced by the
arrest, detention, and prosecution of the defendant. But there was
not assent from the people. This was evidenced by the protest of the

defendant and the five hundred other citizens at the BACC on 23 May 2014 and throughout the entire period in which the NCPO governed, as well as the accompanying arrest and prosecution of those who protested.[84] The Court for the People wishes to emphasize this point: the arrest and prosecution of Apichat Pongsawat itself reflected the incomplete status of the coup's success.

The question of the success of the coup is significant because it affects the status of the legal instrument, NCPO Announcement No. 7/2557 (later Head of the NCPO Order No. 3/2558), under which the defendant's protest was criminalized. Prior Supreme Court decisions have asserted that once a coup is successful, the junta becomes the sovereign and then any orders and announcements issued by the junta acquire the immediate status of law. The Court of First Instance and the Appeal Court ruled in this manner. The Supreme Court declined to rule on this matter, noting that it was a question of fact, not law, and the Supreme Court rules only on matters of law. This was a de facto affirmation of the ruling by the Court of First Instance and the Appeal Court. In the specific case of the NCPO, Article 47 of the 2014 Interim Constitution and Article 279 of the 2017 Constitution also affirmed the legal status of all NCPO orders and announcements until revoked.[85] Despite these measures, both the legality of NCPO Order No. 7/2557 and the announcement of martial law for the entire country, on which the NCPO relied for the authority to issue the order, remain uncertain. Martial law was declared for the entire country on 20 May 2014 but through an order of the Royal Thai Army, not a royal proclamation.[86] NCPO Order No. 7/2557 was announced through the television on 22 May 2014 but was not published in the *Ratchakitchanubeksa* until 26 May 2014.[87] This means that, at best, the defendant was arrested, accused, and prosecuted of a crime on the basis of the retroactive application of the law, which contravenes Article 2 of the Criminal Code. At worst, the defendant was arrested, accused, and prosecuted under an order that was illegally issued and not law.

The Court for the People additionally takes up the matter of the protections of the right of the defendant to protest provided in domestic and international law. Article 4 of the 2007 Constitution, abrogated by the NCPO on 22 May 2014, stipulated that "the human dignity, right, liberty and equality of the people shall be protected"; Article 4 of the 2014 Interim Constitution, promulgated by the NCPO on 22 July 2014, stipulated that, "subject to the provisions of this Constitution, human dignity, rights, liberties and equality previously enjoyed by the Thai people with the protection under Thailand's constitutional convention of the democratic regime of government with the King as Head of State and Thailand's existing international obligations shall be protected under this Constitution"; and Article 4 of the 2017 Constitution, promulgated on 6 April 2017, stipulated that, "human dignity, rights, liberties and equality of the people shall be protected. The Thai people shall enjoy equal protection under the Constitution." Article 21 of the International Covenant on Civil and Political Rights (ICCPR), to which Thailand became a state party in 1996, stipulates that "the right of peaceful assembly shall be recognized. No restrictions may be placed on the exercise of this right other than those imposed in conformity with the law and which are necessary in a democratic society in the interests of national security or public safety, public order (*ordre public*), the protection of public health or morals or the protection of the rights and freedoms of others." The defendant testified that he acted out of his duty to protect nation, religion, king, and democratic rule, according to Article 70 of the 2007 Constitution, which notes, "Every person shall have a duty to uphold the nation, religions, the King and the democratic regime of government with the King as Head of State under this Constitution."[88] Samchai Srisant, defense witness, testified that the defendant's actions were not a crime because a coup is the destruction of a constitutional system, and it is the duty of every citizen to oppose coups. As a student of Thammasat University, the defendant was particularly bound to do so, as protection of the constitution is a key part of the ideals upon which the university was founded.[89] Jaran Kosanan, defense witness, testified that citizens have the right to disobey a state that has acquired power illegally. Citizens have the right to disagree with coup orders. The witness's view was that the defendant's actions were protected from criminalization under Article 68 of the Criminal Code, which stipulates that, "any person who is compelled to commit any act to defend his or her own or other person's rights against an imminent danger arising from unlawful violence shall, if the act committed is proportionate to the circumstances, not be guilty and such act shall be a lawful defence."[90]

But the Appeal Court ruled that the defendant's actions were protected by neither the 2007 Constitution nor the ICCPR.[91] The 2007 Constitution had been abrogated at the time of the defendant's actions and so could not be cited in the defendant's defense. The ICCPR can be derogated for reasons of national security, which was also the justification for the coup. The view of the Court for the People is that the Appeal Court did not provide evidence of sufficient weight for the derogation of rights protections provided by the ICCPR or any of the constitutions relevant across the life of this case. The Court for the People further wishes to praise the defendant for fulfilling his constitutional duty to defend democracy despite the risks and persecution he faced.

The final point the Court for the People wishes to raise is the revocation of the law under which the defendant was convicted, Head of the NCPO Order No. 3/2558. By the time the case reached the Supreme Court, the order had been revoked ahead of planned elections. At the time the decision was being written, the election had been held. Article 2 of the Criminal Code mandates that "any person shall be criminally punishable when an act committed by him or her is provided to be an offence and the punishment is defined by the law in force at the time of such commission, and the punishment to be imposed on such offender must be those provided by law. If, under the law subsequently provided, such an act is no longer an offence, the person committing it shall be exempt from being an offender. If there is a final judgment imposing the punishment, such person shall be deemed to have not been sentenced to such judgment. If he or she is undergoing the punishment, such punishment shall be terminated." With respect to the text of the law, the defendant is no longer guilty. Yet the Supreme Court ruled that, although Head of the NCPO Order No. 3/2558 would not be appropriate during the time of the decision, given the need for the political participation of the people during the new period of democracy, at the time of the defendant's actions, conditions were different and therefore it was appropriate that the defendant was prosecuted for his actions. The Court for the People holds a different view. To judge the defendant guilty once the order has been revoked is contrary to the spirit of the law. Convicting him of its violation once it has been revoked is not in line with need for the political participation of the people during this new period of democracy that the country has entered.

The charges against the defendant are dismissed and the fine ordered returned to the defendant.

Note: The Court for the People is unable to rule on the innocence or guilt of General Prayuth Chan-ocha and the National Council for Peace and Order on the matter of carrying out the coup because it is beyond the scope of this case. A separate case is necessary.[92] The Court for the People is also unable to do what the defendant wished the court to do, which was to provide an amnesty to him and others who protested.[93] This is a matter for Parliament to take up.

THREE

REFUSAL TO REPORT

Beginning on the evening of the coup, the NCPO drew on its authority under martial law to first summon, and then detain, individuals for up to seven days without the need to consult a judge or even offer a potential violation of the law as a reason.[1] Citizens were summoned to report to the Army Club on Thewet Road in Bangkok "to preserve order and properly resolve the problems of the country."[2] Lists of names of those summoned scrolled down television screens and interrupted free-to-air programming at irregular intervals during the first weeks and months after the NCPO seized power. A total of 472 citizens were publicly summoned in this manner through a series of orders between May and July 2014.[3] Those whose names were included on the lists were politicians from the government ousted by the coup; former political prisoners; dissident activists, writers, and professors; and many others whom the NCPO identified as potential opponents.

No details were offered about what would transpire after one reported oneself, but a general picture soon emerged from those who were released. One would be transported, perhaps blindfolded, to a military base. One would not be permitted to contact a lawyer or one's family. One would be interrogated, perhaps politely, perhaps rudely, perhaps accompanied by torture or threats of torture.[4] One might sleep on the floor in a cell with bars or in a bed in an air-conditioned room, but one would definitely be locked in, with soldiers stationed outside the door. One might be released on day 2; on day 8, after the full seven days of arbitrary detention permitted under martial law; or even weeks later, in cases in which the authorities opted to act in excess of the terms of martial law. Upon release, one might be handed over to the police to be criminally charged with lèse-majesté, sedition, or other crimes, or one might be let go after one signed a document disavowing any further political action.[5] Displeased by the negative connotation of the word *detention*, the NCPO spokesperson requested that *attitude adjustment (prap thasanakhati)* be used instead, seemingly without any awareness of its Orwellian connotation.

The name of Thanapol Eawsakul, the editor who accompanied Apichat Pongsawat when he was the first to be arrested for protesting the coup whose case is examined in the previous chapter, was on a list of those summoned to report themselves that was broadcast while he was in military custody.[6] The morning after the arrest, the soldiers handed Apichat over to the police to prosecute him for protesting and delivered Thanapol to the Army Club. He was detained for seven days and then released without being charged. A few days later, Thanapol wrote and published an account of his detention in which he noted, parenthetically, "I kept returning to the question, if I was not already in custody, what path would I take? 1. Report myself; 2. Flee; or 3. Live life normally, and if they came to arrest me, let them."[7] He offered no clear answer but shared his account because he realized that many others were likely contemplating what to do if they were summoned. The soldiers treated him well but made him aware that he had long been under surveillance and that, if he opted not to cooperate, unspecified harsh consequences would follow.

Reticence to report to such a summons is understandable, admirable, and wise. The NCPO had just illegally toppled a democratically elected government. The Thai military has a long history of committing human rights violations with impunity, including torture, prolonged detention, and disappearance, and those whose names were listed in the NCPO summons had no assurance that they would be safe if they complied. But for those who chose not to report when summoned, the harsh consequences were swiftly specified and codified in the junta's growing corpus of orders, which were treated as law by police and judges. NCPO Announcement No. 41/2557, proclaimed four days after the coup, made not reporting to a summons a crime punishable by a fine of up to forty thousand baht, two years of imprisonment, or both a fine and imprisonment.[8] Then, on 25 May, the NCPO announced that all cases of violation of NCPO orders and announcements would be placed within the jurisdiction of the military court.[9] Those summoned before 25 May 2014 who did not report were subject to prosecution in the (civilian) criminal court system, but those summoned on or after that date were subject to prosecution in the military court system with an attendant loss of rights, including appeal of the decision rendered upon them.[10] The legal status of the orders and announcements was cemented two months after the coup when the NCPO issued the 2014 Interim Constitution. Complementing Article 48, which provided the NCPO with amnesty for carrying out the coup, Article 47 designated all NCPO announcements and orders as legal, constitutional, and final.[11]

A total of fourteen people were prosecuted for not responding to the summons.[12] Three among them—Sombat Boonngamanong, Siraphop Kornarut, and Worachet Pakeerut—exemplify both the range of methods the junta's opponents used to challenge and unsettle coup rule and how the junta deployed the law as a tool to attempt to silence and terrorize them. Sombat, a longtime civil society activist, used social media to organize anti-coup protests and dare the authorities to apprehend him until the evening he was arrested. Siraphop, a construction contractor and writer critical of the monarchy and military, went on the run once his name appeared on the list of those summoned, aiming to seek asylum abroad, but he did not make it to the border. Worachet, a professor who led the Khana Nitirat, a group of seven members of the Faculty of Law at Thammasat University who organized to make law and justice accessible to all, was outside the country seeking medical care when he was summoned. While the reason the NCPO summoned any given person must remain only speculative, Sombat's humor, Siraphop's direct criticism, and Worachet's philosophy of law for the people were potent weapons challenging and offering an alternative to the vision of the polity presented by the junta.

Rather than being silenced by the NCPO, Sombat, Siraphop, and Worachet exposed the cynical and unjust use of the law through their defenses. Their cases spanned the civilian Criminal Court system, the Bangkok Military Court, and the Constitutional Court over a seven-year period that continued after the NCPO ceased to exist.[13] Siraphop was the only one of the fourteen to be prosecuted who was sentenced to a prison term that was not suspended.[14] Sombat was sentenced to a suspended term and a fine. Worachet's case was dropped after the Constitutional Court ruled in 2020 that the junta's prosecution of people for not reporting when summoned was unconstitutional. The nearly full suspension of sentences and the Constitutional Court ruling in Worachet's case may seem to be a victory for the people. But the cases were key sites of the creation and maintenance of the jurisprudence of impunity, inflected here as injustice that relied on drawn-out prosecution, adherence to a definition of law, and practice of procedure that favored the junta over the people and the repeated lack of recognition of opposition to the coup.

Sombat, Siraphop, and Worachet all submitted petitions to the Constitutional Court to examine the constitutionality of summons to report to the NCPO and the prosecution of civilians in the military court system, but only in Worachet's case, and only after a significant delay, did the Constitutional Court take it up. The Constitutional Court tentatively queried the legitimacy of the coup, but it did so six years after the coup and a year after the NCPO ceased to exist. The Constitutional Court questioned the impact of the junta's restrictions of rights and liberties only after hundreds of citizens were criminally charged for peacefully dissenting against the coup and thousands more were intimidated and harassed. The Constitutional Court stopped short of challenging coups directly, by noting that the restrictions on rights were appropriate during the coup years but not at the time they examined the case.

Justice delayed is justice denied. When the Constitutional Court finally ruled in 2020 that the NCPO summonses were unconstitutional, the ruling resulted in the criminal case against Worachet being dropped a year later in 2021, seven years after he was arrested. The Constitutional Court should have ruled in 2014, when the petitions were first submitted. Tracing the three cases of Sombat, Siraphop, and Worachet reveals how this did not happen and why it would be significant if it had. As in the case brought against the junta by Resistant Citizen and Apichat Pongsawat's fight to affirm his right to defend democracy, the question of when a coup becomes successful and therefore a junta and its orders lawful and legitimate, is central to all three cases. Devaluing the dissent of the people, which is a way of refusing their claim to sovereignty, legitimizes the coup.

Making the legitimacy of coups unquestionable is an essential accomplishment of the jurisprudence of impunity. Undoing this legitimacy, then, is essential, but not sufficient, for building a jurisprudence of accountability. Resistance to coups—and expressions of the people's sovereignty, what it means for the people to be the supreme power in the land—takes multiple forms. Recognition of this multiplicity is itself a foundation for accountability. Inspiration for the new Constitutional Court for the People ruling comes precisely from Sombat's irreverence, Siraphop's refusal to back down, and Worachet's faith in the law. All three live and fight their cases as if the law were just, enacting a utopian vision in sharp contrast to the injustice they each experience. The new ruling, which would have been issued in 2014, reworks the very meaning of law to be a tool to protect the rights of the people rather than one that dispossesses them of their very claim to the polity.

SOMBAT: DISRUPTION

The NCPO ordered Sombat Boonngamanong to report to the Army Club by 10 am on 23 May 2014.[15] Sombat was aware of the summons but chose not to report because he viewed himself and other citizens as the owners of sovereignty, not the junta.[16] Sovereignty here is the ability to decide whose authority one will cede to, and Sombat resolutely refused to cede to the NCPO: "In truth, I don't know this entity, never heard of it. This NCPO, what is it? And then, out of nowhere, it summons us to do this, do that, and we've done nothing wrong. I don't understand why they summoned me. And why do I have to go? It's like when someone says, 'Hey Sombat, come here.' I have the right not to go, right? And especially an entity that has seized power and summons me to report myself. No way am I going. If I go, it is the acceptance of their power."[17]

Sombat refused to accept the NCPO's power from the moment he was summoned and continued even after the Supreme Court convicted him of not reporting when summoned by the NCPO. Sovereignty is not only a lofty matter of statecraft but also the terrain of everyday struggle between the people and the state in a time of coup rule.

Sombat announced via Facebook post that he would not report and went on the run. In a series of posts laced with playful humor and sarcasm, he refused the authority of the NCPO by organizing opposition and taunting them. His posts during the last six days before he was tracked to the home of a friend in Chonburi province are also a record of the opposition to the coup whose existence the courts repeatedly denied in his trial and that of others.

His posts from 30 May:

- "A big fish told me it is impossible to topple the NCPO. I still don't want to come to this conclusion. From this Sunday on, I will propose activities to 'topple the NCPO.'"

- "When Prayuth goes on television, he greets the people but does not lift his hands to *wai* them. Plus, he wrinkles his brow a lot. Totally incredible."

- "When General Prayuth say that society needs to be brought under the law, I wonder whether or not he has skipped over himself?

- "Those who oppose the coup are bad people. Those who carried out the coup are good people. It's exhausting."

From 31 May:

- "Demonstration against the coup tomorrow. There will be no sound system, no leaders. It will be like a market. Everyone wear masks and bring signs. A masked party."

- "A demonstration against the coup cannot topple the NCPO. But it is the declaration of the stance of this group of Thai people who do not agree with military dictatorship."

- "The operations of the various projects of the military dictatorship government will not have the words unconstitutional or unlawful not because they are just, but because whatever the dictatorship does is right."

From 3 June:

- "If you forbid it and the people stop, then you win. If you forbid it, and the people resist, then you lose."

From 4 June:

- "The victory monument was built as a memorial to the soldiers who fought and were victorious over the French 70 years ago. Today, the soldiers are celebrating victory over the people of what nation in this world? If you have to keep coming to celebrate in the center of the city like this, do you think you have triumphed over the Thai people?"

- "We have no rights, we have no freedom, but you say we are happy. All messed up."

- "The Thai soldiers are using the same model that was unsuccessful in southern Thailand and inflicting it upon Thai people around the country. It failed once and will fail again. Soldiers are not fit for political work, I assure you."

- "The three-finger protest will be held at 12-noon sharp on Sunday, 8 June. If you agree, click like. If you will join, click share."

- "I say it again clearly, in case they are brain dead. I will not report to those rebels who stole the power of the people. If [you] want me, come catch me. I'm in your very country."[18]

Sombat was defiant and articulated both the people's claim to sovereignty and his criticism of the legitimacy of the junta. He was unable to attend the protest he called for on 8 June, because the Technology Crime Suppression Division tracked down his location through the IP address of one of the posts. The house where he was staying was raided on the evening of 4 June. He was already in his bedroom for the evening when the knock came on the door. He opened the door and came face-to-face with a uniformed soldier pointing a gun at his head. Dozens of uniformed and plainclothes soldiers and police searched the house and seized his electronic devices. Soldiers blindfolded him and took him to a military base. They did not tell him where he was being held or allow him to contact a lawyer or his family. Sombat was held incommunicado for nine days, two days longer than that permitted under martial law, and was transferred to police custody on 12 June 2014.[19]

The NCPO brought two criminal charges against Sombat: failure to report when summoned and sedition. The failure to report case was within the jurisdiction of the Dusit District Court because the summons order was issued before cases against the crown and state were placed within the jurisdiction of the military court. But the sedition case, or violation of Article 116 of the Criminal Code, which arose from Sombat's Facebook posts, was assigned to the Bangkok Military Court. During the NCPO's rule, sedition became a catchall accusation used to criminalize criticism of the junta and at least 124 individuals were prosecuted.[20]

The speed with which the NCPO began summoning people to report for arbitrary detention indicates both that the coup was planned and that identifying potential opponents was part of the planning. Sombat's history of opposition to previous coups is a reasonable explanation for why he was summoned. He forged his ideas of how to resist coups over two decades of dissent, beginning with the May 1992 coup, civil society activism for missing and other disappeared people, opposition to the 19 September 2006 coup, and activism refusing the erasure of those killed in the state crackdown on the Red Shirts in April and May 2010.[21] In an interview during the years between the 19 September 2006 and the 22 May 2014 coups, Sombat called for opposition at once playful and sharp: "I want to propose, given that opposition in recent instances has led to great losses, a method of opposition that I call 'disrupt.' We remain stuck in a frame of opposition that requires direct confrontation to the death. . . . I want to propose a method of opposition like disruption, which is to ruin the apparatus and the legitimacy of the ruling class."[22] Irreverence and discomfort productively unsettle injustice, particularly when those who hold power do not imagine that anyone will dare to question them.

At the first hearing in his sedition case in January 2015, his lawyer submitted a petition requesting that the Constitutional Court examine whether prosecuting civilians in the military court system contravened the 2014 Interim Constitution. Just as when the same request was brought by Siraphop's and Worachet's lawyers, the Bangkok Military Court refused to forward the petition to the Constitutional Court on the basis that there was no procedural path for the military court to do so. Under both the 2007 and 2017 Constitutions, any citizen who felt that his or her constitutionally protected rights and liberties were violated by the enforcement of a law could submit a petition through the court in which he or she was prosecuted to the Constitutional Court. While the 2014 Interim Constitution retained the Constitutional Court, affected citizens could not submit petitions, and matters could be referred only by a meeting of the Supreme Court or the Supreme Administrative Court.[23] The witness hearings in Sombat's sedition case stretched across six years and began in the Bangkok Military Court; they were then transferred to the Bangkok Criminal

Court after the NCPO ceased to exist. On 30 July 2020, more than six years after he was arrested with a gun to his head, the sedition case against him was dismissed.

His refusal to report when summoned case was slightly less delayed but resulted in a guilty verdict that was maintained across all three levels of the civilian criminal courts. Witness hearings were held between August 2014 and June 2015. Throughout the prosecution and appeal process, Sombat remained unyielding in his stance against the coup. He pled not guilty because he viewed the coup as the overthrow of a democratic government and the NCPO as ruling without the consent of the people. Similar to Apichat Pongsawat, he held that it was his duty as a Thai person to protect the constitution against criminal insurrection.[24] His own testimony, as well as that of Jantajira Iammayura, another defense witness, challenged the prosecutor and judges to reflect on who held sovereignty in the Thai polity, the meaning of the law, and the role of the court in determining the answers to both of those questions.

Reflecting the utopian attitude common to defenses under the NCPO, Sombat testified as if the law were a tool to actively protect the rights of the people rather than the actually existing tool to dispossess one of rights, which he encountered. First, Sombat refused the authority of the NCPO to accuse and prosecute him. The coup was an illegal and unconstitutional action, as the 2007 Constitution that was in force at the time of the coup stipulated that the executive branch must be elected. He acknowledged that the 2014 Interim Constitution provided amnesty to the junta for carrying out the coup but noted that at the time he was arrested, the Constitution and the amnesty did not yet exist and the NCPO remained criminal. He was also summoned before even the king's formal appointment of the government and the order's printing in the *Ratchakitchanubeksa*. Further, any limitations on the rights and freedoms of the people must derive authority from the law, and NCPO orders were not law given the NCPO's illegitimacy.[25] Further, despite the abolition of the 2007 Constitution, he viewed his rights and liberties as inseparable from his humanity. The junta could plunder the constitution, but not his humanity. He looked toward the future, asserting that the illegal and illegitimate actions of the junta would have to be nullified upon a return to democracy.[26]

Jantajira Iammayura, a lecturer in the Faculty of Law at Thammasat University and a member of the Khana Nitirat, also testified as if the court would act in defense of human rights. When asked if the coup was successful on 22 May 2014, she said no, as the facts did not indicate that the junta was in control of all state apparatuses. Citizens, including Sombat, expressed opposition. At that time, the junta was not the sovereign and the order Sombat was summoned under did not have the status of law. But at the time she gave testimony, on 19 June 2015, the junta was the sovereign.[27] With regard to the legality of the orders Sombat was summoned under, Jantajira testified that, according to the tradition of governance in Thailand, the orders that mentioned Sombat's name were all issued on 23 and 24 May, before the junta was appointed by the king in the *Ratchakitcha-nubeksa* on 26 May, which means that they were issued without authority and without being able to be enforced.[28] Until 26 May, the junta's status remained unclear and unknown.[29] She testified that, although she was aware that the Supreme Court had ruled that once a coup is successful, a junta's orders and announcements are law, her view was that such an assessment was outdated, and the court had evolved to being more in line with democracy at the time of her testimony.[30] She made that claim despite having very little evidence of the court's evolution and instead copious evidence of the court's continued antidemocratic stance, including in the very case at hand.

Jantajira's most utopian action was to submit a written copy of a 2009 dissenting opinion by Kirati Kancharin, a judge in the Supreme Court's Division of Political Officeholders. The case was related to an allegation that Yongyuth Tiyapairat, former minister of natural recourses and environment in the former government of Prime Minister Thaksin Shinawatra, ousted in the 19 September 2006 coup, had provided a false declaration of assets. The majority found him guilty. Kirati wrote a dissenting opinion out of opposition to coups and the coup as an action that led to the case being initiated. Although his opinion had no impact on the decision, he was the first judge in any court in Thailand to take a clear stance against coups. He offered a defense of democracy and the role of the people in a democracy, as the owners of sovereignty. By submitting a copy of it with her testimony, Jantajira ensured that the judges had to read an opinion from one of their colleagues that resonated with the perspective of the person on trial in their courtroom. Kirati wrote:

> The sovereignty belongs to the people. The court is one of the sovereign powers, which is of the people. The court must therefore exercise the aforementioned power for the people by making rulings in cases in order to expand the protection of rights and freedom of the people. And if the court does not serve the people, it will cause the legal system and judicial process to be challenged and shaken. In addition, the court should have a role in preserving the legitimacy of law, including the obligation to protect the rights and freedom of the people from the illegitimate exercise of power and the obligation to protect democracy as well. The exercise of power in governing the country by undemocratic means, or in other words, securing power without the consent of the majority of the people, is equivalent to the overthrow of democracy. A revolution or a coup is the overthrow of the constitution and is a crime according to Article 113. It is a way of obtaining power to govern the country by undemocratic means. If the court affirms the power of individuals or a group of individuals who carry out a revolution or a coup to be the sovereign state, it is equal to the court not serving and protecting the people from the exercise of illegitimate authority, and being indifferent to the protection of democracy as above. . . . The facts that are generally-known are that at present, in the trend of globalization, the majority of civilized countries are democracies, which do not accept power that comes from a revolution or coup. Therefore, as the times have changed from the past, the court should therefore not acknowledge the power of individuals or groups of individuals who carry out a revolution or a coup as the sovereign state. When the facts are generally known that the petitioners along with the committee are the result of the CDRM [Council on Democratic Reform Under Monarchy, junta that carried out the 19 September 2006 coup],

but the CDRM is the group of individuals that carried out the revolution or a coup, which is a crime according to Article 113 of the Criminal Code and is a method of obtaining power that is not democratic, it should not be held to be the sovereign state, even if it has received an amnesty.[31]

Kirati articulated a clear role for judges in condemning coups and protecting the people's sovereignty. In departing from sixty years of jurisprudence, he illustrated what was possible, even as the marginal status of his dissent showed the difficulty of making it real.

But the courts were impervious to the testimony and did not embrace the future of standing on the side of the people that Sombat, Jantajira, and Kirati had each articulated. All three levels of the civilian criminal courts found Sombat guilty and affirmed the legitimacy of the coup. In the Dusit District Court decision, on 21 September 2015, the court refused the argument that Sombat was opposing an illegal coup. The coup was not illegal because the 2014 Interim Constitution provided an amnesty for it. He was found guilty of violation of Article 368 of the Criminal Code, defying an order of a state official, and fined five hundred baht. He was not convicted of violating NCPO Announcement Nos. 25/2557 and 29/2557 because the court viewed this as the punishment being set after the fact and the announcements as targeting particular individuals.

In a decision a year later, on 16 May 2016, the Appeal Court ruled to punish Sombat Boonngamanong more harshly and to explicitly affirm the success of the coup and the position of the NCPO as the sovereign state. The Appeal Court found Sombat guilty of violating NCPO Announcement Nos. 25/2557 and 29/2557 and increased the punishment to a fine of three thousand baht and imprisonment of two months, suspended for one year. The Appeal Court argued that it was merely Sombat's opinion that the coup was illegal. He could be found guilty of violating NCPO Announcement Nos. 25/2557 and 29/2557 even though they were promulgated after the order summoning him, because of the constitutional measure making all orders and announcements of the NCPO legal. Sombat's argument that he was defending democracy did not hold because the NCPO was the sovereign state and the 2007 Constitution was no longer in force.

In an interview after the Appeal Court decision, Sombat highlighted the dangers to the polity of how the Appeal Court characterized governance. The Appeal Court judged the NCPO to have successfully become the sovereign state despite contravening the Constitution in force at the time, violating the law and being undemocratic. He further noted: "Interpreting the recognition of the coup as having the status of being the sovereign state by merely looking at one group of soldiers who used force to seize power and proclaimed the successful seizure of power will create peculiar effects. This will make the governance (of the country) insecure and unstable. It can easily change and transform, because the status of the junta is uncertain, whether it is the sovereign state or rebels, because there might arise opposition until the junta fails."[32] In addition, he noted that recognizing the coup as immediately successful and the junta as the sovereign state made Articles 69 and 70 of the 2007 Constitution, the measures outlining the duty of the Thai people to defend the constitution and democracy, meaningless in practice, "because there is no period of time in which opposition can arise. Such interpretation creates a standard to promote having coups and destroys the rule of law system and the principle of the separation of powers."[33]

The Supreme Court left the logic and decision of the Appeal Court unchanged, but Sombat was found guilty only of violating NCPO Announcement No. 25/2557. The decision again turned on understandings of the coup, success, opposition, and sovereignty. On 1 June 2017, the Supreme Court ruled that the fact that the NCPO issued orders and announcements indicated that it had successfully seized power and was the sovereign state.[34] Articles 69 and 70 did not apply because the NCPO was successful as soon as it seized power and the 2007 Constitution was abrogated. Most significant, the court said of the two provisions, "There was no actual use [of the two articles] because there was no period at all in which the people or any state unit was able to oppose the seizure of power in the country."[35] In his petition, Sombat requested that the Supreme Court take into account opposition from the people and the delay between the coup and when the order from the king appointing the junta as the government was printed in the *Ratchakitchanubeksa*. The Supreme Court responded: "There was not any opposition from the people or state against the seizure of governing power this time until the NCPO was unable to administer the country in any way. Regarding that there has to be a constitutional amnesty or a royal proclamation supporting the status of the NCPO, this is merely the understanding of the defendant himself. There is no set standard that the aforementioned must have happened before the seizure of governing power of the country is considered successful as the defendant petitioned."[36] Here, the Supreme Court unwittingly acknowledged that there was no standard for when a coup is successful, and so the Court became the figure that made that decision. But how does it do so? Commenting on this decision, Worachet Pakeerut asked:

> I really ask, on the day that they announced the seizure of power, in that second, can anyone say that they have successfully seized power? When the court decides, the court has to return to that point, and ask, at the point of the announcement of the seizure of power, did they know that the coup had succeeded? Or did they take the events that arose later to apply to those that arose before when the situation still remained uncertain? If it is the latter, then it is not fair to those who have been prosecuted. The law must be clear and certain when a case is prosecuted. If people are going to be punished, there must be definite criteria for when the court is going to say a coup was successful. This is equivalent to the court being the entity that says if a coup has succeeded. I believe that in terms of the facts at that point, no one could say whether or not the coup had succeeded.[37]

The rule of coups and the history of coup jurisprudence in Thailand to date has left no space for uncertainty. But why have the courts been so unwilling to display uncertainty when the situation remains uncertain? Why have they been so unwilling, or afraid, to side with the people?

Worachet further addressed this point of the clarity of the standard used in the case:

> If you ask if the standard that Khun Sombat cited was clear or not, I think that it had a level of clarity. A royal proclamation appointing the Head of the NCPO printed in the *Ratchakitchanubeksa* is a legal document that can be said to support the status of success of the coup in the clearest way. But that the court said that there was no opposition, is this the understanding of the court itself or not? Have they decided that each person has their own individual understanding? Khun Sombat's understanding is this. The court's understanding is this. This indicates that the court has a different understanding than Khun Sombat, so will punish him? Should the court punish Khun Sombat in a case like this or not?[38]

The court claimed that Sombat was partial without considering its own partiality. Given the power to punish wielded by the court, this was elision with grave consequences.

The consequence was not only the punishment of Sombat but also the erasure of the people's opposition to the coup. The court raised the issue of opposition to the coup as part of the standard it set and yet said that there was no opposition.[39] Piyabutr Saengkanokkul, another member of the Khana Nitirat, queried how that could be the conclusion when there was opposition after the coup that required the military to use armed force: "How did the Supreme Court maintain that the NCPO successfully carried out the coup and became the 'sovereign state' even though in the period of those aforementioned days and after that there were still a very large number of individuals who demonstrated against the coup?"[40] The conclusion he reaches is that the coup became sovereign when the Supreme Court said that it had succeeded. There is no standard of when a coup becomes successful and the junta the sovereign, but rather an antistandard that leaves the meanings of both always uncertain and the people perpetually insecure.

SIRAPHOP: CIVIL DISOBEDIENCE

Similar to Sombat, Siraphop Kornarut chose not to report when the NCPO summoned him to the Army Club by 3 June.[41] A construction contractor by day and an online political critic by night, he was living and working in Hat Yai province in southern Thailand at the time of the coup. He viewed the coup as illegal and illegitimate, and the NCPO as a band of criminal rebels. As soon as he was summoned, he went on the run and planned to request asylum from the United Nations High Commissioner for Refugees.[42] A few weeks later, he was tracked down by the NCPO, arrested, detained, interrogated, and then prosecuted.

But the similarities to Sombat's case end there. How Siraphop was apprehended, what happened after his apprehension, and his prosecution in the military court all diverge from Sombat's experience. What made the difference was that Siraphop was charged with three counts of lèse-majesté, or violating Article 112, along with not reporting when summoned by the NCPO. The NCPO cast itself as a protector of the monarchy and acted swiftly to prosecute anyone who had been critical of the monarchy in the years since the 19 September 2006 coup. Like others accused of lèse-majesté, Siraphop was repeatedly denied bail for nearly five years. But he remained unbowed. In his case on the refusal to report, which was examined separately from his lèse-majesté case, Siraphop turned his defense into a site of struggle over the kind of dissent that is permitted citizens.

Siraphop told no one where he went when he went on the run. He asked his two daughters, twenty and twenty-three years old, to fly from Bangkok in order to stay with his seventeen-year-old son in Hat Yai.[43] He used his mobile phone to contact and instruct his work team of approximately twenty workers and changed his SIM card daily.[44] When three weeks had passed without Siraphop appearing, the authorities decided to simultaneously raid every possible place he might be on 24 June 2014. Approximately ten soldiers and police went to the construction site in Hat Yai and claimed to be searching for migrant workers. A unit went to his mother's house in Bangkok and searched every nook and cranny; she was alone and unwell.[45]

Approximately forty armed soldiers and ten police arrived at two o'clock in the afternoon and raided and searched his house in Hat Yai. When they did not find Siraphop, they arrested everyone present—his three children and his oldest daughter's ten-month-old son. They were taken to a military base forty kilometers away. The authorities also took one computer central processing unit, three one-terabyte hard drives, five smartphones, and an ordinary mobile telephone. They were released at midnight, but the computers and telephones were not returned.[46] Ploy, Siraphop's middle daughter, his primary support during the period he was detained, commented of the arrest: "At that time, I was really shocked but could not do anything. So I tried to stay calm. In my heart I wondered, was it really that grave of an issue? It was like we had gone and murdered someone. Like a very, very serious case, like drugs or another crime. It was a really, really big issue."[47] There are no provisions in the Criminal Code of Thailand or the Martial Law Act of 1914 that permit the authorities to take a suspect's family members when the suspect cannot be found. Targeting families of dissidents to pressure dissidents and spread terror became a regular practice under the NCPO.

The next day, Siraphop was captured while he was on his way to Udon Thani province in northeastern Thailand, where he was going to contact the UN High Commissioner for Refugees. He was waiting at an intersection in the urban area of Kalasin province. June is peak rainy season, and it was pouring. A Toyota Fortuner truck cut him off in front, and a van parked behind him. Five middle-aged men carrying Tavor assault rifles got out and ran toward him. With their hands on the triggers, they yelled at him to give up and not fight. Siraphop and the driver got out of the vehicle with their arms up. They were forced to lay face down on the wet road.[48]

Siraphop was held by soldiers for one night at Siharat Dechothai Camp in Khon Kaen province. The next day, he was sent to the Eleventh Army Region Base in Bangkok. He slept in an air-conditioned room, but there were two soldiers with M16s outside the door to ensure that he did not leave.[49] He was interrogated by officials from the NCPO, Internal Security Operations Command, Department of Special Investigation, Judge

Advocate General's Department, Office of the Attorney General, the First Army Region, and the Technology Crime Suppression Division.[50] They were polite and did not use obscene language. They had been following his writing since 2009.[51] Siraphop had been active online under the pen name "Rungsila" since 2004. He wrote poems and articles challenging conservatives on the *Prachatai* web board and then later on his own website and Facebook. During the ten years between 2004 and the 2014 coup, he wrote more than one thousand articles on the political situation and the military.[52] He did not know how the authorities figured out his identity, because he had told only two people that he was Rungsila.[53]

On 2 July 2014, he was sent to the Crime Suppression Division and formally accused of violating the order to report himself and so also of violating NCPO Announcement No. 41/2557.[54] He was released on bail but immediately rearrested for lèse-majesté, in which an NCPO official had made a complaint on 30 June. Three pieces of his corpus were selected as criminal: a satirical poem posted on the *Prachatai* web board on 4 November 2009, a cartoon and song lyrics posted on the Rungsila Facebook page on 15 December 2013, and an article and image posted on his blog on 22 January 2014.[55] Siraphop confessed that the pen name "Rungsila" belonged to him and that he was behind the Facebook account and the blog. But he maintained that the poems he wrote were about ordinary political issues and that he talked about unjust power in Thai society but did not mean the king. In a procedural decision repeated throughout the period when civilians accused of crimes against the crown and state were placed within the jurisdiction of the military court system, Siraphop's lèse-majesté case was placed there even though he made all the posts long before the coup. The courts claimed that as the posts were still online, the crime remained ongoing.

Siraphop requested bail with four hundred thousand baht in cash, but as in other Article 112 cases, the Bangkok Military Court denied bail on the basis that the crime was grave and he might flee if given the opportunity, because of the potential for a harsh punishment. He requested bail another six times, and it was denied each time. By the time of the 24 March

2019 election and the pending end of the NCPO, only three witnesses had testified.[56] He was finally granted bail on 11 June 2019 after being detained while awaiting and undergoing trial for four years and 353 days and only after the UN Working Group on Arbitrary Detention sent a query on his case to the Thai government.[57] He was ultimately found guilty of lèse-majesté on 18 January 2021 and sentenced to prison for four and a half years, a sentence he had already served while awaiting and undergoing trial.

Siraphop's trial for not reporting to the NCPO summons took place entirely during the time he was being held without bail in his Article 112 case. When hearings in the case began on 11 November 2014, his lawyer submitted a petition to the Bangkok Military Court requesting that the matter of whether prosecuting civilians in the military court system was in violation of Article 4 of the 2014 Interim Constitution and the International Covenant on Civil and Political Rights (ICCPR) be sent to the Constitutional Court for examination. The Bangkok Military Court did not forward the petition to the Constitutional Court because it claimed that the 2014 Interim Constitution provided it with no authority to do so. Instead, the military judges offered their own assessment at the next hearing on 22 January 2015. Trials in the military court system did not violate the rights protections in the 2014 Interim Constitution or the ICCPR, because even though the military court system is under the Ministry of Defense, the judges are independent. Regarding the lack of ability to appeal, the judges asserted that the ICCPR gives state parties the right to abstain from the protection of some rights during emergencies. Once martial law was proclaimed in Thailand and the Thai government informed the United Nations, there was no contravention of the ICCPR.[58]

Despite the judges' assertion that the military court system was independent, there were multiple obstacles to a fair trial. Siraphop's case was examined very slowly with hearings for nine witnesses stretching between November 2014 and August 2016. The witness hearings were each held several months apart, and prosecution witnesses frequently failed to appear without prior notification.[59] The military court judges did not allow anyone to take notes, even though the hearing was not held in camera.[60] They also did not allow the lawyers to make copies of some orders and other case documents.[61]

Within this context of injustice, and the denial of its unjustness, Siraphop challenged the legitimacy of the coup in his testimony through both direct criticism and his practice of civil disobedience. For him, beginning with the 1971 coup, coups were events that increased conflict in society rather than productively resolving it. He testified that he saw the coup as an insurrection that failed, and he highlighted his participation as a plaintiff in the Resistant Citizen case brought against the NCPO (see chapter 1). He testified about his summons order: "I do not think it was law. It was an order issued by a band of rebels. Law must be promulgated with the king's signature. If I reported myself, it would be participation in the insurrection and I would be punished as well."[62] He did not report himself for those reasons and would not report himself were there to be another coup and he were summoned again.[63]

Siraphop further framed his refusal to report as an act of civil disobedience. He testified: "I resisted the coup through consistently peaceful ideas. When the coup arose, I therefore acted in civil disobedience. I did not accept the authority of the group of individuals that used armed force to seize and overthrow the rule of the government that came from the people, which was ruled by democracy with the king as head of state."[64] He further noted: "I did not believe that the junta, or as is called by another name, the band of rebels, would be able to hold on to power for very long. So I chose to protect rights and freedom and the constitution, through ahimsa and using nonviolence by not cooperating with the aforementioned group of rebels."[65] During cross-examination, the prosecutor tried to claim that one had to publicly announce one's planned civil disobedience before beginning for it to have an impact. Siraphop responded that his own reading and interpretation caused him to understand civil disobedience as the refusal of illegitimate authority. There was no rule necessitating that one publicly announces one's civil disobedience before engaging in it.[66] The prosecutor's decision to try to advance a different definition of civil disobedience seems almost immaterial to the case. It is not as though the prosecutor would recognize Siraphop's dissent as legitimate if he had somehow publicly announced it before going on the run. But when the coup, and the five years of persecution inside and outside the courts, is understood as an attempt to reshape the very ways citizens could participate in the polity, then the attempt to deny Siraphop's civil disobedience as civil disobedience makes perfect sense.

Resonant with Apichat Pongsawat's case, the military court judges had a particular idea of the questions that should be asked and those that should not be asked during the trial. The judges objected to Siraphop testifying about the raid on his family's home and his own apprehension on the rainy night in Kalasin province on the basis that it was irrelevant. Yet this was precise evidence of the NCPO's actions beyond the law.[67] The judges also objected to a question Siraphop's lawyer asked Lieutenant Colonel Saiyan Khunkachee, a prosecution witness from the Army's Judge Advocate General's Department. The question was whether the NCPO had legitimacy in issuing and enforcing law. The judges claimed that the question was irrelevant, but the defense argued it was a matter for their case. The judges would not relent and answered for the witness! They said that the NCPO was the sovereign and so the announcement and orders of the NCPO were all legal.[68] In this moment, the judges foreshadowed the decision they would ultimately render.

The Bangkok Military Court decision was issued both in the name of the king, like all court decisions in Thailand, and under the "rule of 22 May 2014." Although there is no description of the "rule of 22 May 2014" provided anywhere, Siraphop's case and others examined in this book provide an idea of its relationship to law and distance from justice and accountability. On 25 November 2016, Siraphop was found guilty and sentenced to one year in prison and a fine of eighteen thousand baht. The sentence was reduced by a third to eight months in prison and a fine of twelve thousand baht because he cooperated with the court. Since he had never been imprisoned before, the prison term was suspended for two years. No appeal was possible because the case was examined in the military court system. Siraphop's response upon hearing the decision was "I don't feel anything at all. I am used to being imprisoned. After this I will go back to being locked up again."[69] He suggested that Article 113 of the Criminal Code should be revoked as meaningless and confusing. Military juntas can carry out coups with impunity, and citizens who act to protect democracy are those who are subject to punishment.

Parallel to his fight inside the courtroom, Siraphop continued writing throughout his time behind bars. His daughter Ploy, who went to every court hearing, explained: "Every time there was a witness hearing at the Military Court, Dad would secretly bring out small pieces of paper. They were articles he had written and poems he had composed. They were accounts of his life."[70] Part of a poem that he wrote on 25 June 2016 expanded on the meaning of *sovereign*, one of the concepts central to his and many other cases during the NCPO years:

> When there are no fundamental rights
> Persecution and being slammed with cases is easy
> The "sovereign" tyrants are dangerous
> They have developed into "full-fledged dictatorship"[71]

Being the sovereign does not mean that one will act justly. He also slipped letters to his children into his political writing that he sent out of the prison. In one of these, he wrote: "I want my children and grandchildren to be free. I want them to be free Thais who stand securely on their two feet proudly and majestically to protect the rights and humanity of themselves and others. To be steadfast in what is right and fair, in order to sustain collective society to be peaceful and content, to divide resources equally and participate in setting the direction of the collective human community to progress forward."[72] This letter, a private letter to those he loved, is a clear continuation of Siraphop's civil disobedience. Bringing the letter out of the prison was a punishable violation of prison rules. Yet he took the risk to write of the Thai polity he wished to see and the roles he wanted his children and grandchildren—the owners of sovereignty—to have in shaping it.

WORACHET: LAW FOR THE PEOPLE

On 19 September 2010, the fourth anniversary of the 19 September 2006 coup, a group of seven law lecturers in the Faculty of Law at Thammasat University unveiled themselves as the Khana Nitirat, or Enlightened Jurists. Led by Worachet Pakeerut, over the following four years up until the coup, they organized regular public seminars on the law. Held in large auditoriums on the Tha Prajan campus of Thammasat University, their events were often standing room only. Their events were about making urgent questions of law—about coups, lèse-majesté, the role of the judiciary in the polity—accessible to the people. Hundreds of people crammed into auditoriums, and the overflow watched monitors to hear the lecturers talk about the law and how it was relevant to their lives. The Khana Nitirat became scholar-activist rock stars of a sort, with people lining up for their autographs after seminars.[73] Their popularity reflects the enduring urgency of the question of the law in Thailand, which is also reflected in the effort the NCPO put into using and reshaping the law.

On the first anniversary of its establishment and the fifth anniversary of the 19 September 2006 coup, the Khana Nitirat published a four-point declaration and proposal to address ongoing political conflict that characterized the coup in stark terms: "The 19 September 2006 coup was an illegal act. The coup destroyed the rule of law and democracy. The coup remains the primary cause of political conflict from then until the present."[74] The coup has become a political institution after decades of being presented as the only solution to resolving conflict. The Khana Nitirat proposal remains a radical reenvisioning of the place of law and the judiciary in redressing impunity and stopping coups.

The first point was to nullify the effects of the 19 September 2006 coup. To do so would entail announcing that the coup and other legal actions of the CDRM were without legal consequence, revoking the amnesty provisions the junta provided for itself, nullifying the actions taken against the previous government, and initiating new cases within existing legal mechanisms. They proposed that this be done through a constitutional amendment and then a referendum. Several months later the group issued a *People's Manual to Topple Coups*, which elaborated on the proposal and traced the creation of legitimacy for coups in laws.[75]

Over the following two years, the Khana Nitirat was active in the campaign to amend Article 112 to reduce punishment for alleged lèse-majesté, campaigning against blanket amnesties for state violence and producing a steady stream of accessible articles about the law on its website. The group had a particularly important role in early 2012 during the effort by the Campaign Committee to Amend Article 112 to collect signatures in support of the law's amendment. Worachet and other members of the Khana Nitirat traveled from province to province to explain the proposed amendment. What was most remarkable about these and other Khana Nitirat events, many of which I attended, was how many different kinds of people came to listen. The majority were not scholars or university students but people from every class and occupation outside the university. Their popularity and impact were also evident in the backlash against them, including vicious online attacks and the physical assault of Worachet outside his office in February 2012.[76] The Khana Nitirat's work to make law accessible was powerful and threatening to those in power in Thailand, where law has long been a tool of and for the powerful.

When martial law was announced on 20 May 2014, the Khana Nitirat issued a statement immediately that it was unconstitutional and illegal.[77] Then, following the coup, two of the members, Sawatree Suksri and Worachet Pakeerut, were summoned. The other five expected to be summoned but were not. Sawatree was released after two days of detention and interrogation, but Worachet was prosecuted.[78] After the coup, the Khana Nitirat went largely out of public view as a collective and issued only one more statement, on the draft constitution in 2016.[79]

Worachet was summoned twice, first on 24 May 2014 by NCPO Order No. 5/2557 and then again on 9 June by NCPO Order No. 57/2557. On 10 June, his wife went to report that he was unwell and unable to report himself. On 16 June, at the airport upon returning from Hong Kong where he had gone for medical treatment, he was taken by soldiers to report himself to the NCPO at the Army Club. He was granted bail on 18 June 2014.[80] Then, on 4 August 2014, he was indicted in the Bangkok Military Court of failing to report in response to a summons by the NCPO. On 24 November 2014, the first evidence hearing, Worachet's lawyer attempted to submit a petition to the Constitutional Court arguing that prosecution of civilians in military courts contravened the ICCPR and the 2014 Interim Constitution.[81]

As they did with Sombat Boonngamanong and Siraphop Kornarut, the military court dismissed the petition. The judges stated that the military court had the authority to examine cases and the 2014 Interim Constitution provided for the protection of civil and political rights. In addition, it did not have the authority to forward a petition to the Constitutional Court.[82]

Witness hearings progressed very slowly in the Bangkok Military Court. By 9 July 2019, when Head of the NCPO Order No. 9/2562 transferred all cases still in the military courts to the civilian courts, only the prosecution witnesses had testified. The first hearing in the Dusit District Court was on 29 July 2020.[83] Worachet's lawyer again submitted a petition to be sent to the Constitutional Court, to examine whether the order to report to the NCPO contravened the 2017 Constitution.[84] The petition queried whether, even though the 2017 Constitution, like the 2014 Interim Constitution, had a measure making all orders and announcements of the NCPO legal (Article 279), the orders to report were truly constitutional?[85] The Dusit District Court forwarded the petition, and examination of the case was placed on hold. The petition was significant because it was the first time that the Constitutional Court examined the constitutionality of an NCPO order.

The Constitutional Court explicitly ruled that both the summons to report and the criminal punishment for not doing so contravened the 2017 Constitution. The NCPO orders contravened the principles of the rule of law (*lak nititham*) and "stipulated a criminal punishment after the fact on the defendant. It is a law that intended to be enforced in particular cases or upon particular individuals specifically. It was not drafted for general use. Both aforementioned NCPO announcements are laws that set disproportionate criminal punishments and contravene Article 26 of the Constitution."[86] The Constitutional Court further explained that the provision of a criminal punishment for not reporting "is threatening, violates human dignity, and unjustly discriminates against individuals. The effect is for people not to receive equal protection according to the law and it contravenes Article 4 and Article 27 of the Constitution."[87] In addition, the two announcements were intended to aid in the preservation of order when the NCPO was in power. Once the NCPO was out of power, the crime of not reporting to the NCPO was no longer a crime, and a person could not be punished for it.

But the Constitutional Court then defended the necessity of the violation of rights and freedom. The assertion that it was necessary to do so is on par with the claim made by every junta that has seized power in a coup in Thailand: illegally overthrowing the existing government is the only solution to political conflict, the spread of communism, corruption, and so on. The judges wrote:

> The examination of law that limits the constitutionally-protected rights and freedoms of individuals must examine the situation of the country and the way of life of the people. The laws were written and enforced in a period when the National Council for Peace and Order had successfully seized the administrative power of the country. On 22 May 2014, they abolished the 2007 Constitution and there was a change of the entity that exercised power. The NCPO exercised both executive and legislative power simultaneously so that the country would become peaceful, orderly, and content. They did so until there was the promulgation of a constitution according to democracy with the king as head of state. In the interim period, when the NCPO performed the duty of administering the country, there was a need for the people to be orderly and not create chaos or impact the security of the country. Therefore, it was necessary to limit some of the rights and freedoms of the people.[88]

The Constitutional Court asserted that the summons to report and criminal punishment for not doing so was appropriate under the coup but no longer appropriate following the promulgation of the 2017 Constitution and the return to an elected government.

The Dusit District Court then dismissed the case against Worachet. But he did not view the decision as a victory. He commented that the decision was analogous to breaking even because so many people were harshly affected by the coup. The junta infiltrated the legal system and used the law as a tool of repression to such a degree that it fundamentally changed the law.[89] May Poonsukcharoen, a lawyer with Thai Lawyers for Human Rights, commented that the possible impact of the Constitutional Court ruling might be that people who were found guilty in cases of not reporting could have their cases expunged or those who went into exile and have an outstanding warrant could be able to return to the country.[90] Or there might be a lack of an impact: "But will it be able to create confidence for people who were summoned to report themselves to return [to Thailand], really? I don't think it will have that effect because in reality, the people who hold power are the same group of people, even though they no longer have the power of the NCPO. But they use the law as an instrument to carry out various matters, including matters beyond the law."[91]

In addition to Worachet's and May's critiques of the limits of the very delayed and insufficient Constitutional Court decision, additional questions remain. Does the derogation of rights create order? If it does, and it is not certain that it does, then for whom and at what cost? The answer to these questions, and who has the authority to decide, is bound up with tension between two forms of sovereignty central to the three cases in this chapter and the broader dissent against the coup of which they were a part. The first is the idea of the people as the owners of sovereignty—the holders of the highest power in the land—which is specified in every Thai constitution, including the 2014 Interim Constitution promulgated by the NCPO. The second is the designation by the courts of the NCPO as the sovereign and therefore able to issue orders and announcements that carry the status of law. This action by judges in courts under the NCPO, and judges in all prior courts, with the exception of Kirati Kanchanarin's 2009 dissenting opinion, was an important contribution to the jurisprudence of impunity because it at once criminalized and erased the people's dissent and their possible claim to sovereignty and participation in shaping the polity.

To contribute to a jurisprudence of accountability, the Constitutional Court would have needed to challenge the NCPO and its legitimacy in May 2014, as soon as it began issuing orders summoning individuals to report and placing civilian cases against the crown and state within the jurisdiction of the military court system. Rather than unquestioningly treating NCPO orders and announcements as the same as laws passed by a democratically elected parliament, the Constitutional Court should have taken a cue from Worachet, who noted: "The court does not view in the sense of procedure of how a law was promulgated or the content of a law, the Court only looks at once power has been seized, whether a law has the name of being junta orders, Head of the NCPO orders, or this or that announcements, they have the same status as that of an act that a parliament in a democracy promulgated. But the question is, is this right? This is the question that we should ask."[92]

The Constitutional Court for the People decision offers a resounding no in response. Informed by the principle of feminist judgment projects to use the law in force at the time of the new decision, and since the examination of the matter of the constitutionality of the NCPO orders should have taken place in July 2014, this means ruling in relation to the 2014 Interim Constitution and the ICCPR. The new decision illustrates how even the junta's own coup-era constitution can be read against the grain to protect rights. In so doing, inspired by the three defendants in the cases in this chapter, the new decision aims to be an example of civil disobedience that disrupts unquestioned ideas of junta sovereignty by imagining that the people, not only the state, have a claim to the law.

THE CONSTITUTIONAL COURT FOR THE PEOPLE

Petitioner: Worachet Pakeerut
Regarding: Whether NCPO Order No. 1/2557, NCPO
    Announcement No. 37/2557 and NCPO Announcement
    No. 41/2557 Contravene Articles 2(1), 3, and 4 of
    the 2014 Interim Constitution and the International
    Covenant on Civil and Political Rights

Article 45 of the 2014 Interim Constitution, promulgated on 22 July 2014, following the coup by the National Council for Peace and Order (NCPO) on 22 May 2014, provides for the Constitutional Court "to determine whether or not a law is contrary to or inconsistent with this constitution," and as specified in Article 5, "such request may be made only upon the resolution of the plenary session of the Supreme Court or the Supreme Administrative Court and only with respect to the trial and adjudication of cases."

Upon observation of the initiation of multiple cases of prosecution for individuals not responding to NCPO orders summoning them to report and the prosecution of civilians in the military court system for this and other crimes against the crown and state, the Supreme Court for the People and the Supreme Administrative Court for the People requested that the Constitutional Court for the People examine whether these orders contravene Articles 2(1), Articles 3 and 4 of the 2014 Interim Constitution, and the International Covenant on Civil and Political Rights (ICCPR), to which Thailand is a state party.

Before turning to these specific orders, the Constitutional Court for the People must first address the foundational act of the coup in relation to Articles 2(1), 3, and 4. Article 2(1) stipulates that "Thailand adopts a democratic regime of government with the King as Head of

State." Article 3 stipulates that "sovereign power belongs to the Thai people. The King as Head of State shall exercise such power through the National Legislative Assembly, the Council of Ministers and the Courts in accordance with the provisions of this Constitution." Article 4 stipulates that "subject to the provisions of this constitution, human dignity, rights, liberties and equality previously enjoyed by the Thai people with the protection under Thailand's constitutional convention of the democratic regime of government with the king as head of state and Thailand's existing international obligations shall be protected under this Constitution." A coup, the illegal seizure of power from—in the case of the 22 May 2014 coup by the NCPO—a democratically elected government, is not compatible with Article 2(1), 3, or 4.

The Constitutional Court for the People finds that, paradoxically, within the 2014 Interim Constitution, there are measures that contradict those measures protecting democracy and the people's human rights, civil rights, liberties, and equality. Article 44 provides the Head of the NCPO with unlimited and unquestioned power and stipulates: "In the case where the Head of the National Council for Peace and Order deems necessary for the purpose of reforms in various fields, for the enhancement of unity and harmony among people in the country, or for the prevention, restraint, or suppression of any act which undermines public order or national security, the Monarchy, the national economy, or State affairs, irrespective of whether such act occurred inside or outside of the Kingdom, the Head of the National Council for Peace and Order, with the approval of the National Council for Peace and Order, shall have power to order, restrain, or perform any act, whether such act has legislative, executive, or judicial force; the orders and the acts, including the performance in compliance with such orders, shall be deemed lawful and constitutional under this Constitution, and shall be final. When those have been carried out, a report shall be submitted to the President of the National Assembly and the Prime Minister for acknowledgement without delay." Article 47 turns the NCPO into a legislative body and stipulates that "all announcements and orders of the National Council for Peace and Order or orders of the Head of the National Council for Peace and Order which had been announced or made between 22nd May BE 2557 and until the date the Council of Ministers takes office under this Constitution, irrespective of their constitutional, legislative, executive or judicial force, including the performance in compliance therewith, irrespective of whether those acts have been performed before or after the date of entry into force of this Constitution, shall be considered lawful, constitutional, and final. Those announcements and orders applicable on the date before the promulgation date of this Constitution shall continue to be in force until there are laws, rules, regulations, resolutions of the Council of Ministers, or orders, as the case may be, issued to amend or repeal them. In the case where the National Council for Peace and Order issues an order appointing any person to assume office or removing from office of any position mentioned in Section 24 before the date this Constitution comes into force, the Prime Minister shall respectfully present to the King for appointing such person to assume office or removing such person from office." Article 48 provides the NCPO with an amnesty for the coup, as well as related prior and subsequent actions, and stipulates that, "in regard to all acts which are performed on account of the seizure and control of State governing power on 22nd May B.E. 2557 by the Head and the National Council for Peace and Order, including all acts of persons incidental to such performance or of persons entrusted by the Head or the National Council for Peace and Order or of persons ordered by persons entrusted by the Head or the National Council for Peace and Order, which have been done for the benefit of the abovementioned performances, irrespective of whether such acts were performed to have constitutional, legislative, executive, or judicial force, including punishments and other official administrative acts, and irrespective of whether the persons performed such acts as a principal, an accomplice, an instigator or an agent and whether those acts have been done on, before or after the aforesaid date, if those acts constitute offences under the laws, the persons who commit those acts shall be entirely discharged from such offences and liabilities."

The Constitutional Court for the People must decide which of the articles to use as a foundation for its interpretation. Articles 44 and 47 are in direct contravention to Articles 2(1), 3, and 4. In making this decision, the Constitutional Court for the People emphasizes that Article 3 stipulates that the judiciary is one of the bodies that exercises the sovereign power, which belongs to the people. The Constitutional Court for the People concurs with the 2009 dissenting opinion in a case in the Supreme Court's Division of Political Officeholders, Kirati Kanchanarin wrote:

The sovereignty belongs to the people. The court is one of the sovereign powers, which is of the people. The court must therefore exercise the aforementioned power for the people by making rulings in cases in order to expand the protection of rights and freedom of the people. And if the court does not serve the people, it will cause the legal system and judicial process to be challenged and shaken. In addition, the court should have a role in preserving the legitimacy of law, including the obligation to protect the rights and freedom of the people from the illegitimate exercise of power and the obligation to protect democracy as well. The exercise of power in governing the country by undemocratic means, or in other words, securing power without the consent of the majority of the people, is equivalent to the overthrow of democracy. A revolution or a coup is the overthrow of the constitution and is a crime according to Article 113 [of the Criminal Code]. It is a way of obtaining power to govern the country by undemocratic means. If the court affirms the power of individuals or a group of individuals who carry out a revolution or a coup to be the sovereign state, it is equal to the court not serving and protecting the people from the exercise of illegitimate authority, and being indifferent to the protection of democracy.

The Constitutional Court for the People views that it is time to join the people who have courageously acted to defend democracy and the constitution against coups. This means that the Constitutional Court for the People must interpret the Constitution on behalf of and in support of the people, and their human dignity, rights, liberties, and equality as stipulated in Article 4. In sum, this further means that the Constitutional Court for the People finds that Articles 44, 47, and 48 do not outweigh Articles 2(1), 3, and 4 to legalize or legitimate the coup and other actions of the NCPO. While determining whether criminal charges should be brought against the NCPO for launching the coup is beyond the mandate of the Constitutional Court for the People, the Court finds that the coup and continued existence of the NCPO are in contravention to the 2014 Interim Constitution.

The Constitutional Court for the People brings this concern to the specific NCPO orders examined in this ruling. NCPO Order No. 1, issued on 22 May 2014, summoned twenty-eight people to report themselves to the NCPO "to preserve order and properly resolve the problems of the country." A series of subsequent orders issued between May and July 2014 summoned a total of 472 individuals in this manner. The orders do not specify why the individuals were summoned. Many of those summoned were then detained for the up to seven days authorized by the Martial Law Act of 1914, although the Constitutional Court for the People is aware of individuals who have been detained in excess of seven days, including Sombat Boonngamanong (nine days) and Kritsuda Khunasen (over one month). Many of those summoned were never informed of why they were summoned or then detained. This practice is in clear contravention of both Article 4 of the 2014 Interim Constitution and Article 9 (1, 2, and 4) of the ICCPR, to which Thailand is a state party, which stipulates:

> 1. Everyone has the right to liberty and security of person. No one shall be subjected to arbitrary arrest or detention. No one shall be deprived of his liberty except on such grounds and in accordance with such procedure as are established by law.
>
> 2. Anyone who is arrested shall be informed, at the time of arrest, of the reasons for his arrest and shall be promptly informed of any charges against him. . . .
>
> 4. Anyone who is deprived of his liberty by arrest or detention shall be entitled to take proceedings before a court, in order that that court may decide without delay on the lawfulness of his detention and order his release if the detention is not lawful.

The next instrument for examination is NCPO Announcement No. 41/2557, issued on 26 May 2014, which stipulated that not reporting to a summons by the NCPO is a crime punishable by up to two years of imprisonment and/or a fine of up to forty thousand baht. Given the problems with the summons to report noted earlier, the Constitutional Court for the People is gravely concerned about the imposition of a criminal punishment for not doing so. Further, the Constitutional Court for the People has become aware of cases brought about individuals who were summoned before the announcement was issued, thereby making their prosecution and any punishment retroactive.

The third instrument the Constitutional Court for the People examines is NCPO Announcement No. 37/2557, issued on 25 May 2014, which placed civilian crimes against the crime and state, which comprised violation of Articles 108–118 of the Criminal Code and violations of NCPO Orders and Announcements, within the jurisdiction of the military court system. Despite assertions of individual military court judges that they are independent, the Constitutional Court for the People is concerned about the guarantee of the independence of military court judges under the command of the Minister of Defense in a government formed and led by a military junta. Further, decisions in the military court system cannot be appealed. This is in direct contravention to Article 14(5) of the ICCPR on the right to a fair trial, which stipulates "Everyone convicted of a crime shall have the right to his conviction and sentence being reviewed by a higher tribunal according to law."

Finally, the Constitutional Court for the People would like to conclude with general observations about the threats to democracy and the Thai polity posed by the 22 May 2014 coup by the NCPO. Many of those summoned to report to the NCPO are those who hold different opinions about coups than the NCPO, including Sombat Boonngamanong, Siraphop Kornarut, and Worachet Pakeerut. Other citizens who have gone into the streets to defend the Constitution and democracy have faced arrest and intimidation. The Constitutional Court for the People would like to remind the NCPO that Article 19(1, 2) of the ICCPR stipulates that:

1. Everyone shall have the right to hold opinions without interference.

2. Everyone shall have the right to freedom of expression; this right shall include freedom to seek, receive and impart information and ideas of all kinds, regardless of frontiers, either orally, in writing or in print, in the form of art, or through any other media of his choice.

The Constitutional Court for the People is aware that these rights can be derogated in cases of emergency of national security, but the NCPO has not yet satisfactorily proven this necessity.

The Constitutional Court for the People rules that NCPO Order No. 1/2557, NCPO Announcement No. 37/2557 and NCPO Announcement No. 41/2557 contravene the 2014 Interim Constitution and the ICCPR.

FOUR

A CONSTITUTION WITHOUT THE PEOPLE

Tearing up the constitution is one of the first actions taken by each junta that has carried out one of the twelve coups since the end of the absolute monarchy in 1932.[1] The constitution creates the legal framework for the relationship between the people and the state in a polity. In a democracy, sovereignty belongs to the people. The constitution stipulates the rights and duties of the people and outlines the methods by which they will be protected by the state. The constitution also prescribes the structure of the state and the mechanisms by which the independence of various branches will be maintained and accountability for state wrongdoing ensured. The constitution supersedes all other law and is the final referent for which actions are legal and legitimate and which violate the people's sovereignty. At four thirty in the afternoon on 22 May 2014, in an announcement less than a page long, the NCPO rendered the 2007 Constitution null and void.[2] In doing so, the NCPO dispossessed the people of their sovereignty and placed itself beyond accountability.

Many who protested the coup framed their actions as an explicit defense of constitutional democracy, a defense that the 2007 Constitution itself compelled.[3] When Resistant Citizen brought its case against the

NCPO, the junta's abrogation of the 2007 Constitution was evidence of the crime of rebellion. When Apichat Pongsawat protested in front of the Bangkok Art and Cultural Center, he did so to protest the theft of the people's sovereignty by an illegitimate junta. When Sombat Boonngamanong and Siraphop Kornarut refused to report when summoned by the NCPO, they did so because they viewed the coup as illegal and unconstitutional. Despite the seeming impossibility of fighting back against the junta, neither the barrel of the gun nor the bars of the prison halted dissent.

But a constitution can be written in the service of dictatorship and the violation of rights just as easily as it can democracy and the protection of rights. The twenty constitutions promulgated since 1932 span a range of relationships between the people and the state, from democracy to dictatorship and many variations between. The well-trodden and often-cited vicious cycle of Thai politics—a junta carries out a coup and abrogates the existing constitution, a new constitution(s) is drafted, elections are held, and the elected government is in power until another junta carries out another coup and the cycle begins again—is the reason for both the high number of constitutions and their impermanence. The NCPO moved swiftly to fill the void it created and promulgated the nineteenth of these on 22 July 2014.[4] The 2014 Interim Constitution amnestied the NCPO for carrying out the coup, designated its orders and announcements as law, and provided the head of the NCPO, General Prayuth Chan-ocha, with absolute power to take any actions he viewed necessary to protect the nation.[5]

Domestic and international calls for a return to democracy grew with every month that the NCPO remained in power. Careful drafting of a new constitution provided the appearance of such a return via the creation of a path toward an election and a civilian government. But the NCPO's assent did not mean a willingness to give up power and transition to democracy. A Constitution Drafting Committee (CDC) handpicked by the NCPO created a charter that entrenched antidemocratic elements, including the preservation of an outsize role for the military in governance and affirmation of the amnesty for the NCPO. The draft was unveiled to the public for the first time on 29 March 2016, and a referendum was set for 7

August 2016.[6] The referendum could have been an important opportunity for the people to participate in setting the direction of the polity. Instead, the creation of a legal framework marked by domination of the people by the state, without any semblance of equality or protection of rights, began from the very moment the draft was released to the public.

The NCPO-appointed National Legislative Assembly passed the 2016 Draft Constitution Referendum Act to set the details of the referendum and foreclose any discussion of the draft. In particular, Article 61(2) was used to criminalize criticism and even discussion of the draft not authorized by the junta: "Any person who disseminates texts, pictures, or sounds in newspaper, radio, television, or electronic media or any other channels that distort the facts or have violent, aggressive, rude, inciting, or threatening characteristics aiming to induce eligible voters to refrain from voting or vote in a certain way or abstain from voting shall be regarded as a person who instigates trouble in order to cause disorder in the voting."[7] Article 60(9) criminalized disorder on the day of the referendum: "Any person who causes disorder in the polling station or commits any act which causes a disturbance or difficulty for voting." The act did not specify what constituted the creation of disorder, which instead was defined through adjudication. Those found guilty of violating either article were subject to up to ten years in prison, a fine of up to two hundred thousand baht, and the potential loss of one's right to vote for ten years. The act was used in combination with existing junta orders to set up the structure under which citizens would participate—or more accurately, not participate—in shaping the future transition to what the junta claimed would be democracy. At least 212 individuals were charged with violating either the 2016 Draft Constitution Referendum Act, with violating NCPO orders, or with sedition in relation to protesting or questioning the draft constitution. Many of the criminal cases stemming from the referendum were ultimately dismissed, and arrests instead aimed to limit the development of opposition to the draft.[8] Strong support for the draft in the referendum would make it possible for the junta to claim a mandate for its continued involvement in governance.

With a turnout of 59 percent of the electorate, the draft passed with

62 percent support, and the new constitution was promulgated on 6 April 2017. Joining the other dissidents who populate this book, two engineers from different generations who were part of the 38 percent against the draft and were both prosecuted for alleged violation of the Draft Constitution Referendum Act illustrate the depth of opposition. Samart Kwanchai, who entered university and came of age politically during the 14 October 1973 movement to oust Field Marshal Thanom Kittikachorn, distributed flyers in July 2016 that read Down with Dictatorship, Long Live the People, Vote No, 7 August. Toto Piyarat Chongthep, who finished university just before the 22 May 2014 coup, tore his ballot in half at a polling station as he yelled, "Down with dictatorship, Long live the people." The phrase they both used—"Down with dictatorship, Long live the people"—was the last phrase uttered by Khrong Chandawong, a socialist activist summarily executed by Field Marshal Sarit Thanarat's government on 31 May 1961, and it has been a rallying cry of activists ever since.[9] The case against Samart was dismissed, and the case against Toto and two friends who filmed his action was the sole referendum case in which a guilty verdict was rendered. Both cases turn on the ambiguity of *disorder* in the Draft Constitution Referendum Act. What unfolded as criminal was nothing that would be recognized as disorder but as participation.

The similarities and differences in the arrests, adjudication, and decisions in these two cases underscore the junta's fear of the people, illustrate how useful legal ambiguity is for authoritarian regimes, and make imagining a different outcome in Toto's case possible. In contrast to the jurisprudence of impunity, which leaves the ambiguity of disorder unspecified, a jurisprudence of accountability demands clarification of a law that could take away an individual's freedom for up to ten years. A key lesson of feminist judgment rewriting projects is that telling a different story and paying attention to context can make a divergent outcome imaginable by providing new information that changes the possible interpretation of law. Beginning with the details of the 2017 Constitution underscores why the NCPO was so adamant in its repression of opposition and why Samart, Toto, and others resisted. Telling the stories of how they opposed the draft constitution challenges the unjust jurisprudence and contributes to tracing the legacy of struggles for democracy of which they are a part. A jurisprudence of accountability affirms participation of the people in the polity rather than criminalizing it. The steadfast, courageous actions of Samart and Toto to dissent and then fight their cases in this context forms the foundation for the Court for the People decision offered here in Toto's case.

UNDEMOCRATIC FROM THE BEGINNING

The draft of Thailand's twentieth constitution was quietly unveiled on 29 March 2016, two months shy of the second anniversary of the coup. The NCPO opted to organize very few sanctioned events and chose not to distribute copies of the draft to all who were eligible to vote in the referendum, as had been done before the referendum on the 2007 Constitution. The antidemocratic content of the draft constitution may have been the reason for the NCPO's reluctance to circulate information about it before the referendum, or the reluctance may have simply been practice that prefigured the content.

But the Draft Constitution Referendum Act meant that circulation of analysis by anyone other than the NCPO, let alone criticism, was very difficult. The lack of criticism of the draft, combined with arrests and prosecutions and how the referendum was carried out, provide a clear reflection of how the 2017 Constitution aimed to consolidate the role of the NCPO in politics rather than be a meaningful step on the path back to democracy. In sum, "the people's right to an informed choice was denied to them and voters were not familiar with the pros and cons of the draft constitution" on which they voted and must live under.[10]

The sharpest analysis of the draft came from the Khana Nitirat, the group of dissident law lecturers at Thammasat University led by Worachet Pakeerut, whose prosecution for not reporting himself when summoned by the NCPO was taken up in the previous chapter.[11] The draft constitution left the absolute power afforded to the Head of the NCPO by Article 44 of the 2014 Interim Constitution intact until the first cabinet entered office.[12] The Khana Nitirat argued that "enacting a constitution with this characteristic makes important measures in the draft constitution, particularly those which pertain to the protection of the rights and liberties of individuals, completely meaningless. This is because the Head of the NCPO is able to use the aforementioned authority to violate the rights and liberties of the people and those whose rights and liberties are violated will be unable to challenge these violations in any way."[13] Yet the NCPO wanted the appearance of protecting human rights.

The draft further set out that for the first five years of the new government, the NCPO and the king would be responsible for appointing 250 senators, to sit with the 500 elected members of the lower house of Parliament.[14] This provided the military with significant power to continue to shape politics and the direction of the polity, and it was an even greater proportion than the 2008 Constitution of Myanmar, which provided the military with a guarantee of occupying 25 percent of seats in parliament.[15] The draft also provided for the ongoing legality of the NCPO Announcements, NCPO Orders, and Head of the NCPO Orders and other actions of the NCPO even after the new constitution was promulgated.[16] The Khana Nitirat noted: "This results in the entirety of actions of the NCPO being constitutional, legal, and beyond contestation, even though they are logically neither constitutional nor legal. The impact of such a constitutional measure is to destroy the status of the constitution as the highest law."[17] These various instruments had to be revoked individually: they did not automatically cease to exist with the promulgation of the constitution.

The draft constitution introduced concerning ambiguity that could further restrict the protection of rights. If a matter arose for which the constitution did not account, action should be taken in line with "the tradition of rule of a democratic regime in which the king is head of state in Thailand."[18] The very uncertainty of the meaning of this kind of rule made this measure equivalent to providing those in power the ability to choose whatever meaning was convenient for their purposes. Further, even though the draft constitution acknowledged rights and liberties, a wide range of ambiguous reasons was provided for their derogation.[19] In particular, rights can be derogated if their protection would have an impact on "national security," "public order," or "the good morals of the people." Without defining those broad terms, the state can violate the rights of the people with little concern. The very interpretations of *disorder* in the Draft Constitution Referendum Act in the cases of Samart and Toto illustrate the danger of such ambiguity.

Given the range of problems in the draft, the restrictions on criticism of the draft themselves demanded to be challenged. The Internet Dialogue on Legal Reform (iLaw), a nongovernmental organization engaged in documenting human rights violations and making information about law accessible to the public, attempted to file a petition with the Constitutional Court that Article 61(2) of the Draft Referendum Act contravened the 2014 Interim Constitution because it was vague and limited the rights and liberties of the people. They argued that the law "describes the offence in such broad and vague terms as 'abusive,' 'aggressive,' and 'seditious,' that have never been defined under any law . . . the punishment for offenders is extreme, and completely unjustified for peaceful expressions of opinion. Prison sentences of up to ten years apply to such offences as manslaughter, or for carrying out an illegal abortion resulting in the death of the mother. Therefore Section 61, paragraph 2 is an unjustified and excessive restriction on freedom of expression."[20] But the Constitutional Court, by unanimous decision and without full examination, maintained that there was no conflict at all.[21]

Instead, there was a rash of cases in which people were charged under several different laws, including NCPO Order No. 3/2558, the Draft Referendum Act, and Article 116 (sedition) of the Criminal Code.[22] Among the 212 individuals who were prosecuted, 36 were prosecuted for distributing flyers and expressing their opinions. This included Samart, as well as a person who yelled out the admonition to vote no in public in Ubon, a person who posted a banner against the draft constitution in Prachinburi, people who distributed flyers in Samut Prakan, people who distributed Vote No stickers in Ratchaburi, and those who made various Facebook posts about the draft. Twenty people were prosecuted for sending letters about the referendum to others. Red Shirt activists set up Anti-Referendum Fraud Centers to monitor the lead-up to the referendum in eight central and northeastern provinces, and 147 were prosecuted in relation to them.[23] Eleven individuals were prosecuted for organizing a seminar about the content of the draft constitution at Khon Kaen University.[24] Three people, Toto and the two friends who accompanied him, were prosecuted for tearing up a ballot. In addition to prosecutions, there was a great deal of intimidation and harassment of activists, including summoning, surveillance, interrupting and shutting down events, and seizing materials such as posters and T-shirts.[25]

When criticized for arresting student activists for distributing flyers, General Prawit Wongsuwan, deputy prime minister, said: "This is a transition period. There will be a lot of time to talk about freedom after the charter draft is ratified. We're now in need of peace and order. So don't ask me again. If anyone breaches the law, I will catch them all." He further noted: "I didn't arrest students, I arrested lawbreakers. There's the law and I do everything in accordance with the law."[26] Prawit ensured that he adhered to the law as written, and in this case, the law that he wrote. But Samart, Toto, and many others were compelled to break the law as written because they operated with a richer idea of law as a tool for creating justice in society.

SAMART: A HISTORY OF STRUGGLE FOR DEMOCRACY

On 21 July 2016, a little over two weeks before the referendum, Samart Kwanchai hopped on his motorbike and drove to Pantip Plaza shopping center in the northern city of Chiang Mai. He parked and made a quick circuit around the parking garage, slipping flyers under the windshield wipers of ten cars. The next morning, sixty heavily armed officials descended upon his home and arrested him. Samart was charged with violating Article 61(2) of the 2016 Draft Constitution Referendum Act. On 24 April 2017, a few weeks after the new constitution was promulgated, the Chiang Mai court dismissed the case against him. But the dismissal came only after he endured being arrested with a show of force comparable to that of the arrest of a drug kingpin or human trafficker, detained for nine days without bail and a trial in which a punishment of up to ten years in prison loomed.

Was the content of the flyers—Down with Dictatorship, Long Live the People, Vote No 7 August as well as the three-finger symbol—so incendiary that distribution of ten of them threatened to create uncontrollable disorder? The series of military and police witnesses for the prosecution revealed that behind the stated concern for order was actually fear of dissent, or even critical thinking by the people. The judges who dismissed the case focused primarily on the prosecution's failure to prove that the flyers fomented disorder but left the vague and antidemocratic Article 61(2) unchallenged, concluding simply that the prosecution did not make a strong enough argument.

Although the dismissal of the case was welcome, it is not enough for the decision to constitute a jurisprudence of accountability. A rich idea of what justice could look like is instead found in Samart's dissent to the referendum and his life of sustained struggle. Despite only rarely encountering democracy in more than forty years, he never stopped living as if it were possible. His commitment is at once powerfully utopian and a stark refutation of NCPO rule, including how the referendum was carried out. While the vicious cycle of Thai politics tidily encapsulates the history of coups, it does not include the opposition that has accompanied every coup. Beginning the analysis of the case with Samart's lifelong resistance invites the imagination of a jurisprudence of accountability by centering the people instead of the state.

Samart's life parallels the political history of the country. Since traveling to Bangkok and joining the 14 October 1973 movement for democracy when he was a first-year student in the Faculty of Engineering at Khon Kaen University, the struggle between dictatorship and democracy were central in his life. Three years later, when the 6 October 1976 massacre and coup ended the period of open politics and activism by students, farmers, workers, and many others, he went into hiding in Khon Kaen. He and many fellow student activists did so because the Communist Party of Thailand, whose existence was one of the reasons the junta cited for launching the coup, was very active in Khon Kaen and across the northeast and they were concerned they would be targeted for arrest or other suppression by state authorities. Many students joined the party, but Samart remained in school and served as a courier between those in the city and those in the jungle. During the next big phase of struggle, in May 1992, after the end of the Cold War and the accompanying counterinsurgent dictatorship, he had returned home to Chiang Mai. Samart, his wife, and their young child joined the nightly protests in Chiang Mai to demand democracy.[27] In 2009 and 2010, Samart traveled to Bangkok to join the Red Shirt protests. He explained: "I was at Ratchaprasong, Ratchadamnoen. I went and ate and slept in front of Government House. When I was tired, I went home to rest [in Chiang Mai] and went back down [to Bangkok]. At home I was comfortable, but was I willing to rough it. Boy, was it hot. Tons of mosquitos. It's not that I was a Red Shirt, but I saw unjust things taking place in this country. I am a 14 October person, and have seen them tyrannize the country over and over again."[28]

Those who came of age politically during the transition to open politics with the 14 October 1973 movement and then experienced the end of democratic possibility with the violence of the 6 October 1976 massacre are often referred to and refer to themselves as "Octobrists." What the meaning of *October* is for members of this generation is heterogeneous, and Octobrists are found on all sides of politics.[29] For Samart, it means continued resistance to domination of the people by the state, and he framed his protest against the NCPO as an Octobrist: "Before, the people who engaged in struggle were the youth. The older people would say, no, don't go out. . . . It has changed to being older people who engage in struggle and the children and grandchildren who discourage it. Don't get too involved. This is a struggle continued from that of an earlier generation. Those who engage in struggle today are those who were young people during 14 October."[30] Samart's lifelong participation in dissent against dictatorship and willingness to endure discomfort for the struggle for democracy is an instance of utopian action. The utopia his life reflects and anticipates is one in which the people take up the struggle for democracy as a duty from which they cannot turn away.

At the time of the coup by the NCPO, Samart was retired from working as an engineer and operated a mosaic shop in Chiang Mai with his wife.[31] After two years, his assessment was that the NCPO was leading the country backward and he had to act.[32] He made his flyers and considered various options for their distribution, such as leaving a pile in a shopping center or letting them flutter to the ground while driving or from the top of a building. But he decided against those options because they were not targeted enough.[33] The flyers might simply be left where they landed without being picked up and read. Samart chose to place the flyers on individual cars as a way to reach those he did not know who might share his desire for change, noting: "My hope was for one flyer that I placed to be seen and picked up by the car's owner, whom I did not know, upon their return. I hoped it would be of use, and would be a spark that catalyzed consciousness. At least they would know that people were fighting. If they disagreed and tossed it aside, no problem."[34] He chose Chiang Mai's Pantip Plaza because he had once rented space there and knew it well. Samart was aware that there were closed-circuit cameras, but he placed his flyers without wearing a hat, mask, or other disguise. Given the potential punishments under the Draft Constitution Referendum Act, wearing a disguise would have been understandable and perhaps even wise. His right leg was weak, and he had a distinctive way of walking with a limp. But Samart's decision to register his dissent openly reflects the democracy he desired.

What Samart viewed as necessary action in the service of democracy was instead immediately treated as a grave crime by the military and police in Chiang Mai. On 22 July 2016, Lieutenant Colonel Phitsanuphong Chaiphut, deputy head of operations and acting head of army intelligence for the Kavila Base, Thirty-Third Army Region in Chiang Mai, received news of Samart's flyers via the Line messaging app. His commanding officer, General Chirawat Chulakul, the deputy commander of the Thirty-Third Army Region, ordered him to file a criminal complaint against Samart. At five o'clock the next morning, sixty military, police, and other government officials assembled and raided Samart's home. They seized the clothes he wore to place the flyers, the backpack he carried, the motorbike he drove, and an additional 405 flyers he had not yet distributed.

Samart cooperated with the officials and did not dispute that he was the person who had slipped ten paper flyers under the windshield wipers of cars parked in the underground garage of Pantip Plaza.[35] He was then held without being informed of his rights or able to contact a lawyer or his family at Chiang Mai city police station for two days before being remanded to the Chiang Mai provincial prison while the investigation continued. He was granted bail only after nine days of detention.[36]

Samart's trial began in February 2017. The very first action of the plaintiff and the prosecutor was to attempt to convince Samart to change his plea. Before testimony began, two soldiers summoned him into the hall and urged him to confess so that the case would end. Confession made sense because he broke the law.[37] The prosecutor also spoke with Samart and his lawyers and warned that the case could result in a prison sentence. Was Samart prepared to accept this? Samart was unswayed. His intentions were good, and he aimed to inspire democratic consciousness among the people.[38] One way to understand these actions is that the prosecutor and the plaintiff continued the attempt to silence dissent even once the trial began. But the other is that they were aware that the repressive, antidemocratic nature of their actions would be revealed and on display in the courtroom.[39] Avoiding such a display and revealing the fiction of the NCPO's and 2017 Constitution's claim to be democratic would be best.

The meaning of the phrase on the flyer—Down with Dictatorship, Long Live the People—was at the center of the hearings. What would happen when people read it? Would people be compelled to go along with it? Would it lead to disorder? In other words, was it a violation of Article 61(2)? Each prosecution witness offered his interpretation of the phrase.

Lieutenant Colonel Phitsanuphong Chaiphut, the accuser and acting head of army intelligence for the Thirty-Third Military Circle, was responsible for keeping track of enemies who were a threat to national security and order.[40] His view was that *dictatorship* referred to the seizure of power to govern the country, *down with* to bringing an end to, the date to the referendum vote, and the three-finger salute was borrowed from the film *The Hunger Games* and was the symbol of those who opposed the government. The phrase "Vote No" constituted persuading the people to be against the constitution, which made the flyer political instigation against the draft constitution.[41] For Police Captain Chaiphon Pha-uprong, a co-accuser and police investigation official in the case, *dictatorship* referred to the government in place at that time, as well as all that arose from coups in other eras. *Down with* referred to complete destruction. He was unequivocal: the message was violent, in opposition to unelected governments, and amounted to political agitation.[42]

But the witnesses for the plaintiff were not united in their assessment of the phrase's power to foment disorder. Police Major Thonsakon Praman, a co-accuser and deputy commander of the Chiang Mai city police station, said that the phrase referred to toppling a dictatorship, and the word *dictatorship* referred to the government that existed at that time that originated with a coup.[43] But he did not feel that he had to go along with it.[44] For Major Sophon Phakdikasem, the commander of a unit of soldiers in Chiang Mai province who was part of the arrest operation, *dictatorship* referred to the government at the time and all governments that came from coups.[45] The three-finger salute was a symbol of those who disagreed with the government. He thought the message might lead to disorder and therefore might be against the Draft Referendum Act. People might go along with the ideas and misunderstand, and there might be disorder and chaos. But on cross-examination, he said no when the defense asked if he would go along with the message upon reading it. On redirect, the prosecutor asked him why, and he said because he held his own opinions. However, people who already disagreed with the government might go along with it.[46]

Despite the prosecutor's valiant efforts, the witnesses' range of responses to the flyer displayed exactly the critical thinking that Samart hoped to spark. The defense strategy refuted both the content and the very premise of the prosecution's argument further by presenting Samart's making and distribution of flyers as the action of a Thai citizen who had rights and freedom, for the people to have a consciousness of democracy and be concerned for it, without any enmity for other people or the country in any way.[47]

Samart was the first witness in his own defense. He began his testimony by explaining, "My dream since I was a university student has been to see the country have full democracy," but that dream had been interrupted by coups over and over, and Thai people rendered without rights or voices.[48] Coups were destructive for the country and bad for the economy, and lowered other countries' esteem for Thailand.[49] If people disagreed with his ideas, they could toss the flyers. If they did so, this was fine with him because he believed that Thai people could think for themselves. He did not see his actions as agitation or criminal in any way.[50] He voted against the draft.[51]

The two other defense witnesses were both academics. Nattakorn Withathanon, a political science professor at Mae Fah Luang University, testified that the phrase on the flyer was used by every movement calling for democracy in every era. The phrase "vote no" or the phrase "vote yes" would not create disorder and so did not fall under the law.[52] The final defense witness was Somchai Preechasinlapakun, a scholar of coups I frequently draw on in this book and law professor at Chiang Mai University. He stressed that the harsh criminal penalty of the Draft Constitution Referendum Act meant that the interpretation in such cases must be very rigorous. Somchai viewed the statement on the flyers as an abstract one, drawn from history and in support of democracy, mentioning no individuals specifically.[53] Phrasing his question in a leading manner, the prosecutor asked during cross-examination whether a person off the street who saw the word *dictatorship* would understand it to mean the current government. Somchai said no, it would refer to all dictatorships, including the current one. Somchai agreed with the prosecutor that a person off the street would conclude that the phrase "down with" would mean destruction. The prosecutor asked if sending the flyer to everyone in the country would cause disorder. Somchai was unequivocal in his response: no, absolutely not.[54]

The defense reiterated that the message on the flyer did not violate the law, and there were irregularities in the officials' testimony and practice in the closing declaration.[55] Most significant, the declaration emphasized Samart's profound respect for the people and his belief that they could think and make their own decisions. The utopian democratic polity that Samart's actions anticipated was not one in which everyone shared his views but one in which everyone had the freedom to think and make their own decisions. The closing declaration noted:

> The defendant testified clearly to the court that he made the flyer. But the reason that he made it is that he believes that it is a fundamental right and freedom of all Thai people to express their political opinions, without any ill intention to any group of individuals, society, or the nation, to create any loss. He only did it to inspire consciousness of all Thai people to love democracy. The defendant did not have the intention to instigate in any way at all. In addition, readers can themselves decide the meaning of the messages of "7 August" and "Vote No" printed on the flyers by the defendant. The prosecution witnesses themselves reflected different opinions upon reading the phrase, both agreement and disagreement. Therefore, the defendant's flyer does not constitute instigation. As regards the accompanying image of holding up three fingers, it is merely a symbol that refers to peace, freedom and fraternity, which are positive, and has no relation to the content of the draft constitution examined in the referendum on 7 August 2016.[56]

They further noted that the only witnesses for the prosecution were the accusers and those involved in the arrest, and there were no experts in linguistics, literature, or law, or anyone else involved in the referendum. Finally, Samart's actions were the expression of rights and freedom guaranteed in the 2014 Interim Constitution, the Draft Constitution Referendum Act, and international conventions to which Thailand is a state party. The defendant's actions were not a threat to society.[57]

Samart was hopeful at the end of the hearings and commented: "Looking at the judge, he seems pretty good. His position means he probably does not really like what I did, but he has to hide his feelings. I did not say everything that I wanted to say at all because the judge had to listen and record it all. If I spoke and he just listened, for let's say an hour, I would say a lot more about the country and the people."[38] Which transformations in the judicial process would be necessary for a judge to be willing to listen to the ideas of a dissident citizen for an hour or more? What would it mean for Samart to speak without restraint in the courtroom, particularly with his words being entered directly into the record rather than interpreted and restated by the judge? Samart was prepared for prison. He said: "I will accept what happens. But I will not accept what they do if it is unjust. I have fought to this degree and see what is what. I cannot not fight because I will not accept defeat."[39] Samart's utopian vision of democracy was one that faced the possibility of suppression but refused to either back down or accept it.

On 24 April 2017, Samart was summoned to the court to listen to the decision. The judges framed the decision by noting that four conditions must be met for an action to be a violation of the 2016 Draft Referendum Act. First, it must be the creation of chaos to make the referendum disorderly. Second, there must be distribution of a message, image, sound in the newspaper, radio, television, electronic media, or other format. Third, it must have the characteristic of being wrong in its facts or violent, aggressive, profane, instigating, or threatening. Fourth, there must be a special intention, which is for those eligible to vote to not exercise their right to vote or to vote in one particular way or another.[60]

As in the witness hearings, the meaning of the statement was central to the decision. Drawing on the Royal Institute Dictionary, the royally and state-sanctioned authoritative guide to the Thai language, the judges wrote:

> The word dictatorship . . . means the decisive exercise of power, the ideology or mode of governance in which there is one leader or a single group of individuals who exercise power decisively in their governance of the country. The phrase "down with," according to the dictionary, means completely damaged, totally damaged. When they are combined, the phrase "Down with Dictatorship" means for those who exercise power decisively in governing the country to be completely damaged or totally destroyed.

This is abstract and general and does not refer to the draft constitution as dictatorial as the plaintiffs charged, but refers to the government that was in power at the time. . . . If a person off the street read the aforementioned, it would not cause them to have feelings or change their feelings to lead them to not exercise their right to vote or vote in a particular way. In addition, those who have the right to vote in the referendum must be not less than eighteen years old on the day of the referendum. They have sufficient maturity to make a decision or not exercise their right to vote, including if they are going to vote to endorse or not to endorse the draft constitution. Merely a message on a leaflet . . . therefore does not carry enough weight to impact the decision of those voting in the referendum. In addition, the message of "Down with Dictatorship, Long Live Democracy," is a longstanding phrase that has been used generally among those who love democracy prior to the defendant's use in the flyer.[61]

The judges further ruled that although several witnesses for the plaintiff testified that the flyer constituted agitation, that was merely their personal opinion and it was not corroborated by expert witnesses in linguistics or elections. The case was dismissed and the 405 leaflets seized were ordered to be returned to Samart because they were not used in a crime.

Samart viewed the verdict as a victory for everyone in the country.[62] He felt as though he succeeded, because he wanted to inspire the people to not be motionless.[63] The judges' defense of democracy was one such instance of not being motionless. Reflecting on his role in politics, Samart said: "I am proud that my thinking has not changed since I was a young man, when I was a first-year university student, up until today. I still dream of democracy in this country. In truth, I am just only one screw. I have not had any great role. But I am a screw that is in motion. Not a screw that is covered in rust and has been tossed in a gutter."[64] Like Samart's life of struggle, the formation of democracy and justice is never static. His metaphor of being a single screw that is part of a bigger, ongoing process leaves space for the participation by a wide range of the critically thinking people so essential to creating both.

TOTO: THE DISORDER OF DEMOCRACY

At eleven thirty in the morning on the day of the referendum, Toto Piyarat Chongthep walked into his polling station in Bangkok and obtained his ballot. He then stood in front of the ballot box and tore his ballot into two halves as he yelled, "Down with dictatorship, long live democracy!" Destruction of a ballot, even one's own ballot, is a crime under Article 59 of the Draft Constitution Referendum Act, and he was immediately taken into custody at the polling station. By eight o'clock that evening, Toto, as well as two friends who had recorded his action, were charged with violation of Article 60(9) of the Draft Constitution Referendum Act for allegedly creating disorder in a polling station.

They maintained their innocence throughout their prosecution and a series of decisions over all three levels of courts that stretched across nearly four years. Toto admitted that he tore his ballot but argued that it was an act of peaceful expression that did not cause disorder. His two friends, Dave Songtham Kaewphanphruk and Jirawat Aekakornuwat, admitted that they filmed their friend's action but denied that it caused disorder. The Court of First Instance agreed with them, but the Appeal Court and Supreme Court found all three guilty and sentenced them to a fine and four months' imprisonment. As the case progressed, it became clear that their crime was their joint effort to record and share Toto's dissent with a broader audience. Disorder was the name given to the crime of participation in politics. Tracing the series of events that led to this designation illustrates how the jurisprudence of impunity was formed and identifies the junctures at which different interpretations could have arisen.

On the day of the referendum, Toto Piyarat Chongthep was a twenty-five-year-old electrical engineer and master's student in the Faculty of Law at Thammasat University. After the coup, he cofounded Friends for Friends Association, a mutual-aid organization for current and former political prisoners, with Ekachai Hongkangwan, a former Article 112 prisoner.[65] Dave was a former student activist at Rajamangala University of Technology Suvarnabhumi who met Toto through antihazing activism.

Jirawat was an activist who organized a protest with Toto in which they walked around in public wearing copies of the uniform worn by prisoners to reflect that the whole country was a prison.[66] The three also operated a business selling miscellaneous plastic items. They had an appointment with a potential customer on the afternoon of the referendum. They decided to meet at the polling station in the late morning, discuss business over lunch, and then go to their appointment.[67]

Upon being arrested, Toto was told to sit in a chair inside the polling station. He asked to be taken outside so he would not get in the way of other voters. The pieces of his ballot were bagged up and taken into custody as evidence of a crime.[68] Toto made a declaration that he posted to Facebook and that was swiftly picked up by independent and mainstream media:

> As regards what happened today, I would like to inform state officials, the media, and the people that I was fully conscious of my actions. I am not mentally ill. I was neither on drugs nor was I drunk. My actions grew out of the consciousness of a citizen who only wishes to demand and stand firm for rights and freedom, which ought to be ours. Whatever the result, I will take responsibility for my actions. I will not run away or hide out of fear. I will fight the case in a court that has used the power of dictatorship to distort the law's legitimacy and democratic principles. I will fight the case in a judicial system that arrests and imprisons those who criticize the constitution draft. This is a draft that destroys the principles of law and the rule of law to such a degree that it will be difficult to find a solution and which lacks security for the liberty and freedom of the Thai people.[69]

Toto chose to tear his ballot to make his view on the referendum and the draft constitution visible and unforgotten. He explained: "Actually, at first, I was going to vote no. Then later I changed my mind and was going to boycott. But in the end, I decided to tear my ballot because I wanted it to be a political milestone, and historical evidence for the future of the illegitimacy of this constitution draft. At least there was one person who did not endorse it. And history must record it."[70] Like Samart, Toto faced his potential punishment without turning away, even though he recognized that the punishment would be unjust.

Dave and Jirawat used their mobile phones to record Toto's protest and uploaded it to Facebook. They were careful to stand outside the polling station, as only voters were permitted inside. The poll workers ordered them to stop filming, and they did so without any resistance.[71] The formation of the jurisprudence of impunity began through a series of events around the arrests. The police asked Jirawat for his phone number so that they could request a copy of the video file. They pressed Dave for information about Toto.[72] Then, as the two friends prepared to follow Toto to the police station, two plainclothes police officers asked if they could ride with them, as all the police vehicles were full.[73]

Toto was taken into an interrogation room with a one-way video camera. Similar to Samart's case, the military was involved, and there were soldiers present in the police station.[74] A plainclothes military officer told Toto that the video camera was a direct link to the NCPO.[75] Dave attempted to take photographs of the soldiers guarding the interrogation room. This angered the police, and they erased the photographs from his phone.[76] By eight o'clock that evening, the interrogation and processing of Toto were almost complete. As Jirawat was walking outside to bring his car to wait for Toto at the entrance, a plainclothes policeman stopped him and said he could not leave because a case was going to be brought against him and Dave for causing disorder.[77] All three were finally released at three o'clock in the morning.[78] They were indicted on 13 December 2016, and each spent two days and one night in prison before bail was granted.[79]

The primary argument that the prosecutor tried to advance was that Toto, Dave, and Jirawat planned the actions ahead of time, which constituted the creation of disorder in a polling station as criminalized in Article 60(9) of the Draft Constitution Referendum Act. But examination of the testimony and the decisions instead indicates that the three were neither prosecuted for creating disorder in a polling station nor for creating disorder in any recognizable way. Instead, similar to Samart's case, they were being prosecuted for daring to participate in politics by sharing their dissent publicly. Disagreeing with the draft constitution was not illegal, and voting against it was not illegal. But recording one's views and sharing them with other people so they could not be forgotten was made illegal. The crime of Toto, Dave, and Jirawat was that their public criticism of the draft constitution and referendum interrupted the order the NCPO wished to create in the country. Just as disorder had an unexpected meaning, so did order. Order for the NCPO was a polity in which the people assented and were silent.

Then, resonant with the prosecution's presentation of different interpretations of the phrase on the flyer in Samart's case, the prosecution presented different versions of the series of events that took place in the polling station centered on whether disorder ensued. Charuwan Srithongchai, the accuser and a polling station official, said during cross-examination by the defense that Toto's actions did not have an impact on anyone else. But on redirect from the prosecutor, she said that both the tearing of the ballot and the video recording of the tearing of the ballot were against the rules and therefore created disorder.[80] Amarin Nonthakotr, the polling station director, testified that he was shocked by Toto's tearing of the ballot. He told Dave and Jirawat that they could not make recordings in the polling station and they refused to move. But then on cross-examination by the defense, he contradicted himself and said that he did not actually see Dave or Jirawat but was informed by other people about them. On redirect by the prosecution, he said that the sheer presence of Dave and Jirawat in the area of the polling station created disorder.[81]

Testimony by other prosecution witnesses cast doubt on this assessment of disorder. Sukanda Khanunthong, a polling station official who witnessed the event, heard a loud sound and turned toward it. She saw someone using a mobile telephone to take pictures and officials leading Toto to sit in a chair. Sukanda said that taking photographs was against the law, created disorder, and was an obstacle that made it impossible for people to vote conveniently. But then on cross-examination by the defense, she said that she continued performing her role without interruption.[82] Nuchanapha Tunchaiphim, another polling station official, testified that she saw Toto tear his ballot because few people were voting at that time. When officials told Dave and Jirawat to stop recording, they did so. There was no interruption of voting.[83] Police Senior Sergeant Major Somporn Phakwongthong, the safety officer at the polling station, testified that voting continued normally at the polling station during and after the tearing of the ballot. Toto did not resist arrest. He further testified that the disorderly loud sounds were made by officials who screamed in surprise, not the defendants.[84] Finally, Police Major Apichoke Khonabadee, the inspector at Bangna Police Station, testified that his assessment from viewing the clip was that there was no disorder during the tearing of the ballot. Voting went on as usual.[85]

The testimony by the three witnesses for the defense—the three defendants—focused on what happened on the day of the referendum and why they protested. Toto testified that he tore his ballot because the rights of those who did not support the draft constitution were violated. They were arrested, detained, and prosecuted. He was aware when he tore his ballot that doing so was against the law. He chose lunchtime, when few people were present, for his action.[86] When he was arrested and the police brought a chair for him to sit in, he asked to move beyond the yellow line that demarcated the area of the polling station.[87] Dave testified that recording his friend was not a crime.[88] On cross-examination, the prosecutor claimed that in the video clip of the events, there was no disorder in the polling station after the ballot tearing, but how could Dave affirm that there was not any disorder outside the view of the camera? Dave said he was prepared to maintain his assertion of the lack of disorder.[89] Jirawat testified that he had asked Police Senior Sergeant Major Somporn, the safety officer, if they could record their friend, and he directed them to remain outside the polling station. They did so for the entire period. When asked by the defense lawyer why he thought they were prosecuted, he said he did not know, as he did not have any enmity with the polling station official who accused him or any of the other prosecution witnesses. He thought that it might be because all three publicly expressed political views that were critical of the NCPO.

On 26 September 2016, the Court of First Instance dismissed all charges of creating disorder because voting had proceeded normally. Toto was found guilty of violating Article 59 of the Draft Referendum Act and Article 358 of the Criminal Code, which criminalizes the destruction of property belonging to someone else. He was sentenced to four months in prison and fined four thousand baht; the prison term was suspended for one year.[90]

Toto was satisfied by the Court of First Instance's decision. Were the situation to arise again, he would take the same actions: "I still stand firm. And I am confident that the process and steps I took did not cause anyone hardship or cause anyone to be unable to exercise their right. I wanted to exercise my right and I exercised my right. Not voting in the referendum does not have to mean that I stayed at home. I did not vote but I expressed my opinion clearly that I did not vote and I did not like the process that arose."[91] He continued: "As far as I understand it, a referendum should take place within an atmosphere of greater democracy and should primarily be for the benefit of the people. But ultimately, the referendum was as many have said: it was a mechanism for the continuation of the power of the junta and a political instrument of one particular group of leaders."[92] Toto did not plan to appeal the decision.

The prosecutor was less satisfied with the decision and submitted an appeal. The prosecutor argued that public posting to social media of the video of Toto tearing his ballot created disorder and was an obstacle to voting.[93] Toto's tearing of the ballot and yelling and the recording affected the order of the state and was not peaceful resistance. The defense response was that voting carried on as expected and the three did not have an impact on or obstruct anyone else's exercise of their right to vote.[94]

The Appeal Court reversed the decision of the Court of First Instance and concluded that the three defendants caused disorder and were guilty of violating Article 60(9) of the Draft Constitution Referendum Act. All three were sentenced to six months imprisonment and a six-thousand-baht fine, which was reduced for their cooperation with the investigation to four months' imprisonment and a four-thousand-baht fine, with the term of imprisonment suspended for one year. But the Appeal Court's explanation of its logic for the guilty verdict did not focus on the creation of disorder in a polling station. Instead, the judges argued that examination of the defendants' public postings to Facebook in the five months before the referendum reflected strong anti-NCPO sentiment. The judges interpreted this to mean that they had planned the action ahead of time and that it was a disturbance of or an obstacle to voting.[95] Because there was no evidence of such an obstacle or disturbance at the specific polling station, the Appeal Court's decision seems incorrect. But upon remembering that the meaning of *disorder* is not what it seems under the NCPO, the decision can be understood as one in which what is made criminal is any view different from that of the NCPO. The jurisprudence of impunity allows for departures from the law, even the law as written, to preserve the fiction of the people's assent to dictatorship. The collective crime of Toto, Dave, and Jirawat was to expose that fiction.

The three defendants responded to the Appeal Court decision with concern. Toto worried that the Appeal Court decision might create a standard about dissent for future referendums. Jirawat noted that all he did was take pictures of his friend's actions, like a citizen reporter. He did not think that what he did was criminal, and he was proud of what he did, but it made getting a job difficult because employers were reluctant to hire those with an outstanding political case. Songtham was surprised by the Appeal Court decision but also aware that anything could happen when one was fighting against dictatorship.[96]

The defense submitted a petition to the Supreme Court. The three responded to the assessment of alleged disorder by arguing that their actions were peaceful and without weapons, and that voting continued without any problems. There was no disorder, no creation of obstacles to voting, no assault of state officials, and they did not resist arrest.[97] Further, neither the Draft Constitution Referendum Act nor any other law prohibited the taking of pictures or making of videos, or putting either on social media.[98] The ICCPR guaranteed Toto's right to peacefully oppose the referendum. Finally, the Appeal Court punishment was disproportionate.[99]

The Supreme Court's decision was read on 21 July 2020, three years and eleven months after the referendum. The Supreme Court left the verdict, logic, and punishment of the Appeal Court unchanged.[100] This was the first and only Draft Constitution Referendum Act to reach the Supreme Court. All other cases were dismissed.[101]

After the Supreme Court decision, Jirawat commented: "I will continue being in movement if there are any interesting points or those that are within the agenda that I support pushing this country to be a real democracy, a full-fledged democracy. It is like many people say, let it end in our generation—I want full-fledged democracy to succeed in our generation."[102] He continued and said, "I think that actually, having a case, or being prosecuted, being imprisoned in a period in which a dictatorship is in power, is something to be proud of. I want to pass on to the younger brother and sister university students . . . that fighting against unjust power, fighting against dictatorship is our duty."[103] Like Samart, Jirawat sees his action, struggle, and suffering as a duty. Samart, Toto, Dave, and Jirawat all chose to oppose the draft constitution despite knowing the punishment they faced and knowing that the judges who presided over their trials were more likely to choose injustice over justice. That they still chose to fight under such circumstances reflects a belief in the possibility of democracy and justice that is at once utopian and necessary if it is to become real.

A Court for the People's decision in Toto, Dave, and Jirawat's case must go beyond dismissing the case to be part of the jurisprudence of accountability. Accountability is not merely the absence of impunity but is substantial in its affirmation of and creation of space for the people to shape the future of the polity. Such a jurisprudence begins by telling a different story about the referendum and offering a different assessment about the meaning and role of dissent. What was conceived of as destructive disorder by the Appeal and Supreme Courts is instead cast in the new decision as the very participation foundational to democracy.

THE COURT FOR THE PEOPLE

Office of the Attorney General, Plaintiff
versus
Piyarat Chongthep, Defendant No. 1
Jirawat Aekakornuwat, Defendant No. 2
Songtham Kaewphanphruk, Defendant No. 3
Charge: Violation of the Draft Referendum Act

The facts indicate that on 22 May 2014, a military junta, the National Council for Peace and Order (NCPO), carried out a coup and illegally ousted the caretaker government of Prime Minister Yingluck Shinawatra. As part of the coup, the NCPO immediately abrogated the 2007 Constitution. The country was without a constitution for two months, until 22 July 2014, when the NCPO promulgated the 2014 Interim Constitution. Simultaneously, the NCPO appointed a Constitutional Drafting Committee (CDC) chaired by Bowornsak Uwanno to draft a new, permanent charter. The NCPO did not approve of the first draft, completed in September 2015. The NCPO appointed a second CDC, chaired by Mechai Ruchuphan. The membership of both CDCs was selected by the NCPO without any public representation or consultation. The second draft constitution was completed in February 2015. The draft was quietly released to the public, and it was announced that a referendum would be held on 7 August 2016. Simultaneously, the National Legislative Assembly appointed by the NCPO passed a law, the Draft Constitution Referendum Act. This law established a set of rules surrounding the debate and discussion of the draft constitution and the referendum. Only the NCPO and those approved by the NCPO were permitted to circulate information and organize public debate about the draft. The draft constitution passed with 61.4 percent support, with the participation of 59.4 percent of eligible voters. The 2017 Constitution was promulgated on 6 April 2017.

On the morning of 7 August 2016, Piyarat Chongthep, Defendant No. 1, an engineer and activist working on behalf of former political prisoners, decided to exercise his right to oppose the draft constitution. He was concerned with both the content of the draft itself and the restrictions of debate surrounding the referendum, which had led to the arrest and prosecution of more than two hundred citizens who attempted to join or create public discussion about the draft. He walked into his polling place and picked up his ballot. Instead of then entering a booth and filling out his ballot, he tore his ballot in half while yelling out, "Down with dictatorship! Long live democracy!" Two of his friends, Jirawat Aekakornuwat, Defendant No. 2, and Songtham Kaewphanphruk, Defendant No. 3, made a video recording of his action with their mobile telephones. They posted this videorecording to social media; Piyarat also posted a written declaration explaining why he tore his ballot to social media. Piyarat was taken into custody immediately after tearing his ballot, and Jirawat and Songtham were arrested later that evening.

All three defendants were charged with violating Article 60(9) of the 2016 Draft Referendum Act, which stipulates "Any person who commits the following acts during the opening of the polls: (9) cause disorder in the polling station or commit any act which causes a disturbance or difficulty for voting . . . shall be liable to imprisonment not exceeding ten years and to a fine of not exceeding 200,000 baht." Piyarat was further charged with violating Article 59, which stipulates "Any person who destroys a ballot paper prepared for voting without authority, or intentionally commits any act to cause a defect or damage to ballot papers, or commits any act to cause an invalid ballot to become valid, shall be liable to imprisonment not exceeding one year and to a fine not exceeding 20,000 baht."

The first matter that the Court for the People must examine is whether the three defendants violated Article 60(9) of the 2016 Draft Referendum Act. In order to do so, it is necessary to determine whether the actions of the three defendants resulted in disorder. The act does not define *disorder*, but the Court for the People understands it to mean a disturbance or interruption of the normal functioning, and in this case specifically, a disturbance of or interruption to voting in the referendum.

The witnesses for the plaintiff offered a range of views about the impact of the actions of the three defendants. Charuwan Srithongchai, the accuser and a polling station official, said that Defendant No. 1's actions did not have an impact on anyone else; she later said that his tearing of the ballot was against the rules and therefore disorder. Amarin Nonthakotr, another polling station official, testified that the act of video recording itself created disorder, although he did not witness it occur. Sukanda Khanunthong, another polling station official, said that taking photographs was disorderly, but she also testified that her role was not interrupted. Nuchanapha Tunchaiphim, another polling station official, said that there were few other voters at the polling station at the time. She testified that neither the tearing of the ballot nor the recording of the action caused an interruption of voting. Police Senior Sergeant Major Somporn Phakwongthong, the safety officer at the polling station, said that voting on the draft referendum continued as normal during the tearing of the ballot and the arrest. He further testified that the loud sounds and any disorder caused arose from the actions of the officials, not any of the three defendants. The final prosecution witness, Police Major Apichoke Khonabadee, was not present at the polling station and only watched a clip of the events. He testified that, from watching the clip, his assessment was that there was no disorder and that voting went on as usual. Jirawat and Songtham, Defendants No. 2 and 3, requested permission to record from Police Senior Sergeant Major Somporn and he granted it, as long as they remained outside the perimeter of the polling station, which they did. The Court for the People observes that the evidence presented by the plaintiff does not support the accusation that the three defendants caused disorder and is therefore untenable.

The second matter that the Court for the People must examine is whether Defendant No. 1, Piyarat Chongthep, violated Article 59 of the 2016 Draft Constitution Referendum Act when he tore his ballot. As he tore his ballot, he yelled, "Down with dictatorship, long live the people." This phrase was first spoken by Khrong Chandawong before his execution on 31 May 1961 and has been used by every successive generation of citizens calling for democracy. In the written statement he released shortly after tearing his ballot, Piyarat acknowledged his responsibility in doing so. He said: "My actions grew out of the consciousness of a citizen who only wishes to demand and stand firm for rights and freedom, which ought to be ours. Whatever the result, I will take responsibility for my actions. I will not run away or hide out of fear. I will fight the case in a court that has used the power of dictatorship to distort the law's legitimacy and democratic principles. I will fight the case in a judicial system that arrests and imprisons those who criticize the constitution draft." Piyarat was aware that tearing his ballot was against the law as written, but he did so anyway to reveal broader problems within the law and the judicial system. The Court for the People observes that the tearing of a ballot into two pieces in this instance was therefore not destruction but expression. Expression is guaranteed in Article 34 of the 2017 Constitution, which stipulates "A person shall enjoy the liberty to express opinions, make speeches, write, print, publicize and express by other means. The restriction of such liberty shall not be imposed, except by virtue of the provisions of law specifically enacted for the purpose of maintaining the security of the state, protecting the rights or liberties of other persons, maintaining public order or good morals, or protecting the health of the people." The Court for the People observes that the evidence presented by the plaintiff does not support the accusation that Piyarat Chongthep destroyed his ballot and is therefore untenable.

All charges against Defendants Nos. 1–3 are dismissed.

FIVE

DISAVOWING RESPONSIBILITY

On 8 September 2015, General Paiboon Kumchaya, the NCPO-appointed minister of justice, issued Ministry of Justice Order No. 314/2558 designating a section of the Eleventh Military Circle Base (MCB) in Bangkok as a prison for civilian defendants in national security cases.[1] Reflecting on the relationship between the NCPO and the people, Thai Lawyers for Human Rights (TLHR) characterized the prison as the culmination of the military junta's intervention in the judicial process. With each step, the NCPO aimed to provide injustice rather than justice, as THLR explained: "It could perhaps be said that the NCPO, which wields power in the present, is the plaintiff or the direct opponent [of the people]. It is an opponent with the power to make its followers, such as military officials, arrest or search without any need for a warrant. Then, the cases of those arrested are prosecuted in military courts which are under the Ministry of Defense, which is under the executive, which is the NCPO. This takes place before they ultimately send their opponents into solitary confinement in a prison on a military base."[2] The provision of injustice by the NCPO—which was accompanied by violation of human rights and the creation of fear—relied on the combination of concentration of power in the hands of the junta, secrecy, and a healthy dose of arbitrariness.

Resonant with the obscured logic of who was summoned to report for detention during the first months after the coup, it was unclear who would be selected for detention at the MCB prison and who would be detained within the existing prison system. Further, similar to the problems that arose with the NCPO's prosecution of civilians in military courts, detention of civilians on a military base beyond the public eye created immediate concerns of safety and protection of rights. Events at the prison soon deepened these concerns. Detainees reported torture, isolation, difficulty of access to lawyers, and other rights violations. Then, less than two months after the prison was established, two individuals accused of lèse-majesté died in custody. On 23 October, Police Major Prakrom Warunprapa allegedly hung himself in his cell. On 7 November, Suriyan Sucharitpolwong died, allegedly due to a blood infection. I use the word *allegedly* deliberately, as neither death was fully investigated, despite the legal requirement for an inquest to be held in all cases of deaths in custody.[3] Rather than protecting detainees from state violence, the law—the Ministry of Justice order, along with other NCPO orders and announcements invoked in the operation of the MCB prison, were all treated as law—made them more vulnerable to it.

Yet as the cases traced throughout this book illustrate, activists never conceded the power over the law to the NCPO. Underlining Noura Erakat's argument that the law is contingent and a site of struggle, the NCPO and activists fought one another on the terrain of the law.[4] The NCPO sought to use the law as a tool to dispossess the people of their rights, while TLHR and the people they represented insisted on the possibility that law could safeguard the rights, and lives, of the people. This contest over the subjects and meaning of the law—who could use the law and for what—was also a contest over the very shape of the polity. Who is permitted to voice their visions for the future, and whose visions are cast as dangerous dissent that must be quashed? Who is protected from the arbitrary exercise of law, and who lives at the will of the more powerful? Most acute, who can kill without being held to account, and who can be killed without any possibility of redress for their families or society? The jurisprudence of impunity answers these questions by refusing their relevance to the law. This refusal increases ambiguity over who holds power and whether and how limits may be placed on it. Ambiguity creates the lacunae—physical, legal, and political—in which violence arises out of public sight and beyond accountability. A jurisprudence of accountability must instead begin with clarity in multiple registers: the importance of safety of person and life, the equality of all members of the polity, and the urgency of ending impunity.

Such a possibility was broached in a petition brought to the Administrative Court challenging Ministry of Justice Order No. 314/2558. The Administrative Court was established in 2001 for the people to bring cases against state officials or agencies that have caused harm to the people or otherwise not carried out their duties appropriately.[5] Pansak Srithep, one of the members of Resistant Citizen who brought the treason and rebellion case against the NCPO in Chapter 1, filed the petition against the minister of justice. He argued that the definition of "national security cases" in which defendants would be subject to detention was vague and that the reports of extensive rights violations at the MCB prison necessitated its closure. The Administrative Court acknowledged the existence of problems at the MCB prison but ruled that they were not caused by the order. It dismissed the petition.

To keep the MCB prison open, the Administrative Court left substantive questions of law, rights, and justice untouched. Rewriting this Administrative Court decision from one that consolidated the jurisprudence of impunity to one that contributes to the creation of a jurisprudence of accountability means actively centering the protection of civilians rather than state officials or agencies. In other words, rather than looking for a legal loophole to absolve the state from responsibility, an Administrative Court for the People would take the mandate of protecting the people and securing accountability for violence against them as paramount. Instead of dispensing with the reports of torture and the unresolved deaths in custody by stating that they were not caused by the order establishing the prison, an

Administrative Court for the People would reflect on what kinds of state structures might safeguard the people rather than render them vulnerable.

Inspiration for the new decision comes from the life of the plaintiff, Pansak Srithep. In addition to being the plaintiff in this and the Resistant Citizen case, he was also a defendant in cases stemming from his actions against the coup. His opposition to the military began when his son, Cher, was killed during the crackdown on Red Shirt protestors in April and May 2010. Rather than halting his dissent when the potential consequences grew grave after the NCPO came into power, he continued his protest and maintained his faith in the possibility of justice. By highlighting Pansak's opposition, my goal is not to romanticize resistance but to examine how persistence in the face of repression itself generates the idea and vision of a just society. This is an instance of what Davina Cooper identifies as the conceptual action of everyday utopias, in which "the utopian is not simply a depiction of another kind of place, but a process or challenge—a mode of striving toward something else that is better—in which questions of imagination, creation, and processes of chance are deeply intertwined."[6] Refusing separation between envisioning change and making it concrete, she explains that "actualization and imagining do not take shape as discrete, separate worlds, but simultaneously interconnect in multiple, complexly tangled ways."[7] Pansak's refusal to stop fighting recurring injustice in his life before and during the regime of the NCPO models the relentless struggle through which the Thai polity can be, and is being, remade. The urgency of this struggle, and ending impunity for state violence, became acute within the context of the rights violations at the MCB prison.

THE VIOLENCE OF AMBIGUITY AT THE MCB PRISON

Ambiguity, the abuse of power, and human rights violations intersected at the MCB prison. From the moment of its inception, who would be held there, and why, was unclear and discretionary. The physical structure and location then moved both prisoners and the authority behind the prison out of view. This eliminated the conditions for the protection of basic rights and created those for their violation. The deaths of Police Major Prakrom and Suriyan soon after the prison opened should have led to its closure but instead loomed as a threat of the violence possible within its walls that generated significant fear for those held there and those who might be held there. The pointedly incomplete investigations into their deaths underlined this fear and became another aspect of the violence perpetrated by the NCPO.

Ministry of Justice Order No. 314/2558 designated the MCB prison as a place to detain those accused in "national security cases" but did not offer any further specification of what this meant. When the order was issued, all cases against the crown and state, including all violations of NCPO announcements and orders, were within the jurisdiction of the military court system.[8] Judges hold the authority to assign places of detention, yet most of those accused in cases in the military court system were not remanded to the MCB prison.[9] In total, during the period between 14 September 2015 and 8 March 2016, forty-seven people, including forty-five civilians, were detained at the MCB prison. They were accused of a range of crimes, including crimes against the crown and state, but also graft, robbery, attempted murder, and drug-related crimes. Sixteen of the civilians were known to be held in four cases, including the bombing of the Erawan Shrine, an attempted attack on a Bike for Dad event in support of the monarchy, and a gun robbery case, in addition to the Article 112 case in which Police Major Prakrom and Suriyan were held.[10] The inclusion of cases that seem distant from national security, including robbery and drugs, suggests that the definition of "national security" was at the discretion of judges.[11] This unexplained exercise of authority in remanding some, but not others, was both emblematic of the NCPO's rule and a component of the violence at the MCB prison. The detention of these forty-seven people, and the deaths of two of them, was overseen by eighty-six people, comprised of six Department of Corrections (DoC) officials and eighty soldiers appointed as temporary correctional officers. Although Minister of Justice Order No. 314/2558 placed the MCB prison officially under the authority of the DoC, the overwhelming ratio of soldiers to DoC officials and its location on a military base means that in practice it was controlled by the military.[12]

To obtain this spare statistical information on detainees and staff at the MCB prison, TLHR had to use the mechanisms in the Official Information Act (OIA).[13] There was no information about, or even reference to the existence of, the MCB prison on the DoC website. TLHR requested information about the number of detainees, the accusations they faced, and the number of staff, but it was initially refused on the basis that it was personal information and would affect state security.[14] TLHR appealed with the argument that it was statistical information and its provision would increase transparency and reduce fear among the public, which was the precise purpose of the OIA.[15] It was successful in the appeal, but the information raised as many questions as it answered. Who were the other thirty civilians detained at the MCB prison who were not known by TLHR? Why were some accused in crimes against the crown and state detained at the MCB prison while others were not? What training were the eighty soldiers working at the MCB prison given? What was accomplished—for the DoC, for the NCPO—by holding them at the MCB prison instead of the Bangkok Remand Prison or other existing prisons? These questions are unanswerable, but what is certain is that those detained at the MCB prison experienced a lack of safety, rights violations, and danger.

The physical conditions at the MCB prison reflected an explicit disregard for rights. The prison was constructed as a temporary structure and was unlike other prisons in Thailand. Rather than the large, open communal cells that are standard in Thailand, the MCB prison had individual cells with an inner layer of four walls of bars and then an outer layer of four concrete walls.[16] The doors were solid without a window or other way for guards to see in or prisoners to see out except when the door was open.[17] Detainees were held in these closed cells for twenty-four hours a day without the opportunity to regularly converse or even encounter other people and so experienced de facto solitary confinement.

Detainees were let out of their cells to meet with their lawyers but under conditions that provided for the further violation of their rights rather than their protection. Benjarat Meetian, a lawyer with clients at the prison, described it by noting: "It is murky for them in the Eleventh Military Circle Base. Everything is murky. They are blindfolded and shackled with chains . . . it is murky for them."[18] The murkiness was caused by both a physical lack of light and a dimness of another order, one in which the boundaries of principles, in this case of rights and justice, were disregarded. There were no provisions for confidential consultation between lawyers and clients. During each meeting, soldiers stood guard in the room and closely listened.[19] Meetings were limited to fifteen minutes and lawyers had to submit the questions they planned to ask ahead of time for the military to review. Open-ended questions were discouraged and often forbidden. Benjarat elaborated on the consequences of the surveillance: "From the very beginning, we have to fight the case without being able to get facts from the defendant because the defendant is in the custody of the NCPO, which is the opposing party, the plaintiff. Even though we can speak, we cannot speak. What is a lawyer going to get from them? As long as they are in MCB, there is no lawyer who can get the truth from the defendants to fight their cases."[20] This expansive disregard of the fundamental rights of those detained in the MCB prison also ensured that they did not have the right to a fair trial.[21]

Intimidation was directed toward lawyers as well. Armed soldiers surrounded the lawyers from the very moment they entered the prison until they left. Chuchart Kanpai, another lawyer with clients in the prison, commented: "There were always armed soldiers around me. If anything happened, I would not make it out. If they ordered me to be shot on the spot, would any soldier dare to be a witness on my behalf? No way. Because they place great importance on orders. They have to follow orders, whether or not the order is legal. This was an assertion made to me by a soldier. He implored me, older brother lawyer, try not to enter the Eleventh Military Circle Base, for your own safety. Older brother, try not to come in here, because if they give the order, I have to do it."[22] Soldiers did not dare to assassinate lawyers but instead exercised their authority to make lawyers' work difficult. Adem, one of Chuchart's clients who was accused of being involved in the Erawan Shrine bombing, was tortured to confess while held at the MCB prison. Adem, an ethnic Uighur from China, admitted that he was guilty of entering the country illegally but denied any involvement in the bombing. Chuchart made a formal complaint on his behalf and gave interviews to the press about the torture. State officials delayed carrying out an investigation into the torture and the deputy national police chief, Police General Srivara Ransibrahmanakul, threatened to prosecute Chuchart. He claimed that Chuchart's comments to the press about the case and torture affected state security and damaged Thailand.[23] Speaking about torture—not the torture itself—was criminal and damaging to the country in Police General Srivara's view. Refusing to investigate the violence at the MCB prison protected direct perpetrators from being held to account, prevented questions from being asked about the structure of authority behind the violation of rights, and enhanced the creation of fear.

The deaths in custody represent the peak of both violence at the MCB prison and the obscuring of that violence. On 16 October 2015, Suriyan Sucharitpolwong, Jirawong Watthanathewasilp, and Police Major Prakrom Warunprapa were arrested and detained under Head of the NCPO Order No. 3/2558, which allowed for up to seven days of incommunicado detention without charge.[24] Then, on 21 October, the three men, who were thought to be close to the then crown prince, were accused of lèse-majesté at the Bangkok Military Court and ordered to be remanded at the MCB prison. Three days later, on 24 October, the DoC reported that at ten o'clock the previous evening, Prakrom used his prison-issued clothing to hang himself from the bars in his cell. He was still alive when he was first found by the guard on duty. They tried to aid in his breathing and took him to the DoC hospital, but he died before reaching the hospital. As explanation for his death, the DoC claimed that given that he was a high-profile person, Police Major Prakrom may have found it difficult to adjust to being locked up. The DoC further noted that the Bangkok Remand Prison had established a committee to determine the facts of what took place in the case and there would be an autopsy in line with criminal procedure law.[25] But the autopsy never took place, and if such a committee was in fact established, its conclusions were never released to the public. On 25 October, Prakrom's family went to obtain his body from the Institute of Forensic Science, where the autopsy would have taken place. But his body was not there: it was never sent. On 26 October, the minister of justice announced that the police, prosecution officials, pathologists, and administrative officials had concluded the cause of death without needing to send the body to the Institute of Forensic Science for an autopsy.[26] His family cremated his body the next day.

Then, on 7 November, the minister of justice announced that Suriyan, a famous fortune-teller also known as Mor Yong, had also died in custody. He claimed that an autopsy had been carried out by the Institute of Forensic Science and determined that the cause of death was "respiratory and blood circulation failures due to blood infection." Like Prakrom, Suriyan's family cremated his body the next day.[27] The lack of an autopsy in Prakrom's case and the swift cremations, which forewent the typical three to seven days of Buddhist prayers for the deceased, raises the question of the veracity of the minister of justice's statements. Did Police Major Prakrom kill himself? Did Suriyan die of a blood infection? Or was the minister of justice covering for murder or other foul play? Further investigation was made difficult, if not impossible, given Police Major Prakrom's and Suriyan's proximity to the then crown prince Vajiralongkorn. Even as crown prince, he was covered by Article 112 and merely raising questions about his possible involvement or even proximity to foul play would be enough for a critic to be charged with violation of the law.

The two deaths reverberated through society as a warning, and especially among other detainees at the MCB prison. One of their lawyers noted: "This is how it appears to the lawyer. I dare to say that they have none of the rights defendants are supposed to have. They don't have the right to meet with the lawyer, just two people. I don't know whether or not there is a clinic in there. The defendants do not have the right to tell their lawyer the truth. Because every time we speak, meet, several soldiers sit and observe. If they speak the truth, danger might befall them. They always say that they are afraid it will be like those who already died."[28] State violence is pedagogical for perpetrators, victims, and witnesses. The lessons in a time of impunity are simple: everyone is a possible victim and perpetrators will not be held to account. This generates the fear of speaking the truth that is a key component of the provision of injustice.

CHALLENGING THE ADMINISTRATIVE COURT

Throughout the years the NCPO was in power, activists worked to expose the truth about how the NCPO's legal structures facilitated state violence and the evasion of accountability. Each time they did so on the terrain of law, they offered the courts an opportunity to act in the service of ending impunity and fostering justice. As the cases in this book illustrate, they rarely did so. But to interpret these as failures would be incorrect. Every challenge by the people to the legality of the coup and the junta's authority was an active reinterpretation of the meaning and purpose of the law and the demonstration of the possibility of justice. Every challenge also forced the junta to face up to its own unjust reinterpretation and practice of the law. In the case of the MCB prison, this meant demonstrating how far the judiciary would go to preserve a place of detention surrounded by ambiguity and secrecy. This struggle was at once personal and political for Pansak Srithep, who was unyielding in his challenges to the junta as both a plaintiff and a defendant.

On 24 June 2014, Pansak laid out his views on the origins of the coup and the destruction wrought by it. In a declaration he made as part of a series of anticoup video clips in its immediate aftermath, he explained that the 2014 coup's antecedent was the 2006 coup, but the path to military involvement in the polity "began far, far before then. This is only the robust, flourishing progress of the seeds of depravity scattered long ago."[29] When his son was killed in 2010, people told him that if he had not left home, he would still be alive. But Pansak retorted: "The problem is not that people left their houses and then died. The question is rather why were ordinary people shot and killed in the streets?"[30] Between 2010 and 2014, a process to bring legal cases against perpetrators of an instance of mass state violence arose for the first time in Thailand. A case was brought against the former prime minister and deputy prime minister in late 2013.[31] But before witness hearings began, the NCPO, whose head, Prayuth Chan-ocha, was commander in chief of the army during the 2010 crackdown, launched a coup. Pansak continued:

> Over and over again, the Army conceals its crimes by fomenting coups to overthrow democratic regimes. This is the nation's wound. The happiness of the people dries up entirely and completely at the hands of the soldiers. The Army claims that all of this is to prevent confrontation from all sides. But instead, they have used every means to suppress and inhibit the processes of justice. Our ears are covered. Our eyes are blindfolded. Our mouths are taped shut. The people are not permitted to investigate the truth. The people are not allowed to critique. The army uses summons to report to threaten and intimidate the people. They arrest and detain all those who come out to oppose them. The people are ordered to believe only what the Army says, and ordered to trust in what the leader wishes us to believe. This includes having confidence in what the Army has done, because they claim that they wish to return happiness to the people.[32]

The NCPO's claim that it aimed to create happiness, which began in the first days after the coup, rings hollow in light of its regime. Pansak concluded by declaring: "The only path that can bring an end to the conflict is to establish the truth and return justice and fairness to society. These events should be able to be studied and comprehended by society as a national tragedy, rather than fading from memory or allowing bias to eclipse and block access to the truth, as the Army has always tried to do. Justice cannot arise when the truth is obscured."[33]

His activism aimed to reveal the obscured truth of the NCPO's actions. In response, the NCPO surveilled and harassed Pansak at every turn. His first criminal charge was violating NCPO Announcement No. 7/2557, which prohibited political assembly of five or more persons, for participating in a protest on Valentine's Day in February 2015, commemorating the

February 2014 election, the last before the coup.[34] The protest, under the title of "My (Dear) Snatched Election," was organized by Resistant Citizen in front of the Bangkok Art and Culture Center, with plans to include the display of ballot boxes and an open-air seminar on elections and democracy. But soldiers and police broke up the protest before it had a chance to begin, and Pansak and three other activists were arrested. Pansak was then summoned to give testimony to the police in March 2015. He announced on social media that he would walk from his home in Nonthaburi province to the police station in neighboring Bangkok. He planned to walk over a period of two days, and his route included passing locations of significance to the struggle for democracy. But the police stopped him after only a few hours and claimed that his solo walk was politically motivated and therefore criminal. He was soon slapped with a second case of violation of NCPO Announcement No. 7/2557, as well as sedition and violation of the Computer Crimes Act.

The two cases against Pansak and their adjudication are emblematic of how the NCPO used the law as a tool to threaten peaceful activists. Both cases began within the jurisdiction of the military court system. While those accused and convicted of violation of Article 112, lèse-majesté, were denied bail and almost always swiftly convicted, the NCPO used the charges of sedition and violation of NCPO Announcement No. 7/2557 to harass activists by making them show up at the court over and over again as their cases stretched out over multiple years, with hearings often separated by many months. When the cases were decided, if a defendant was convicted, the prison sentence was almost always suspended. The punishment was instead the hassle and uncertainty. Each defendant wondered, Will the pattern change with me? Will my bail be revoked? Will my prison term not be suspended?

Pansak was granted bail in both cases and both were ultimately dismissed. The NCPO revoked Announcement No. 7/2557 in advance of the election and so the election commemoration case was dismissed on 15 February 2019 because the law that he and other activists allegedly violated no longer existed.[35] After the appointment of a new cabinet on 9 July 2019 following the election, all civilian cases remaining in the military court system were transferred to the civilian criminal court system, including Pansak's walking case.[36] On 16 December 2020, the Criminal Court dismissed all remaining charges against Pansak on the basis that the actions in question were the peaceful exercise of his constitutionally protected rights.[37] But none of this was certain when he was arrested in 2015.

Pansak brought his Administrative Court case in the context of his sedition case. After Ministry of Justice Order No. 314/2558 came into force, Pansak was concerned that he might be detained at the MCB prison were his bail to be revoked. On the basis of the possibility of detention, he brought a petition detailing the known rights violations at the prison and arguing that the order should be revoked and the MCB prison closed.

Pansak submitted his case to the Administrative Court on 9 December 2015, less than four months after the prison opened and less than two months after the two deaths in custody. The Administrative Court took eleven months before finally accepting the case on 3 November 2016.[38] Pansak began by explaining his raison d'être in bringing a case. Given the laws he was accused of breaking, he was concerned that he might be detained at the MCB prison if his bail were revoked. He had the right to bring the case because detention would cause him to experience dangers to his liberty, human dignity, body and life.[39]

Pansak then explained the injustice generated by the order. First, he argued that Ministry of Justice Order No. 314/2558 was not sufficiently clear to be understood. Did "national security cases" refer to those crimes detailed in the second chapter of the Criminal Code, Articles 113–118, which included lèse-majesté and sedition? Did it include violation of NCPO Announcements and Orders, the 2015 Public Assembly Act, weapons-related charges, or other violations?[40] What about peaceful protests that were illegal according to the NCPO but legal under international law? What about Computer Crimes Act cases?[41] His questions were evidence that the meaning of "cases related to state security is unclear to the degree that it cannot be understood in terms of what cases it includes."[42] The phrase "related cases" was even less clear without a definition of "national security cases."

The problem with this lack of clarity was that it gave officials the authority to use their power arbitrarily.[43] Pansak acknowledged that the Corrections Act gave the authorities the ability to designate special categories of prisoners to be detained in particular locations but noted that it was not clear what characteristics necessitated separate detention in this instance.[44]

Second, the order was issued dishonestly and for political reasons. General Paiboon Kumchaya, the minister of justice, was appointed by General Prayuth and previously held a commanding position in the army. The NCPO announced its "clear political intention to want to use power to deal with groups of individuals who were a danger to state security" from the very beginning of the coup and the order seemed to serve this goal rather than a legitimate need accounted for in the Corrections Act.[45]

Third, the order contravened constitutional provisions of equality. Creating a special prison for those who allegedly committed security crimes, which were political cases, was selective and discriminatory. While the Corrections Act gave the minister of justice the authority to set special locations of detention, they must not conflict with the provisions of Article 4 of the 2014 Interim Constitution, which provided guarantees for human dignity, liberty, and equality.[46] The reports from detainees and lawyers indicated that conditions at the MCB prison did not conform to these guarantees.[47] In addition, the physical structure of the prison meant that the officials were unable to ensure safety and those who were detained were at additional risk for anxiety because of a lack of communication with others and natural light. This put detainees in danger of harm and self-harm.[48] The deaths of Prakrom and Suriyan confirmed these problems and further illustrated how the physical structure made it difficult for assistance to be provided in a timely manner to detainees in distress.[49]

Fourth, Pansak turned to the problems of access to justice caused by the MCB's location on a military base and under the authority of the commander in chief of the army. The overwhelming number of soldiers working as staff in the MCB prison and their interference and surveillance when detainees were consulting with their lawyers was a direct violation of the right to a fair trial. Without the ability to confidentially consult, lawyers could not obtain the information they needed to mount the best defense.[50]

In summary, the temporary MCB prison was an exercise of discretion by the minister of justice that was disproportionate and had caused harm to the people. Pansak petitioned, "The minister of justice is able to use his discretion to choose other measures that are appropriate that would have a lesser impact on the rights and liberties of detainees and would achieve the purpose of guaranteeing the safety and safeguarding appropriateness in detention."[51] He concluded by noting that the order was unjust and illegal.[52] In contrast to the injustice, discrimination, and arbitrariness that Pansak argued was created by Ministry of Justice Order No. 314/2558, his petition calling for the revocation of the order and the closure of the MCB prison held to an idea of the law as intended to protect the people. By bringing the Administrative Court petition despite not (yet) being detained there, Pansak Srithep expressed care for fellow members of the polity. This concern formed the foundation for the indictment's transformative potential. While the NCPO aimed to isolate people, the utopian future envisioned by activists using the law treats the polity as a place where people care for one another.

Administrative Court cases primarily proceed through a series of written responses by the parties rather than hearings. The minister of justice appointed Thawatchai Plengsombat, who worked in the administrative case department of the Office of the Attorney General, to respond on his behalf.

Thawatchai responded to Pansak's petition by refuting his criticism of the MCB prison and, most important, denying his right to bring a case. He argued that as Pansak had not been detained at the MCB prison, his rights had not been affected and he therefore could not bring a case.[53] This illustrates a profoundly narrow idea of the polity and protection of its members in contrast to the generous one which advocates used.

Thawatchai then methodically argued against the request to revoke the order and close the prison. The genesis of the temporary prison was that the Bangkok Remand Prison was full at the time, and the Department of Corrections proposed that the accused in national security and related cases were a special category who should not be held with regular prisoners.[54] There was no lack of clarity in the order, as evidenced by the petitioner's own bringing of the case as a person possibly affected.[55] In response to Pansak's assertion that the order was political, he argued that it was not but instead was in response to practical concerns of overcrowding and a large number of cases related to national security.[56] Thawatchai claimed that detainees had free time, a clinic, and leisure activities, and that DoC staff were present at the MCB prison as well.[57] He further claimed that everything proceeded according to the law and to criminal procedure with regard to visits with lawyers. He concluded his response with the assertion that there was no unjust discrimination and safety of detainees was guaranteed. The minister of justice had acted appropriately; therefore, the petition should be dismissed.[58] Thawatchai left the specific questions of torture, death, and other suffering and rights violations unmentioned.

Pansak then responded to Thawatchai's refutation in writing. He acknowledged that he had never been held in the MCB prison, but as an accused person in a sedition case, his temporary release could be revoked at any time. He could be detained at the MCB prison and therefore had the right to bring the case as someone whose rights and liberties could be affected.[59] He refuted Thawatchai's assertion regarding the clarity of the phrase "national security" and argued: "[It] is an abstract word that is used broadly. There are no clear or certain criteria and the meaning is highly unspecific. Even though the minister of justice claimed that the phrase appears in other laws, for example, the Criminal Code, its meaning is not specified. Most important, the phrase has never been used to enact a law that limits the rights and freedom of the people in the legal code."[60] In the case of Ministry of Justice Order No. 314/2558, it was being used to limit the rights and freedoms of the people and so the unclarity and ambiguity were particularly problematic. Pansak reiterated the political, not legal, goals of the order: "On 22 May 2014, the National Council for Peace and Order seized power in a coup. The purpose of carrying out the coup was to use power to deal with groups of individuals who thought differently than the NCPO by claiming that these groups of individuals were a danger to state security. Therefore, the intention in issuing the order . . . is to respond to the political reasons of General Paiboon Kumchaiya, the person who issued the order, which is the distortion of the exercise of power which is not in line with the purpose of the law."[61] He critiqued the comment about overcrowding by noting that there were only forty-seven prisoners in the temporary prison at the time.[62] He reiterated the problem about not being able to consult lawyers freely due to the presence of soldiers.[63] In the conclusion, he argued that the order was illegal because it was not clear enough to understand, it was in conflict with the principles of equality in the law and constitution, and it was political in nature.[64] In challenging the order by naming it as political, Pansak Srithep refuted the very logic of the necessity of the coup that recurred across court decisions during the time of the NCPO.

The Administrative Court ruled on 26 April 2019 and dismissed Pansak's petition. The court stuck to an interpretation of the law that was at turns textually faithful and contradictory but consistently devoid of substantive justice. The first matter the court ruled on was whether or not Pansak could bring a case. The court ruled that he could, even though he had not been detained at the MCB prison, because he might be given the case against him. At this moment, the Administrative Court, perhaps unexpectedly, provided some clarity about the order and the meaning of national security cases.[65] The second point that the court ruled on was whether the order was lawful. Acknowledging the provision for human dignity, liberty, and equality in the 2014 Interim Constitution, the court noted that the Corrections Act provided for special conditions in which there could be separation of prisoners. The Administrative Court claimed that the minister of justice used his discretion in setting up the temporary prison and thought about the safety of the prisoners and the staff. The Administrative Court then offered an intriguing explanation of national security cases, highlighting their special status under the NCPO and noting: "There is a motive in wrongdoing that is different than other cases of wrongdoing, as well as arising in a period in which the National Council for Peace and Order has seized the governing power of the country, which is an abnormal time. Such instances therefore have a characteristic different from other offences, or cases of the aforementioned offences in normal times."[66]

With regard to Pansak's argument about the lack of clarity about the offenses included, the Administrative Court ruled that it included all crimes in the second volume of the Criminal Code, meaning Articles 107–377, or all felony crimes. The Administrative Court then provided further leeway, noting, "In general principle, a commander is unable to stipulate all the details for those under his command to follow in every instance."[67] The order was therefore neither unclear nor ambiguous and not in conflict with administrative law. The Administrative Court here legitimated the unclarity and ambiguity in the law. The court further noted that the majority of those among the forty-seven held in the MCB prison were accused of drug violations and their presence was due to the actions of the criminal justice system rather than the order.[68] The contradictions were left unexplained.

With regard to the complaint about the prison not conforming to human dignity, the Administrative Court asserted that each prisoner had a bed and a toilet, even though there were no windows. The documented rights violations that arose at the prison—the two deaths and the torture—were not related to the order that established the temporary prison. In closing, the Administrative Court ruled that the detention of drug offenders indicated that the MCB prison was not political and not intended to "hold individuals who hold different opinions than the National Council for Peace and Order and is not the dishonest exercise of power as the plaintiff claimed."[69]

The Administrative Court's dismissal of the case deepened and further muddied the meaning of the Ministry of Justice's order rather than clarifying it. Attempting to legitimize the Ministry of Justice's order by dismissing the human rights violations that took place at the MCB prison as resulting from the order, the Administrative Court confirmed the problems at the MCB prison. By then choosing to leave those problems unaddressed, the Administrative Court sacrificed its own legitimacy in service of defending the Ministry of Justice instead of protecting the people from the excessive and arbitrary exercise of state power. In this instance, the Administrative Court contributed to the jurisprudence of impunity by choosing to stand with and defend another state agency against the people at all costs. The ruling is reminiscent of Chuchart's comment on soldiers: "They have to follow orders, whether or not the order is legal."[70]

In contrast, a jurisprudence of accountability offered by an Administrative Court for the People would name the exercise of power in establishing and running the MCB prison as unjust and in need of redress. A jurisprudence of accountability would begin with the recognition that the state is not in an adverse relationship with the people. An Administrative Court for the People would take its role as protecting the people particularly seriously in a time of abnormal times, such as under the NCPO, rather than taking this as an invitation to disavow its mandate and role. This begins by taking as foundational Pansak Srithep's point that "justice cannot arise when the truth is obscured." To reveal the truth of state violence, or even simply refuse to cover it up, then becomes the first step to stopping it and holding those responsible to account.

THE ADMINISTRATIVE COURT FOR THE PEOPLE

Pansak Srithep, Petitioner
versus
General Paiboon Kumchaiya, Minister of Justice, Defendant
Regarding: The issuance of an illegal order,
**   Ministry of Justice Order No. 314/2558**

The petitioner in this case, Pansak Srithep, has been charged in the military court in two cases. The first case is for violating NCPO Announcement No. 7/2557 for participating in a protest in February 2015 about the February 2014 election and the obstacles to democracy. The second case arose in relation to the first case. Pansak was summoned to report himself to the Pathumwan police station in March 2015. He chose to walk from his home in Nonthaburi province to report himself. He announced this intention and his route via social media. The police arrested him shortly after he began his walk, and he was charged with anther count of violation of NCPO Announcement No. 7/2557, as well as violation of the Computer Crimes Act and Article 116 of the Criminal Code. Both cases arose from peaceful actions and the exercise of the petitioner's constitutional rights. Both cases arose during the first year following the coup by the NCPO. Martial law was in force and civilian cases against the crown and state were placed within the jurisdiction of the military court. Pansak was charged in the Bangkok Military Court and granted bail. Then, on 8 December 2015, Minister of Justice General Paiboon Kumchaiya issued Ministry of Justice Order No. 314/2558, which established a temporary prison on the Eleventh Military Circle Base (MCB) on Nakorn Chaisri Road in Bangkok. The order specified that that the prison would be used for those accused in "national security and related cases." Within a few months after the opening of the MCB prison, two people detained at the prison died. Police Major Prakrom Warunprapa hung himself, and Suriyan Sucharitpolwong died following a blood infection. Other rights violations, including torture, poor sanitary conditions, difficulty accessing lawyers, and others were soon reported. Pansak grew concerned that were his bail to be revoked, he might be detained at the MCB prison. If that happened, he would face dangers to his freedom, dignity, and rights. Concerned with this possibility, he submitted a petition to the Administrative Court against the minister of justice, General Paiboon Kumchaiya, on the basis that Ministry of Justice Order No. 314/2558 was an illegal and unjust order.

The Administrative Court for the People asked the minister of justice to respond in writing to the petition, and then for Pansak to respond to this response. The Administrative Court for the People has taken into account these documents as well as additional facts and evidence about the MCB prison.

Before turning to the specifics of this case, the Administrative Court for the People wishes to comment on its role following a coup. The role of the Administrative Court is to review the legality of administrative acts by state officials and state agencies. A coup is an illegal ouster of the existing government. While the Administrative Court for the People notes that the Supreme Court for the People and the Constitutional Court for the People have yet to rule on the legality of coups, the Administrative Court for the People recognizes the period following a coup as a moment of particular uncertainty and danger for the people from state officials and state agencies. The Administrative Court for the People must be very circumspect in its actions at all times, but particularly in a time of a coup.

The first matter that the Administrative Court for the People must examine is whether Pansak Srithep has the right to bring a case against the defendant. The minister of justice argued that Pansak Srithep could not bring a case because he was not an injured party, as he had not been held at the MCB prison. The view of the Administrative Court for the People is that Pansak's concern that he could be held at the MCB prison is reasonable.

The second matter which the Administrative Court for the People must examine is whether the issuance of Ministry of Justice Order No. 314/2558 was an unjust exercise of discretion by the minister of justice.

The view of the Administrative Court for the People is that there are significant problems with Ministry of Justice Order No. 314/2558 and the MCB prison. First, there is a lack of clarity about who is to be held there. The order specifies that those accused in "national security and related cases" are to be held at the MCB prison. This is confusing, as noted by Pansak. According to the information provided by the Department of Corrections, the majority of the forty-seven detainees are accused in drug-related cases. The Administrative Court for the People is unclear about how these detainees fall within the category of "national security and related cases." The majority of detainees and prisoners in Thai prisons are held in drug-related cases and in the regular prison system. With respect to those held at the MCB prison accused in terrorism or Article 112 cases, the Administrative Court for the People also notes that most accused in these cases are held in the regular prison system. This indicates that the guidelines for who is to be held at the MCB prison are unclear. Although the minister of justice claimed in his response to Pansak's petition that the meaning of the category in the order could be understood, it is not clear. If the Administrative Court for the People does not understand the category, it is similarly impossible that Pansak or any other citizen would know the meaning of the category and therefore whether they might be held there.

The Administrative Court for the People observes that the pervasive poor conditions at the MCB prison are well documented. The prison is temporary and was constructed in a hurry. Fundamental concerns of physical and sanitary safety are left unaddressed and unaccounted for. The cells are designed to be like solitary confinement cells. The walls and doors are all solid, so it is difficult for prisoners to see one another or to be seen by guards. This makes it difficult for prisoners to request assistance or to have social interaction. This is compounded by the lack of exercise or other recreational facilities or designated times for detainees to leave their cells to go outside.

The Administrative Court for the People further observes that there are no provisions for private consultation with lawyers. Soldiers are always present during the consultation and further demand review of the questions to be asked by lawyers before the consultation, with the capacity to veto any questions they do not approve of. In addition, one lawyer reported being threatened by soldiers at the prison. This means that detainees and their lawyers cannot adequately prepare for their trials. Article 14(b) of the International Covenant on Civil and Political Rights (ICCPR), to which Thailand is a state party, guarantees that those accused of crimes, shall "have adequate time and facilities for the preparation of his defense and to communicate with counsel of his own choosing." The procedures at the MCB prison are in direct contravention of that guarantee.

The Administrative Court for the People also observes reports of torture at the MCB prison. Adem Karadag, a detainee accused in the bombing of the Erawan Shrine, reported being tortured while in custody. When his lawyer made a report about the torture, state authorities, rather than commencing an investigation, threatened the lawyer with a criminal defamation case. Article 7 of the ICCPR stipulates "No one shall be subjected to torture or to cruel, inhuman or degrading treatment or punishment." Both torture and the general conditions at the MCB prison are not in compliance with Article 7.

The Administrative Court for the People notes that the most concerning report about the MCB prison are the two deaths in custody. Police Major Prakrom Warunprapa allegedly hung himself in his cell on 23 October 2015 and Suriyan Sucharitpolwong died due to an alleged blood infection on 7 November 2015. Both men were remanded to the MCB prison after being accused of violating Article 112 and indicted in the Bangkok Military Court. Although the Criminal Procedure Code mandates that a postmortem inquest must be carried out when a person dies in state custody, an inquest was not carried out in the case of Police Major Prakrom and was rushed in the case of Suriyan. Both men were rapidly cremated, foreclosing any additional investigation into their deaths. The view of the Administrative Court for the People is that as soon as the two deaths occurred, the use of the MCB prison should have been paused and a full investigation carried out by the Ministry of Justice.

The Administrative Court for the People further observes with concern that, although Ministry of Justice Order No. 314/2558 placed the MCB prison under the administration of the Department of Corrections (DoC), the small number of DoC staff, six, and large number of soldiers, eighty, indicates that it was under the control of the military. The combination of the role of the military in administering the MCB prison and its location on a military base may mean that there are additional detainees who were not reported to the Department of Corrections and who remain unknown to the public.

The view of the Administrative Court for the People is that although none of these rights violations were specified in Ministry of Justice Order No. 314/2558, the vagueness and brevity of the order created a great deal of leeway for those administering the MCB prison to act as they saw fit. When the people's rights are being restricted, such as in the instance of detention, the conditions must be explicitly defined. This protects the people's rights as guaranteed in Thai law and with respect to Thailand's international human rights obligations and further ensures that the responsibilities of involved state officials and agencies are clear.

The Administrative Court for the People orders the revocation of Ministry of Justice Order No. 314/2558 and the immediate closure of the MCB prison. Anyone still detained there should be transferred to the Department of Corrections regular prison system.

EPILOGUE

JUDGMENTS THAT CANNOT BE REWRITTEN

On 16 July 2019, following promulgation of the 2017 Constitution and the first general election since the coup, the National Council for Peace and Order (NCPO) formally exited power when a new cabinet was formed. Yet General Prayuth Chan-ocha remained prime minister, dissidents remained under attack, and the legacy, and impunity, of the NCPO remained intact.

But in July 2020, several weeks before the Supreme Court decision was read in in the case of Piyarat Chongthep, who tore up his referendum ballot, a new movement for democracy emerged. Led by university students and other young people who had grown up in a polity shaped by the 2006 and 2014 coups, the movement began with three primary demands. First, for General Prayuth Chan-ocha to resign and new elections to be held. Second, for a new constitution to be drafted. Third, for the state to stop threatening dissidents. In August 2020, a fourth demand was added: the institution of the monarchy must be reformed. This demand was first spoken aloud in public on 3 August 2020 by Arnon Nampha, a human rights lawyer and one of the plaintiffs in the case brought against the junta for treason and rebellion rewritten in chapter 1. The protest was a Hogwarts-themed demonstration organized by students activists from Kasetsart University at the Democracy Monument in Bangkok. Dressed as Harry Potter, Arnon said: "Out of honor and respect for myself, and to honor and respect the brothers and sisters who have come to listen, and with the greatest honor and respect for the monarchy, it is of the utmost necessity that we speak about how the monarchy is involved in Thai politics today. We have shoved this problem under the carpet for many years, brothers and sisters. There is no mention of the actual problem, which means that the solutions miss the mark."[1] Then, one week later, at a protest at Thammasat University, Panusaya Sitthijirawattanakul, an activist from the United Front of Thammasat and Demonstration, read a ten-point list of specific demands for reform of the monarchy.[2] For decades, the monarchy had exercised political, economic, and legal influence, but the combination of Article 112 and persistent royalism kept that from either becoming known in detail or discussed openly. Royalists, whose power has waxed and waned but never disappeared since 1932 and grew stronger under the NCPO, immediately reacted. Many sympathetic to the movement worried that it would endanger activists and frighten many from joining them in the streets.[3]

Instead of the bold demands emptying the streets, the opposite happened. For a few months, demonstrations spread throughout the country and drew a broad, diverse cast of people. Reform of the monarchy, perhaps even a republic, seemed both possible and imminent. Even when police began to crack down on protests in October 2020, using the need to contain COVID-19 as an excuse, the streets did not empty. But then in November 2020, the authorities turned to the law to shut down the protests. Between 24 November 2020 and 10 November 2023, at least 262 people were charged with violation of Article 112.[4] Although the measure has been part of the Criminal Code since its last major revision in 1957, it was used rarely until the 19 September 2006 coup. Since then, the use of the law has expanded in an always-increasing trajectory. The only crime of those prosecuted has been peaceful expression of opinions and asking questions about a key political, social, and economic institution whose precise role and power has remained ambiguous since the end of absolute monarchy.

There is no presumption of innocence in these cases. To be accused is to enter already the realm of the guilty. Bail is nearly always denied to those accused of lèse-majesté, at least initially, with the explanation that the crime is a grave one and that the accused may flee given the lengthy possible punishment of three to fifteen years per count. This was the experience of Apichat Pongsawat and Siraphop Kornarut, who appear in this book, and were denied bail for 32 and 1,813 days, respectively. In cases since 2020, even once bail has been granted, it has tended to come with strict conditions, such as wearing an electronic monitoring anklet, being prohibited from participating in protests, and being warned to refrain from impugning the monarchy.

In the early days of this crackdown, an activist imaginary of a different kind of judiciary, one resonant with the Court for the People I fantasize into being in this book, fleetingly appeared in front of the Criminal Court on Ratchadaphisek Road in Bangkok. During a demonstration on 6 March 2021, protestors leaned a tall sign up against a larger-than-life photograph of Rama 10, Maha Vajiralongkorn, the current king.[5] Mirroring the design of an official court judgment, the phrase "In the Name of the People" was printed in large, bold letters across the top of the sign rather than that across the top of official court judgments, which are issued "In the Name of the King." That evening, the people directed their complaint on "the use of illegitimate power to lock up the innocent" to "the court and all the powers of justice." Writing in the voice of the Court *of* the People, they retold the story of the protests that began in July 2020. The people who called for democracy were peaceful and unarmed, but they were met with violence. Clubs, rubber bullets, tear gas, water cannons, and the law rained down upon their bodies and lives. Rather than preserving justice, the court and related units instead used the law to further dispossess those who dissented of their rights. They marched to the Criminal Court that night because their fellow protestors had been held without bail for nearly a month after being indicted for violation of Article 112.

They continued by noting that the Court of the People judges that by arresting the activists and denying them the right to be released on bail before trial to prepare their defense, the judges of the Criminal Court had destroyed the balance of the scales of justice by serving "the feudal over-lords as their unceasingly faithful servants." In choosing to identify the presence of feudalism, the Court of the People highlighted the absolutism that lingered in Thailand despite the nominal transition from absolute to constitutional monarchy.

The Court of the People called for the release of all those being held in political cases. Civil servants should respect their own honor and dignity, which will come "when they perform their duties with loyalty and honor to the people alone, not the feudal overlords and the institution of the mon-archy." Those who administer the unjust judicial system, not only those subject to it, were being harmed by the dispossession of the people in the service of the alleged protection of the monarchy. In calling on the judicial system to be just, the Court of the People called for a new relationship between the rulers and the ruled, and highlighted the essential role of the courts in creating it. The poster-sized judgment of the Court of the People, issued in the name of the people, rested against the portrait of Vajiralong-korn for less than an hour before it was confiscated by the police.

In the three years since the Court of the People briefly appeared, activ-ists have continued to be indicted in Article 112 cases, and they and their supporters have continued to call on the judiciary to act in the service of justice. Nightly protests are held for one hour and twelve minutes (to refer-ence Article 112) in front of the Supreme Court in Bangkok, Tha Pae Gate in Chiang Mai, Ubon Ratchathani University in Ubon, and other loca-tions to call for the immediate release of political detainees and prisoners. Detainees held in pretrial detention have gone on hunger strike in protest of the denial of their and others' right to bail.[6] Speeches and debates on the judiciary and its unjust actions are a staple of every protest that occurs. The poster and ongoing calls from activists for the judiciary to act justly indi-cate that the long-standing position of the judiciary on the side of those with power is no longer accepted as an unchanging status quo.[7] The people are aware of the jurisprudence of impunity that punished them for participating while leaving state violence, including coups, unaddressed. They demand otherwise.

Although I write for the people, rather than presuming to write in the name of the people, this book has taken the seemingly impossible premise of creating a jurisprudence of accountability as a necessary beginning. The future I write toward is one in which the participation of the people in the polity is valued, state officials and institutions are held to account for their crimes, and justice is itself treated as a guiding principle of adjudication in the courts. Writing in the voice of a judge and the form of a decision has been full of discomfort, uncertainty, and fun. Doing so has made the contingency of the law and the possibility of different outcomes palpable. The contest over law has gone from being theoretical and hopeful to being real and present on the page. Writing for the people, not the king, has made it possible to center the people, not the king or the state, and cast the judge as having a role other than legitimizing the junta. The rule of coups has ceased to appear inevitable. Instead, it is clear that it is the result of a series of particular and deliberate interpretations and narrative decisions by judges. As I struggled, sentence by sentence, to rewrite the original decisions, the legal decision ceased to be only a source of evidence for the history I write and became a very site from which to imagine the future anew.

This is a future in which the court would examine and judge a case brought against a junta for carrying out a coup, such as the case brought by Resistant Citizen against the NCPO. Protests against coups would be taken as a sign that the people do not assent to the coup. The right to demonstrate of those who join such protests, such as Apichat Pongsawat, who did so the day after the 22 May 2014 coup, would be protected, not derogated. The creation of fear through summoning and arbitrary detention, such as that experienced by Sombat Boonngamanong, Siraphop Kornarut, and Worachet Pakeerut, would cease to occur. Prosecution of civilians in all cases, even the gravest of national security cases, would remain in the civilian court system with active protection of the right to bail and the right to a fair trial. The Constitution, the highest law in the land, is one that should be drafted with citizen input and rigorous exchange of ideas. Distributing flyers about a draft, as Samart Kwanchai did, or tearing up one's ballot, as Toto Piyarat Chongthep did, would not be crimes. In such a future, if prisons still exist, they would have clear provision for the safety and protection of the rights of prisoners, unlike the Eleventh Military Circle Base in Bangkok. If reports of torture or deaths in custody arose, the Department of Corrections, the Administrative Court, and other relevant bodies would place the protection of the people, not the state, at the forefront.

But there is one category of decisions that cannot be rewritten as part of imagining such a future. Despite—and due to—the prevalence of Article 112 cases under the NCPO, I do not take them up in this book. Without speaking openly about and reforming the monarchy, as Arnon said in his clarion call, the struggle for democracy cannot succeed. The reason I do not rewrite any of the many convictions for lèse-majesté during the NCPO years is not because I disagree with the law and think that it should be revoked and all those currently held under it released, although I do. Instead, my reason is far simpler. As Thongchai points out in his concept of the royalist rule of law, and the spatial organization of every courtroom in Thailand communicates, the monarchy is above the law and above justice. What this means in practice was eloquently broached inside a courtroom in 2017 by a lawyer, Prawais Praphanukul. In 2008, Prawais took on the pro bono defense of Daranee Charnchoengsilpakul, one of the first to be accused of violation of Article 112 after the 19 September 2006 coup.[8] Then, in 2017, Prawais himself was accused of multiple counts of lèse-majesté in relation to a series of social media posts. He refused to appoint a lawyer or to participate in his own trial. He instead made a series of declarations to the court:

> The Thai judiciary has always declared itself to be the court of the king as can be seen from its proclamation of "acting in the name of the king." As the accusation in this case is the insult, defamation or threatening of the king, the king is therefore the directly injured party. The Thai judiciary proclaims itself to be acting in the name of the king, which is the declaration of itself as the court of the king, which is therefore the an-

nouncement of itself as the court of the directly injured party in this case. The judiciary is therefore in the position of being an organ of the injured party. The judiciary then has a vested interest in the outcome and is therefore devoid of impartiality. As the Thai judiciary is devoid of impartiality, it lacks the legitimacy to examine and rule in cases of insult, defamation, and threat according to Article 112 of the Criminal Code. As the Thai judiciary is without the legitimacy to examine and rule in this case, I therefore declare that I do not accept the process of the trial of this case in the Criminal Court. I will not participate in the trial. I will not testify. I will not appoint a lawyer to take part in the case, cross-examine witnesses, or present defense witnesses. I will not sign any court documents.[9]

Although a Court for or by the People would not have the constraints of partiality, there would also be no reason for any one individual, the king or anyone else, to be privileged. Changing the evidence presented, foregrounding the people, and paying attention to context—the tools of feminist judgment projects—are not enough to tell a different story about the monarchy in the Thai polity. There can be no Court for the People, as I write it, or a Court of the People, as the activists imagined on 6 March 2021, until the law that places one individual, and an entire institution along with him, beyond question and accountability, is no longer the law. This is the everyday utopia that Arnon, Panusaya, and all the activists who call for reform of the monarchy, at great personal risk, insist upon. Despite how impossible it seems, especially as Article 112 cases rise, living as if it is possible is necessary for it to one day be so. Scholars, too, must write as if another history, and the justice imagined and forged within it, is possible.

SOURCES FOR COURT DOCUMENTS IN THAILAND

Judgments and other court documents occupy a semipublic, semiprivate space in Thailand. Summaries of Supreme Court judgments are available online (http://deka.supremecourt.or.th), and selected full-length decisions are published in reference books by year available in the National Library and university libraries in Thailand. Rulings of the Constitutional Court and Administrative Court, both established following the promulgation of the 1997 Constitution, are disseminated publicly. For the Constitutional Court, rulings are both on their website (http://www.constitutionalcourt. or.th) and, in some cases, in the *Ratchakitchanubeksa* (https://ratchakitcha. soc.go.th). For the Administrative Court system, rulings are sometimes disseminated online (https://www.admincourt.go.th) and are otherwise available at the Administrative Court Library in Chaeng Watthana.

But for criminal cases, including those examined and rewritten in this book, there is no archive at the Ministry of Justice or the specific military or civilian criminal courts. At the National Archives, material for selected historical cases is available across the records of various reigns before the end of absolute monarchy and the Ministry of Justice and other relevant government departments, but it is not comprehensive in terms of either time or topic. Instead, judgments and other court documents become public when published: by parties in a case, by legal scholars and commentators, and most relevant here, by human rights lawyers and activists. As I explain in the prologue, I chose to write about cases already in the public sphere in this book for two reasons. The first is that I did not want to expose those who would rather not be for the purpose of academic analysis. The second is so that readers who are inspired to write their own new judgments can find the materials needed to do so. In the main text I cite court judgments by court, case number, and date. Below I provide a chapter-by-chapter guide of where readers can find these judgments. For materials available online, the information was current as of the writing of the book; online materials can be fleeting, as website storage capacity and priorities of organizations change. Readers may contact me via email at tyrell.haberkorn@ wisc.edu with any questions.

An additional note is that, as explained in chapter 2, there are no verbatim transcripts made of court proceedings in Thailand. The court reporter types the judge's restatement and summary of testimony instead. This record is read out each day in the court, and parties can request amendments. However, this means that the official record is partial, incomplete, and sometimes incorrect. Part of the work carried out by journalists and human rights activists during the NCPO years was court observation. The court observers both served as an important reminder to the judges that they were being watched and created an essential record of what took place in the court. Throughout this book I cite and draw on the observations made by those working with *Prachatai*, the Internet Dialogue on Legal Reform (iLaw), and Thai Lawyers for Human Rights (TLHR). In particular, I urge readers to explore the rich material available in the public databases of human rights cases curated and maintained by iLaw (https:// freedom.ilaw.or.th/) and TLHR (https://database.tlhr2014.com/).

INTRODUCTION: HISTORY AND JURISPRUDENCE

Supreme Court, Judgment No. 1874/2492.

Supreme Court, Judgment No. 1153–1154/2495.

Supreme Court, Judgment No. 45/2496.

Supreme Court, Judgment No. 1512–1515/2497.

The four Supreme Court judgments related to the 1947 coup can all be found in abbreviated version on the Supreme Court website and in full-length version in the printed books of Supreme Court judgments.

CHAPTER 1: THE IMPOSSIBILITY OF THE PEOPLE

Criminal Court, Judgment, Black Case No. 1291/2515, Red Case No. 1295/2515, 13 March 2515 [1972].

The Criminal Court dismissal of the complaint of rebellion against Field Marshal Thanom Kittikachorn for carrying out the November 1971 coup brought by Uthai Pimchaichon, Anan Phakpraphai, and Boonkerd Hirankham, the three members of parliament, can be found in Phairoj Chaiyanam, *Constitutions: Laws and Important Documents in the Politics of Thailand* (Bangkok: Thammasat University Press, 2519 [1976]), 798–802.

Head of the Revolutionary Council Order No. 36/2515, 22 June 2515 [1972].

The Revolutionary Council's summary judgment of Uthai, Anan, and Boonkerd can be found immediately following the Criminal Court dismissal in Phairoj above, 802–209.

Criminal Complaint, Mr. Pansak Srithep et al. v. General Prayuth Chan-ocha et al., 22 May 2558 [2015].

Supreme Court, Judgment, No. 1688/2561, 27 March 2561 [2018].

I translated both documents into English for TLHR, and links to both translations can be found at the end of Thai Lawyers for Human Rights, "The Owners of Sovereignty: Resistant Citizen, the Supreme Court, and the 2014 Coup," 3 March 2019, https://tlhr2014.com/en/archives/11291.

CHAPTER 2: COUPS AND COUPOCRACY

Pathumwan District Court, Judgment, Black Case No. Or. 363/2558, Red Case No. Or. 134/2559, 11 February 2559 [2016].
Appeal Court, Judgment, Black Case No. 1097/3559, Red Case No. 9075/2559, 6 June 2559 [2016].
Pathumwan District Court, Judgment, Black Case No. Or. 363/2558, Red Case No. Or. 134/2559, 19 December 2559 [2016].
Appeal Court, Judgment, Black Case No. 559/2560, Red Case No. 2247/2561, 20 February 2561 [2018].
Supreme Court, Judgment, No. 3055/2562, 9 September 2562 [2019].

All decisions in Apichat Pongsawat's case were included as part of an online briefing by the Human Rights Lawyers Association, previously available at http://naksit.net/2019/01/casedata/. The second Appeal Court decision is included in Anon Chawalawan, "'[I] Do Not Accept Illegitimate Power': The Struggle of Apichat Pongsawat and the Court That Constructed 'Coupocracy,'" in *The People Rebel: Nine Cases of Opposition to the Coup during the NCPO Period*, edited by Noppon Archamas (Bangkok: Thai Lawyers for Human Rights, 2562 [2019]), 35–78.

CHAPTER 3: REFUSAL TO REPORT

Supreme Court, Judgment, 3578/2560, 1 June 2560 [2017].

The Supreme Court judgment in Sombat Boonngamanong's refusal to report to the NCPO summons is included in Mutita Chuachang, "Sombat Boonngamanong: Unconventional NGO Worker and the 'Sovereign State' Acknowledged by the Court," in *The People Rebel: Nine Cases of Opposition to the Coup during the NCPO Period*, edited by Noppon Archamas (Bangkok: Thai Lawyers for Human Rights, 2562 [2019]), 79–114.

Constitutional Court Ruling No. 30/2563, 2 December 2563 [2020].

The Constitutional Court Ruling in the petition about the constitutionality of summoning and detaining civilians submitted by Worachet Pakeerut was published in *Ratchakitchanubeksa*, Book 137, Part 104 Ko, 22 December 2563 [2020].

CHAPTER 4: A CONSTITUTION WITHOUT THE PEOPLE

Chiang Mai Provincial Court, Judgement, Black Case No. Or. 3542/2559, Red Case No. Or. 1531/2560, 24 April 2560 [2017].

The court judgment in the case of Samart Kwanchai's distribution of flyers urging people to vote against the draft constitution in 2016 is included in Wirawat Somnuk, "The Referendum, Cases, and Those Who Rose Up to Press for 'Justice,'" in *Dissident Citizen: Nine Cases of Opposition to the Coup during the NCPO Period*, edited by Noppon Archamas (Bangkok: Thai Lawyers for Human Rights, 2562 [2019]), 260–88.

Prakanong Provincial Court, Judgment, Black Case No. Or. 5952/2559, Red Case No. 3789/2560, 26 September 2560 [2017].
Appeal Court, Judgment Black Case No. 523/2562, Red Case No. 6884/2561, 7 June 2561.

The two judgments in the ballot-tearing case of Toto Piyarat Chongthep are included in iLaw's electronic database and are available here at "Piyarat: Tore Referendum Ballot," *Freedom of Expression Documentation Center*, https://freedom.ilaw.or.th/case/732.

CHAPTER 5: DISAVOWING RESPONSIBILITY

Central Administrative Court, Judgment, Black Case No. 2132/2558, Red Case No. 453/2562, 26 April 2562 [2019].

The Administrative Court judgment dismissing the petition to close the prison at the Eleventh Military Circle Base is not available in their online database but can be read in person at the Administrative Court Library in Chaeng Watthana.

ACKNOWLEDGMENTS

This book began in June 2019 in the Thai Lawyers for Human Rights (TLHR) office in Bangkok. For three months, May Poonsuk Poonsuk-charoen and Sorawut Wongsaranon made it possible for me to read in the TLHR archive. They met my shock at what took place under the NCPO with two reminders. One, the human rights situation could get worse, as it has. Two, the struggle for justice will continue, as it has. Over the past four years, May has continued to offer advice, collaboration, and encouragement. My deep gratitude to and respect for May, Sorawut, and everyone else at TLHR for their support of this project, especially Sirikan Charoen-siri, Noppon Archamas, Montanaa Duangprapa, and Yaowalak Anupan.

I started writing *Dictatorship on Trial* while a fellow at the Institute for Advanced Study at Central European University in Budapest in the spring of 2021. My gratitude to Agnes Bendik and Agnes Forgo for making it possible to travel to and live in Budapest in the midst of the COVID-19 pandemic. Nadia Al-Bagdadi created a warm and generous intellectual community at IAS, and conversations with István Pál Ádám, Mary Cox, Zsuzsa Hetényi, and Mostafa Minawi were insightful. Walks through Budapest—where we talked about activist scholarship and crammed before Hungarian class—with Gina Caison brought both inspiration and laughter. I finished writing during the 2021–2022 academic year, with generous support from a John Simon Guggenheim Fellowship. The fellowship enabled me to spend eleven months in Bangkok as a visiting researcher at the Institute for Human Rights and Peace Studies (IHRP) at Mahidol University. Colleagues at IHRP, especially Bencharat Sae Chua, made my work possible and reminded me of the urgency of human rights scholarship. Additional funding for research travel to Thailand between 2018 and 2023 was provided by the University of Wisconsin–Madison Office of the Vice Chancellor for Research and Graduate Education, with funding from the Wisconsin Alumni Research Foundation.

I began working on this book shortly after joining the Department of Asian Languages and Cultures at the University of Wisconsin–Madison. Steve Ridgely and John Dunne facilitated my research leave and provided crucial encouragement. I feel very lucky to have an office at UW-Madison next to Hieyoon Kim, whose commitment and clarity sparkle. I worked out the initial ideas, a rough outline, and then the nearly finished manuscript in three lectures over five years as part of the Center for Southeast Asian Studies Friday Forum series. I am grateful to Mary McCoy, Alfred McCoy, Katherine Bowie, Neeranooch Malangpoo, Nam Kim, Mike Cullinane, Anne Hansen, Ian Baird, Ni Guh Lede Sri Pratiwi, Chris Hulshof, and Veronika Kusumaryati for their challenging questions and unstinting support.

Parts of this book were also presented at Naresuan University, Prince of Songkhla University-Hat Yai, Thammasat University, Yale University, JETRO Institute of Developing Economies, University of North Carolina at Chapel Hill, University of Michigan, University of California Los Angeles, Central European University, University of Toronto, Columbia University, Kyoto University, Council on Thai Studies, and the annual meeting of the Canadian Council of Southeast Asian Studies. Audiences in each of these places challenged me with questions about method and the difficulties of securing accountability after dictatorship.

Working with Stanford University Press has been a great gift as a thinker and writer. From the very beginning, conversations with Dylan Kyung-lim White make me want to write and write and write. His support made finishing this book possible, and his questions have made me a better writer. Two anonymous readers for the press offered two rounds of feedback pushing me to think in new ways about both law and history and have improved the book. Tim Roberts shepherded the book through the publication process and Katherine Faydash's copyediting smoothed the prose. J. Naomi Linzer created an index that made me see the book with new eyes.

In addition to the readers for Stanford University Press, Tamara Loos, Doreen Lee, Hieyoon Kim, Scott Straus, Duncan McCargo, Beth Drexler, Tom Ginsburg, Samson Lim, Alexandra Dalferro, Nick Cheesman, Nattapoll Chaiching, John Roosa, Ben Tausig, Khorapin Phuaphansawat, Puangchon Unchanam, Eli Elinoff, Chanida Chitbundit, Chaipong Samnieng, Tze Loo, Thannapat Jarernpanit, Anthony Irwin, Erik Kuhonta, Haley Duschinski, Andrew Harding, Khemthong Tonsakulrungruang, Frank Munger, Maitrii Aung-Thwin, Andrew Harding, Diana Kim, Patrick Pierce, Penchan Phoborisut, Puangthong Pawakapan, Jane Ferguson, Ana Dragojlovic, Eef Vermeij, and Thongchai Winichakul asked hard questions and offered productive advice. Craig Reynolds provided an elegant solution to a thorny organizational problem when I could not see the forest for the trees.

My greatest gratitude is to those in Thailand who let me join them in the struggle against dictatorship. Somyot Prueksakasemsuk, Jatupat Boonpattararaksa, Arnon Nampha, Chaipong Samnieng, and many who cannot be named shared their experience of being targeted by the NCPO with me. Sarayut Tangprasert offered endless advice, ideas and solidarity. Writing encouragement from Coeli Barry, Chiranuch Premchaiporn, Ida Aroonwong, Peera Songkunnatham, Unchalee Maneeroj, Mutita Chuachang, and Prontip Mankhong means more than I can articulate. May Poonsuk Poonsuksharoen, Waddao Chumaporn, Anna Lawattanatrakul, and the collective of the People's Constitutional Court who collaborated to rewrite the Constitutional Court's homophobic and patriarchal ruling shared the liberatory power of law with me. The Khana Comrades bring verve, and *khana*, to documenting and reporting on state repression and opposition to it.

Joy exists alongside, and is necessary, for the struggle both in the streets and in the writing of this book. At the beginning and end of every day is Ben. Her unflagging support made this book possible and her courage inspires me constantly. Many days while I was writing this book at home in Bangkok during 2021 and 2022, we would stop working before evening to join the protests against dictatorship and for reform of the monarchy. She is the person whom I want to fight beside.

NOTES

PROLOGUE

1. Entrenched political conflict began in the lead-up to the 19 September 2006 coup that ousted Prime Minister Thaksin Shinawatra, Yingluck's older brother. Although the day of the coup itself was bloodless, it catalyzed polarized and polarizing color-coded contention between primarily urban royalist-nationalist Yellow Shirts willing to sacrifice democratic process for the protection of the monarchy and primarily rural populist-democrat Red Shirts, who included strong supporters of Thaksin's universal health care and other pro-poor and pro-working-class policies, as well as radical democrats who were critical of Thaksin but did not think the solution was to be found in military interventions into politics. A series of unelected prime ministers coexisted with ongoing clashes in the streets until March 2010, when several hundred thousand Red Shirt protestors from around the country occupied Bangkok to demand a new election. As their presence grew, so did the animosity of the middle- and upper-class Yellow Shirt residents of Bangkok. At the time, Abhisit Vejjajiva was the appointed prime minister, supported by the Yellow Shirts. A sustained crackdown by the military in April–May 2010 led to the deaths of at least ninety-four and more than two thousand injuries. A year later, an election was finally held, and Yingluck was elected prime minister. But the same pro-monarchy and pro-military forces began to mobilize almost immediately and worked to obstruct democratic process to set the stage for 22 May 2014 coup. On the Yellow Shirt movement, see Aim Sinpeng, *Opposing Democracy in the Digital Age: The Yellow Shirts in Thailand* (Ann Arbor: University of Michigan Press, 2021). On the Red Shirt movement, see Benjamin Tausig, *Bangkok Is Ringing: Sound, Space, and Media at Thailand's Red Shirt Protests* (Oxford: Oxford University Press, 2019). On the April–May 2010 crackdown, see People's Information Center, *Truth for Justice: A Fact-Finding Report on the April–May 2010 Crackdowns* (Bangkok: PIC, 2017). On the period bracketed by the 2006 and 2014 coups, see Pavin Chachavalpongpun, ed., *Coup, King, Crisis: A Critical Interregnum in Thailand* (New Haven, CT: Yale University Center for Southeast Asian Studies, 2020).

2. At least 162 individuals were prosecuted for alleged violations of Article 112. At

least 92 individuals were prosecuted for alleged violation of Article 116, the measure regarding sedition. NCPO orders criminalizing public assembly were used to prosecute those who joined demonstrations, with 378 cases initiated; Thai Lawyers for Human Rights, "Public Statement on the Fifth Anniversary of the Seizure of Power by the NCPO," 17 July 2019, https://www.tlhr2014.com/?p=13027&lang=en. On the monarchy and Article 112, see David Streckfuss, *Truth on Trial in Thailand* (London: Routledge, 2010); Thongchai Winichakul, *Thailand's Hyper-Royalism: Its Past Success and Present Predicament*, ISEAS Trends in Southeast Asia 7 (Singapore: Institute of Southeast Asian Studies, 2016); and Tyrell Haberkorn, "Under and beyond the Law: Monarchy, Violence, and History in Thailand," *Politics & Society* 49.3 (September 2021), 311–36.

3. Prajak Kongkirati, "Overview: Political Earthquakes," *Contemporary Southeast Asia* 41.2 (2019): 163–69.

4. Tyrell Haberkorn, *In Plain Sight: Impunity and Human Rights in Thailand* (Madison: University of Wisconsin Press, 2018).

5. Frank Munger has written extensively on legal struggle and the role of lawyers in defending rights in Thailand. See Frank Munger, "Constructing Law from Development: Cause Lawyers, Generational Narratives, and the Rule of Law in Thailand," in *Law and Development and the Global Discourses of Legal Transfers*, ed. John Gillespie and Penelope Nicholson (Cambridge: Cambridge University Press, 2012); Frank Munger, "Revolution Imagined: Cause Advocacy, Consumer Rights, and the Evolving Role of NGOs in Thailand," *Asian Journal of Comparative Law* 9 (2014): 29–64; Frank Munger, "Thailand's Cause Lawyers and Twenty-First-Century Military Coups: Nation, Identity, and Conflicting Visions of the Rule of Law," *Asian Journal of Law and Society* 2.2 (2015): 301–22; and Frank Munger, "Trafficking in Law: Cause Lawyer, Bureaucratic State and Rights of Human Trafficking Victims in Thailand," *Asian Studies Review* 39.1 (2014): 69–87.

6. Jules Lobel, *Success without Victory: Lost Legal Battles and the Long Road to Justice in America* (New York: New York University Press, 2003).

7. For example, Piyabutr Saengkanokkul, *The Court of the Coup: The Judiciary, Dictatorship and the Rule of Coups* (Bangkok: Fa Diew Kan, 2560 [2017]); and Noppon Archamas, ed., *The People Rebel: Nine Cases of Opposition to the Coup during the NCPO Period* (Bangkok: Thai Lawyers for Human Rights, 2562 [2019]).

8. Diana Majury, "Introducing the Women's Court of Canada," *Canadian Journal of Women and the Law* 18.2 (2006): 6.

9. Ibid., 5.

10. Ibid., 9–10.

11. Ibid., 5.

12. The feminist judgment-rewriting projects include the following: Rosemary Hunter, Clare McGlynn, and Erika Rackley, eds., *Feminist Judgments: From Theory to Practice* (Oxford: Hart Publishing, 2010); Kathryn Stanchi, Linda Berger,

and Bridget Crawford, eds., *Feminist Judgments: Rewritten Opinions of the United States Supreme Court* (Cambridge: Cambridge University Press, 2016); Troy Lavers and Loveday Hodson, eds., *Feminist Judgments in International Law* (Oxford: Hart Publishing, 2019); Sharon Cowan, Chloë Kennedy, and Vanessa Munro, eds., *Scottish Feminist Judgments: (Re)creating Law from the Outside In* (Oxford: Hart Publishing, 2019); Máiréad Enright, Julie McCandless, and Aoife O'Donoghue, eds., *Northern/Irish Feminist Judgments: Judges' Troubles and the Gendered Politics of Identity* (Oxford: Hart Publishing, 2017); Heather Douglas, Francesca Bartlett, Trish Luker, and Rosemary C. Hunter, *Australian Feminist Judgments: Righting and Rewriting Law* (Oxford: Hart Publishing, 2014); and the Indian Feminist Judgments Project (https://www.indianfeministjudgmentsproject.com/). Two human rights–focused judgment-rewriting judgment projects have also resulted in collections: Eva Brems and Ellen Desmet, eds., *Integrated Human Rights in Practice: Rewriting Human Rights Decisions* (Cheltenham, UK: Edwin Elgar, 2017); and Eva Brems, *Diversity and European Human Rights: Rewriting Judgments of the ECHR* (Cambridge: Cambridge University Press, 2015).

13. Rosemary Hunter, Clare McGlynn, and Erika Rackley, "Feminist Judgments: An Introduction," in *Feminist Judgments: From Theory to Practice*, ed. Rosemary Hunter, Clare McGlynn, and Erika Rackley (Oxford: Hart Publishing, 2010), 5.

14. Ibid., 8.

15. Erika Rackley, "The Art and Craft of Writing Judgments: Notes on the Feminist Judgments Project," in *Feminist Judgments: From Theory to Practice*, ed. Rosemary Hunter, Clare McGlynn, and Erika Rackley (Oxford: Hart Publishing, 2010), 46.

16. Rosemary Hunter, "An Account of Feminist Judging," in *Feminist Judgments: From Theory to Practice*, ed. Rosemary Hunter, Clare McGlynn, and Erika Rackley (Oxford: Hart Publishing, 2010), 36.

17. Ibid.

18. Ibid., 37.

19. Hilary Charlesworth, "Prefiguring Feminist Judgment in International Law," in *Feminist Judgments in International Law*, ed. Troy Lavers and Loveday Hodson (Oxford: Hart Publishing, 2019), 480.

20. Ibid., 493.

21. Davina Cooper, *Everyday Utopias: The Conceptual Life of Promising Spaces* (Durham, NC: Duke University Press, 2013), 25.

22. In writing the civilian Criminal Court decisions, I drew heavily on a reference book used by judges: Phairoj Wayuphap, *Judgment Writing and the Language of Writing* (Bangkok: Banaratch, 2564 [2021]). Thank you to May Poonsuk Poonsukcharoen for finding and giving me a copy of this book.

23. The method I followed is that I wrote the decisions in English first and then

translated them into Thai. I then circulated the drafts to lawyer colleagues for comments, and then revised them in English again.

24. The three-finger salute originated in the first weeks following the 22 May 2014 coup. In response to the banning of street protests of five or more persons during the first weeks following the coup, activists responded by developing symbolic protests that could be carried out individually or in small groups in public, including eating sandwiches, or raising three fingers in a salute like that used by the actors and actresses in *The Hunger Games.* This logo was first designed with a rainbow colorway for a collaborative judgment-rewriting project I was part of with TLHR and feminist activists in early 2022 in which we rewrote a Constitutional Court decision on same-sex marriage. See Alexandra Dalferro, "The 'People's Court' Supports and Celebrates Marriage Equality in Thailand," *Fulcrum,* 31 May 2022, https://fulcrum.sg/the-peoples-court-supports-and-celebrates-marriage-equality-in-thailand/. Ben Winitchakul designed that logo and generously designed the black-and-white logo I use here.

25. Article 112 of the Criminal Code stipulates "Whoever defames, insults or threatens the King, Queen, the Heir-apparent or the Regent, shall be punished (with) imprisonment of three to fifteen years." The code does not elaborate further on the meaning of what falls within the scope of defamation, insult, or threat. Is it a violation of the law to rule for the people as part of critiquing the law? Perhaps. But the uncertainty is precisely, analytically and politically, why it must be done.

26. Audre Lorde, *Sister Outsider* (Trumansburg, NY: Crossing Press, 1984), 112.

27. Saidiya Hartman, "Venus in Two Acts," *Small Axe: A Journal of Criticism* 26 (2008): 11.

28. Ibid.

INTRODUCTION

1. Bhumipol Adulyadej (Rama 9) ruled from 9 June 1946 until his death on 13 October 2016. His son, Maha Vajiralongkorn (Rama 10), has ruled since then.

2. Duncan McCargo has written insightfully about the cultural political milieu of judges and how it affects their adjudication. See Duncan McCargo, *Fighting for Virtue: Justice and Politics in Thailand* (Ithaca, NY: Cornell University Press, 2020), esp. 56–79.

3. Puey Ungpakorn, "Violence and the Military Coup in Thailand," *Bulletin of Concerned Asian Scholars* 9:3 (1977): 4–12.

4. Thongchai Winichakul, "The Legal Privileged State and Royalist Rule of Law: History of the Genealogy of Thai-Style Rule by Law," 17th Puey Ungpakorn Special Lecture, 9 March 2020 (Bangkok: Way Magazine, 2563 [2020]), 79.

5. Ibid., 193.

6. Somchai Preechasinlapakun, "The Coup Rule of law," in *The 19 September Coup: Coup for Democracy with the King as Head of State*, edited by Thanapol Eawsakul (Bangkok: Fa Diew Kan, 2550 [2007]), 192.

7. Thanapol Eawsakul, ed., *The 19 September Coup: Coup for Democracy with the King as Head of State* (Bangkok: Fa Diew Kan Press, 2550 [2007]).

8. Arjun Subrahmanyan, *Amnesia: A History of Democratic Idealism in Modern Thailand* (Albany, NY: State University of New York Press, 2021).

9. Chris Baker and Pasuk Phongpaichit, *A History of Thailand* (Cambridge: Cambridge University Press, 2014), 118.

10. Pridi Banomyong, *Pridi by Pridi: Selected Writings on Life, Politics, and Economy*, trans. Chris Baker and Pasuk Phongpaichit (Chiang Mai: Silkworm Books, 2000), 124–25.

11. "Royal Amnesty Act on the Occasion of the Transformation of the Country, B.E. 2475," *Ratchakitchanubeksa*, 26 June 2475 [1932], Book 49, 165.

12. Nattapoll Chaiching, *Dream the Impossible Dream: Counter-revolutionary Movements in Siam (1932–1957)* (Bangkok: Fa Diew Kan Press, 2556 [2013]).

13. See Pridi, *Pridi by Pridi*, 83–123, for the text of the Outline Economic Plan. A commission cleared Pridi's name, and he returned to the country.

14. "Amnesty Act for Arranging the Resignation of the Cabinet to Open Parliament According to the B.E. 2476 Constitution," *Ratchakitchanubeksa*, 25 June 2476 [1933], Book 50, 391.

15. "Amnesty Act for Those Who Carried Out the Coup B.E. 2490," *Ratchakitchanubeksa*, 23 December 2490 [1947], Book 64, Part 62, 743–44.

16. "Amnesty Act for Those Who Reinstated the 2475 B.E. Constitution B.E. 2494," *Ratchakitchanubeksa*, 31 December 2494 [1951], Book 68, Part 80, 28.

17. "Amnesty Act for Those Who Seized the Administrative Power of the Country on 16 September B.E. 2500," *Ratchakitchanubeksa*, 26 September 2500 [1957], Book 74, Part 81, 1–3.

18. "Amnesty Act for Those Who Carried Out the Revolution on 20 October B.E. 2501 B.E. 2502," *Ratchakitchanubeksa*, 3 April 2502 [1959], Book 76, Part 41, 3.

19. The coup "will respect and protect human rights according to the Universal Declaration on Human Rights made by the assembly of the United Nations. [The coup] will not do anything out of step or to violate the Declaration, other than if there are situations in which it is truly necessary to do so in order to ensure the safety of the nation." *Ratchakitchanubeksa*, Special Issue, Book 75, Part 81, 20 October 2501 [1958], 14.

20. "Amnesty Act for Those Who Carried Out the Revolution on 17 November B.E. 2514 B.E. 2515," *Ratchakitchanubeksa*, 26 December 2515 [1972], Book 79, Part 197, 235–36.

21. The most insightful analysis of the intersection of the monarchy and law is in

Eugénie Mérieau, *Constitutional Bricolage: Thailand' Sacred Monarchy Vs. the Rule of Law* (Oxford: Hart Publishing, 2022).

22. David Morell and Chai-anan Samudavanija, *Political Conflict in Thailand: Reform, Reaction, Revolution* (Cambridge, MA: Oelgeschlager, Gunn and Hain, 1981).

23. Thongchai Winichakul, *Moments of Silence: The Unforgetting of the October 6, 1976, Massacre in Bangkok* (Honolulu: University of Hawai'i Press, 2020). Puey Ungpakorn notes that the NARC said that 41 were killed, several hundred injured, and 3,037 arrested: "Sources at the Chinese Benevolent Foundation, which transported and cremated the dead, it was revealed [*sic*] that they handled 'over a hundred corpses' that day"; Puey, "Violence and the Military Coup in Thailand," 8.

24. "Amnesty Act for Those who Seized the Administrative Power of the Country on 6 October B.E. 2519 B.E. 2519," *Ratchakitchanubeksa*, 24 December 2519 [1976], Book 93, Part 156, 44–45.

25. The actions that needed to be amnestied extended beyond the administrative action of the coup that displaced the civilian government. This was an amnesty not only for the coup but also for the massacre of students at Thammasat University that preceded it, and the drafters were confident that that the temporal language in the amnesty made its coverage universal. Brutal and lethal violence against the people was made legal, if not legitimate in a broader sense, as part of the defense of the institution of the monarchy. This cannot be discerned from the text of the law itself, but it is clear in the file from the Office of the Juridical Council file about the drafting process and the minutes from the debate in the assembly. See Tyrell Haberkorn, "The Hidden Transcript of Amnesty: The 6 October 1976 Massacre and Coup in Thailand," *Critical Asian Studies* 47.1 (2015): 44–68.

26. "Amnesty Act for Those Who Committed Offences against State Security Inside the Kingdom between 25 and 26 March B.E. 2520 B.E. 2520," *Ratchakitchanubeksa*, 3 December 2520 [1977], Book 94, Part 121, 7.

27. "Amnesty Act for Those Who Seized and Controlled the Administrative Power of the Country on 23 February B.E 2534 B.E. 2534," *Ratchakitchanubeksa*, 3 May 2534 [1991], Book 118, Part 79, 2–3.

28. Physicians for Human Rights and Asia Watch, *"Bloody May": Excessive Use of Lethal Force in Bangkok, the Events of May 17–20, 1992* (New York: Physicians for Human Rights, 1992).

29. Erik Martinez Kuhonta, "The Paradox of Thailand's 1997 'People's Constitution': Be Careful What You Wish For," *Asian Survey* 48.3 (2008): 373–92.

30. Pasuk Phongpaichit and Chris Baker, *Thaksin: The Business of Politics in Thailand* (Chiang Mai: Silkworm Books, 2004).

31. "Interim Constitution of the Kingdom of Thailand, B.E. 2549," *Ratchakitchanubeksa*, Book 123, Part 102 Ko, 1 October 2549 [2006], 13–14.

32. Article 47 stipulated "All announcements and orders of the National Coun-

cil for Peace and Order or orders of the Head of the National Council for Peace and Order which had been announced or made between 22nd May B.E. 2557 [C.E.] 2014 and until the date the Council of Ministers takes office under this Constitution, irrespective of their constitutional, legislative, executive or judicial force, including the performance in compliance therewith, irrespective of whether those acts have been performed before or after the date of entry into force of this Constitution, shall be considered lawful, constitutional and final. Those announcements and orders applicable on the date before the promulgation date of this Constitution shall continue to be in force until there are laws, rules, regulations, resolutions of the Council of Ministers, or orders, as the case may be, issued to amend or repeal them." "Interim Constitution of Thailand, B.E. 2557," *Ratchakitchanubeksa*, Book 131, Part 55 Ko, 22 July 2557 [2014], 16. The translation I use for this and other provisions of the 2014 Interim Constitution was provided by the Legal Opinion and Translation Section of the Foreign Law Bureau of the Office of the Juridical Council.

33. Tayyub Mahmud, "Jurisprudence of Successful Treason: Coup d'État and Common Law," *Cornell International Law Journal* 27.1 (1994): 137.

34. Ibid., 53.

35. Supreme Court, Judgment No. 1874/2492, 1073; and Somchai Preechasinlapakun, "Some Problems of Law Related to Coups," Master's thesis, Faculty of Law, Thammasat University, 2539 [1991], 96–97.

36. It is tempting to identify this challenge to the 1947 coup as a challenge to the legitimacy of coups. However, because the defendants themselves attempted a coup, it is not.

37. Supreme Court, Judgment No. 1153-1154/2495, 841.

38. See Nattapoll Chaiching, *The Military Chief, the Feudal Lord, and the Eagle* (Bangkok: Fa Diew Kan, 2563 [2020]), esp. 59–65, for details about protests against the 1947 coup.

39. Somchai Preechasinlapakun argues that this decision is the first in which the court rules that if a junta is able to carry out a coup and keep opposition at bay, then it is considered to be successful and legal. Somchai, "Some Problems of Law Related to Coups," 98.

40. Supreme Court, Judgment No. 45/2496, 57–58.

41. Ibid., 58.

42. Ibid., 59.

43. Ibid., 63.

44. Ibid., 58. This idea of success being equated with the ability to capture and hold state power is very close to Hans Kelsen's idea of revolutionary legality, which was heavily drawn on in common-law cases about coups beginning with the 1958 coup in Pakistan. The Supreme Court of Pakistan used and even cited Kelsen. The Thai Supreme Court never cites Kelsen or any other legal theorists. Sasipa Pruksa-

dachan persuasively finds ideas resonant with both Hans Kelsen and John Austin with respect to sovereignty and coup success in Thai Supreme Court decisions but proposes that the ideas were already present in Thai legal thought rather than being imported. See Sasipa Pruksadachan, *The Law May Be the Law* (Bangkok: Illuminations Editions, 2564 [2021]), 219.

45. A note about courts and coups by Yut Saeng-uthai, an important Thai legal scholar whose ideas still form a major part of what is taught in Thai law schools, appended to the decision signals its importance and offers further elaboration of the logic behind the rule of coups. In his first sentence, he explained that this was an exemplary case in which to consider whether or not the courts "must affirm revolutions or coups which have been successful and those who did it become those with real, firm power in the state." Supreme Court, Judgment, No. 45/2496, 64–65. He then turned to a German Supreme Court decision about the 1918 Revolution and explained that he saw similarities to the 1947 coup in Thailand. The laws issued by the German revolutionary government were "complete and legally binding because, even though the government which issued the law arose through a revolution which used force, it has still been able to substantiate its own position of power. Therefore, constitutionally, there must be an acceptance of the power of such a government." Yut then cited the German Supreme Court, noting that once a revolutionary entity has been able to take power and is able to "eliminate groups of the people who are opposed to it through the application of means of the power of that government which is successful and absolute. Just this is enough for the power of the government to be true and to be sanctioned legally." He then interpreted this in his own words to "show that a revolution or coup d'état is at first illegal but whenever the perpetrators have successfully and fully carried out the revolution or coup d'état, they are then able to legitimize their power as true, through the suppression and pacification of the former government or group of individuals who are opposed to it, and thus are able to have state authority and [exercise] the highest power in the state. Therefore, they are in a position that enables them to grant a new constitution, repeal the original laws, and enact new laws according to their wishes." Yut amplified the key slippage between the people providing their assent and a junta government being able to suppress them that is present in this decision and remained a feature of decisions following the 22 May 2014 coup. Similar to the acquisition of state power, the means by which acceptance and respect are secured by a junta, and whether they are freely given or coerced, is not important. Ibid., 63–64.

46. Supreme Court, Judgment, No. 1512–1515/2497, 1328.

47. Ibid.

48. Ibid.

49. Streckfuss, *Truth on Trial in Thailand*, 121.

50. Robert Cover, "Violence and the Word," *Yale Law Journal* 95 (1985): 1601.

51. Tom Ginsburg and Tamir Moustafa, *Rule by Law: The Politics of Courts in*

Authoritarian Regimes (Cambridge: Cambridge University Press, 2008); Jothie Rajah, *Authoritarian Rule of Law: Legislation, Discourse and Legitimacy in Singapore* (Cambridge: Cambridge University Press, 2012); and Nick Cheesman, *Opposing the Rule of Law: How Myanmar's Courts Make Law and Order* (Cambridge: Cambridge University Press, 2015).

52. Noura Erakat, *Justice for Some: Law and the Question of Palestine* (Palo Alto, CA: Stanford University Press, 2019), 7.

53. Thai Lawyers for Human Rights, "A Conversation with 'Polka Dot Editor' on a Day on Which He Has No Doubts about Why the Country Is Not a Democracy," 30 July 2563 [2020], https://tlhr2014.com/archives/20010.

54. Peter Leyland, "Genealogy of the Administrative Courts and Consolidation of Administrative Justice in Thailand," in *New Courts in Asia*, ed. Andrew Harding and Penelope Nicholson (London: Routledge, 2010), 231–50.

CHAPTER 1

1. Thongchai Winichakul, "The Legal Privileged State and Royalist Rule of Law: History of the Genealogy of Thai-style Rule by Law," 17th Puey Ungpakorn Special Lecture, 9 March 2020 (Bangkok: Way Magazine, 2563 [2020]).

2. For example, former heads of juntas and junta-appointed prime ministers and cabinet members are often appointed to the Privy Council. This is a position of proximity to the institution of the monarchy rich in both symbolic and material capital.

3. Theorizing this alliance, variously identified as the "network monarchy" by Duncan McCargo and the "deep state" by Eugénie Mérieau, is beyond the scope of this book. However, times of coups and military dictatorship are those in which this shifting alliance is formulated and comes into view. See Duncan McCargo, "Network Monarchy and Legitimacy Crises in Thailand," *Pacific Review* 18.4 (2005): 499–519; and Eugénie Mérieau, "Thailand's Deep State, Royal Power, and the Constitutional Court (1997–2015)," *Journal of Contemporary Asia* 46.3 (2016): 445–66.

4. Criminal Complaint, Mr. Pansak Srithep et al. v. General Prayuth Chan-ocha et al., 22 May 2015, 13–14.

5. Craig Reynolds, *Thai Radical Discourse: The Real Face of Thai Feudalism* (Ithaca, NY: Southeast Asia Program Publications, 1994), 34. On Field Marshal Sarit Thanarat's rise to power and rule, see Thak Chaloemtiarana, *Thailand: The Politics of Despotic Paternalism* (Bangkok: Social Science Association of Thailand, 1979).

6. See Kasian Tejapira, *Commodifying Marxism: The Formation of Modern Thai Radical Culture, 1927–1958* (Kyoto: Kyoto University Press, 2001); and Suthachai

Yimprasert, *The Plan to Plunder the Thai Nation: On the State and Opposition to the State during the Second Regime of Field Marshal Phibun Songkhram (2491–2500 BE)* (Bangkok: 6 October Commemorative Press, 2553 [2010]), originally published in 2531 [1988].

7. Tyrell Haberkorn, *In Plain Sight: Impunity and Human Rights in Thailand* (Madison: University of Wisconsin Press, 2018), 63–76.

8. Jaran Kosanan, *Law, Rights, and Liberties in Thai Society: Parallel Lines from 1932 until the Present* (Bangkok: Coordinating Group on Religion and Society, 2528 [1985]), 77–95.

9. "Revolutionary Council Announcement No. 6," *Ratchakitchanubeksa*, Book 88, Part 124, 18 November 2514 [1971], 13–15.

10. "Amnesty Act for Those Who Carried Out the Revolution on 17 November B.E. 2514 B.E. 2515," *Ratchakitchanubeksa*, 26 December 2515 [1972], Book 79, Part 197, 235–236.

11. Criminal Court, Judgment, Black Case No. 1291/2515, Red Case No. 1295/2515, 13 March 2515 [1972], 798.

12. Ibid., 799.

13. Ibid., 801.

14. Ibid., 802.

15. Philip Abrams, "Notes on the Difficulty of Studying the State (1977)," *Journal of Historical Sociology* 1.1 (March 1988): 58–89.

16. "Head of the Revolutionary Council Order No. 36/2515," 22 June 2515 [1972], 805.

17. Ibid.

18. Ibid., 806.

19. Ibid., 807.

20. Throughout this discussion I have made Field Marshal Thanom the subject of the actions taken in this order because he signed the order and this reflects the stated authorship. However, I suspect that a team of legal experts, perhaps in the Office of the Juridical Council, the Supreme Court, or the Judge Advocate General's Department, were the actual authors. Most of the records from the Thanom regime are not yet available in the National Archives of Thailand, so proving or disproving this suspicion will have to wait.

21. "Head of the Revolutionary Council Order No. 36/2515," 22 June 2515 [1972], 809.

22. Wirat Toariyamitr, ed., *Imprinted on the Heart: Perspectives, Ideas and the Political Life of "Uthai Pimchaichon"* (Bangkok: B-Yes Press, 2002 [2545]), 57.

23. "Act Revoking Head of the Revolutionary Council Order No. 36/2515 Issued on 22 June 2515, B.E. 2517," *Ratchakitchanubeksa,* Book 91, Part 11, 25 January 2517 [1974], 1–3.

24. Thannapat Jarernpanit, "The Rule of Authoritarianism and the Justice Prob-

lem through the Life of Anan Phakprapai," *Political Science and Public Administration Journal* 11 (July–December 2020 [2563]): 87.

25. "'Uthai Pimchaichon' and Resistance to the 17 November 1971 Coup: Interview with Uthai Pimchaichon," in *People against Coups*, ed. Jessada Chotikitphiwat and Withayakorn Boonruang (Bangkok: Laizen, 2012 [2555]), 79.

26. Ibid., 77–78.

27. Wirat, *Imprinted on the Heart*, 55.

28. Ibid., 37–38.

29. Thai Lawyers for Human Rights, "The People Have Never Been Able to Convict: Looking Back at Rebellion Lawsuits against Juntas from the Time of Field Marshal Thanom to the NCPO," 19 June 2561 [2018], https://tlhr2014.com/archives/7831.

30. Piyabutr Saengkanokkul, *The Court of the Coup: The Judiciary, Dictatorship and the Rule of Coups* (Bangkok: Fa Diew Kan, 2560 [2017]), 133.

31. Ibid.

32. Mutita Chuachang, "When 'Citizens' Resist the NCPO: The Rebellion Lawsuit and the Court's Ruling in 2014," in *The People Rebel: Nine Cases of Opposition to the Coup during the NCPO Period*, ed. Noppon Archamas (Bangkok: Thai Lawyers for Human Rights, 2562 [2019]), 235.

33. Piyabutr, *Court of the Coup*, 135.

34. Prachatai, "'Chalad Worachak' Opens Up about His Hunger Strike Opposing a Coup (Once Again) at Age 71," 8 June 2557 [2014], https://prachatai.com/journal/2014/06/53872.

35. Mutita, "When 'Citizens' Resist the NCPO," 235.

36. Prachatai, "'Chalad Worachak' Opens Up."

37. Ibid.

38. Davina Cooper, *Everyday Utopias: The Conceptual Life of Promising Spaces* (Durham, NC: Duke University Press, 2014), 4.

39. Criminal Complaint, Mr. Pansak Srithep et al. v. General Prayuth Chanocha et al., 22 May 2558 [2015], 2.

40. Ibid., 1–2.

41. The Center for the Resolution of the Emergency Situation was established in early April 2010 following the proclamation of the emergency decree by then prime minister Abhisit Vejjajiva to coordinate the dispersal of Red Shirt protesters.

42. This translation is from the Office of the Juridical Council, "Martial Law Order Buddhist Era 2457 (1914 AD)," https://www.icj.org/wp-content/uploads/2012/12/Thailand-Martial-Law-1914-eng.pdf.

43. Criminal Complaint, Mr. Pansak Srithep et al. v. General Prayuth Chanocha et al., 22 May 2558 [2015], 6.

44. Ibid., 6–7.

45. Ibid., 7.

46. Ibid., 8.

47. Ibid.

48. They hoped for a total of 113 plaintiffs, to reference Article 113, but only 15 people were prepared to come forward. Prachatai, "Apichat-Pansak-Rangsiman-Piyabutr: Debate on 'The Judiciary in a Special Situation,'" 22 February 2559 [2016], https://prachatai.com/journal/2016/02/64214.

49. Criminal Complaint, Mr. Pansak Srithep et al. v. General Prayuth Chanocha et al., 22 May 2558 [2015], 9.

50. Ibid., 9–10.

51. Ibid., 10. When demonstrations of five or more persons were banned following the coup, activists defined other activities as protest of the coup. This included distributing and eating sandwiches and reading, especially dissident books such as *1984*, in public. The NCPO reacted by arresting and removing those doing so from public space, though often not charging them with any violations of the law.

52. Ibid.

53. Ibid.

54. Ibid., 10–11.

55. Ibid., 11.

56. Ibid.

57. Ibid., 12.

58. Ibid.

59. Ibid.

60. Ibid., 13.

61. Ibid.

62. Ibid., 13–14.

63. Ibid., 14.

64. Ibid, 14.

65. Article 44 of the 2014 Interim Constitution stipulates "In the case where the Head of the National Council for Peace and Order deems necessary for the purpose of reforms in various fields, for the enhancement of unity and harmony among people in the country, or for the prevention, restraint, or suppression of any act which undermines public order or national security, the Monarchy, the national economy, or State affairs, irrespective of whether such act occurred inside or outside of the Kingdom, the Head of the National Council for Peace and Order, with the approval of the National Council for Peace and Order, shall have power to order, restrain, or perform any act, whether such act has legislative, executive, or judicial force; the orders and the acts, including the performance in compliance with such orders, shall be deemed lawful and constitutional under this Constitution, and shall be final. When those have been carried out, a report shall be submitted to the President of the National Assembly and the Prime Minister for acknowledgement without delay."

66. Ibid., 15–16.

67. Ibid., 17.

68. Thai Lawyers for Human Rights, "Not Yet at the Beginning: Reviewing 3 Years of Resistant Citizen's Rebellion Lawsuit against the NCPO before the Supreme Court Rules," 12 June 2561 [2018], https://tlhr2014.com/archives/7744.

69. Thai Lawyers for Human Rights, "Appeal Court Upholds the Ruling and Dismisses the Case of Resistant Citizen against Prayuth and Others for Overthrowing the Government," 18 February 2559 [2016], https://tlhr2014.wordpress.com/2016/02/18/resistancecitizen-appeal-prayuth-dismiss/.

70. This appeal was permitted according to Article 221 of the Criminal Procedure Code. Prachatai, "Appeal Court Dismisses Resistant Citizen Case against 'Prayuth and Co.' for Overthrow, Explains That the Constitution Has Already Provided Amnesty," 18 February 2559 [2016], https://prachatai.com/journal/2016/02/64149.

71. Cooper, *Everyday Utopias*, 5.

72. Quoted in Mutita, "When 'Citizens' Resist the NCPO," 244.

73. Ibid.

74. Thai Lawyers for Human Rights, "The Owners of Sovereignty: Resistant Citizen, the Supreme Court, and the 2014 Coup," 12 March 2019, https://tlhr2014.com/en/archives/11291.

75. Supreme Court, Judgment, No. 1688/2561, 27 March 2018.

76. Quoted in Mutita, "When 'Citizens' Resist the NCPO," 236.

77. Somchai, "Coup Rule of Law," 197.

78. Worachet Pakeerut, a legal scholar whose case is taken up in chapter 3, provocatively queries whether the courts should be viewed as able to fight coups. The law is no longer the law, he argues, because the junta is more powerful than the courts. See Krisada Suphawanthanakul, "Worachet Pakeerut: On the Judiciary and Coupocracy," *Prachatai*, 10 July 2561 [2018], https://prachatai.com/journal/2018/07/77786.

CHAPTER 2

1. Anon Chawalawan, "'[I] Do Not Accept Illegitimate Power': The Struggle of Apichat Pongsawat and the Court That Constructed 'Coupocracy,'" in *The People Rebel: Nine Cases of Opposition to the Coup during the NCPO Period*, ed. Noppon Archamas (Bangkok: Thai Lawyers for Human Rights, 2562 [2019]), 38.

2. Ibid., 35–36. Law in Thailand is a four-year undergraduate degree. Thammasat University was founded in 1934 by Pridi Banomyong, the civilian leader of the People's Party that fomented the transformation from absolute to constitutional democracy.

3. Anon, "'[I] Do Not Accept Illegitimate Power,'" 36.

4. NCPO Announcement No. 7/2557, *Ratchakitchanubeksa*, 26 May 2557 [2014], Book 131, Special Part 84 Ngo, 8.

5. Thanapol Eawsakul, "Approximately 20 Hours with Apichat Pongsawat: From the BACC to the Military Camp to the CSD," *Prachatai*, 23 May 2558 [2015], https://prachatai.com/journal/2015/05/59441.

6. Noppon Archamas, "Consider Military Junta's Order to Ban of Political Gatherings as State Repression in Thailand," *Nithisangkhomsat* 12.2 (July–December 2562 [2019]).

7. Ibid., 8–17.

8. Ibid., 19.

9. Martial law was revoked with a royal proclamation on 1 April 2015; "Announcement of Revocation of Martial Law," *Ratchakitchanubeksa*, 1 April 2558 [2015], Book 132, Part 25 Ko, 1. The revocation of martial law was greeted with relief by many as a possible easing of restrictions on rights. Martial law had provided General Prayuth and the NCPO with the authority to issue orders and announcements that functioned with the force of law unilaterally. However, they then relied on Article 44 of the 2014 Interim Constitution to issue orders to effect the same rights violations. See "Head of the NCPO Order No. 3/2558," *Ratchakitchanubeksa*, 1 April 2558 [2015], Book 132, Special Part 73 Ngo, 1–4. Head of the NCPO Order No. 3/2558 left the definition of the crime of assembly unchanged but reduced the punishment to a maximum imprisonment of six months and/or a fine of ten thousand baht.

10. Noppon, "Consider Military Junta's Order," 17.

11. Ibid., 20–21.

12. Anon, "'[I] Do Not Accept Illegitimate Power,'" 38.

13. Thanapol, "Approximately 20 Hours with Apichat Pongsawat."

14. Thai Lawyers for Human Rights, "The Defense on Which the Court Did Not Rule: Case File of 'Apichat Pongsawat,'" 11 February 2559 [2016], https://tlhr2014.wordpress.com/2016/02/11/aphichart_acquit/.

15. Thanapol, "Approximately 20 Hours with Apichat Pongsawat."

16. Thanapol Eawsakul's account of this night is important as a historical record of both the arbitrary violence of the military and the generosity of citizens to one another in the face of this violence. He writes that one of the two others arrested had been beaten by the soldiers: "He arrived without shoes because his fell off during his beating. I immediately took off my shoes and gave them to Khun Wirayuth to wear. I walked barefoot for the time being." Thanapol, "Approximately 20 Hours with Apichat Pongsawat."

17. Ibid.

18. Ibid.

19. Ibid.

20. Thanapol was never charged with violating NCPO Announcement No.

7/2557. He was held for seven days on the base in Ratchaburi and wrote an account of his detention in Thanapol Eawsakul, "An Account of Reporting Oneself," *Prachatai*, 3 June 2014, https://prachatai.com/english/node/4080. He was held for an additional four days between 5 and 9 July 2014; Reporters without Borders, "With the Military Junta Monitoring Facebook, a Political Message There Can Put a Journalist Behind Bars," 9 July 2014, https://rsf.org/en/news/military-junta-monitoring-facebook-political-message-there-can-put-journalist-behind-bars.

21. Prachatai, "Case Dismissed against 'Apichat' for Holding Up Sign against the NCPO, Court Notes That CSD Did Not Have Authority to Bring Case," 11 February 2559 [2016], https://prachatai.com/journal/2016/02/63996.

22. Thanapol explained this unusual and unexpected decision by noting: "The opinion of the Court was that the accused was currently studying and had a duty to complete the writing of his thesis. The accused had a stable place of employment and the authorities could keep track of him. If he underwent further detention, he might be fired and would be unable to take care of his mother. He might have difficulties in completing his studies. These are effects for which the state would be unable to compensate him for later." Thanapol, "Approximately 20 Hours with Apichat Pongsawat."

23. He returned to work one day after being released and was subject to investigation because he was absent for more than fifteen days. He explained that he did not intend to skip work, but was in custody due to the order of the court; Prachatai, "Case Dismissed against 'Apichat.'"

24. *Prachatai*, "'Apichat' Fights Case of Violation of NCPO Order for Assembly in Front of BACC, Evidence Hearings on 10 June," 20 May 2558 [2015], https://prachatai.com/journal/2015/05/59353.

25. Prachatai, "Case Dismissed against 'Apichat.'"

26. Prachatai, "'Apichat' Fights Case of Violation of NCPO Order."

27. Ibid. Article 78 of the Criminal Code of Thailand stipulates that a sentence may be reduced by half if the defendant confesses.

28. Prachatai, "Feelings of 'Bond Apichat,' Defendant in the Case of Holding Up a Sign to Protest the Coup," 10 February 2559 [2016], https://prachatai.com/journal/2016/02/63990.

29. Ibid.

30. Davina Cooper, *Everyday Utopias: The Conceptual Life of Promising Spaces* (Durham, NC: Duke University Press, 2014), 4.

31. On 25 May 2014, NCPO Announcement Nos. 37/2557 and 38/2557 established that cases against the crown and state, including all violations of NCPO orders and announcements, would be prosecuted in the military court system. See "NCPO Announcement No. 37/2557," *Ratchakitchanubeksa*, Book 131, Special Part 92 Ngo, 30 May 2557 [2014], 3; and "NCPO Announcement No. 38/2557, *Ratchakitchanubeksa*, Book 131, Special Part 92 Ngo, 30 May 2557 [2014], 4. On 12

September 2016, the NCPO ceased the initiation of new civilian cases in the military court system. On 30 June 2019, all civilian cases still in process in the military court system were transferred to the civilian criminal court system.

32. On the 6 October 1976 case, see Somyot Chuathai, *The Historical Case of 6 October: Who Are the Murderers?* (Bangkok: People's Legal Assistance Fund, 2531 [1987]).

33. Thai Lawyers for Human Rights, "Prosecution Witness Hearings in Case of Apichat Violating Prohibition on Assembly, Court Dismisses Petition on Legal Matter—Suggests Defendant Confess," 15 September 2558 [2015], https://tlhr2014.wordpress.com/2015/09/15/apichart/.

34. Ibid.

35. Prachatai, "11 February 2016 Set for Decision in Case of 'Apichat' Who Held Up a Sign Opposing the Coup, He Fights to Create a Norm," 5 November 2558 [2015], https://prachatai.com/journal/2015/11/62300.

36. iLaw, "Apichat: Protest against the Coup," *Freedom of Expression Documentation Center*, https://freedom.ilaw.or.th/case/679.

37. Ibid.

38. Ibid.

39. Ibid.

40. Ibid.

41. Thai Lawyers for Human Rights, "The Defense on Which the Court Did Not Rule."

42. Ibid.

43. iLaw, "Apichat: Protest against the Coup."

44. Ibid.

45. Ibid.

46. Ibid.

47. Prachatai, "11 February 2016 Set for Decision."

48. iLaw, "Apichat: Protest against the Coup."

49. Thai Lawyers for Human Rights, "The Defense on Which the Court Did Not Rule."

50. Ibid.

51. Quoted in Thanapol, "Approximately 20 Hours with Apichat Pongsawat."

52. The independent media website Prachatai then disseminated the text of Apichat's statement to its broad audience of readers. Apichat Pongsawat, "From the Heart of 'Bond Apichat' before the Court Decision, Defendant in Case of Holding Up a Poster against the Coup," *Prachatai*, 10 February 2559 [2016].

53. Ibid.

54. Prachatai, "Case Dismissed against 'Apichat.'"

55. Thai Lawyers for Human Rights, "The Defense on Which the Court Did Not Rule."

56. Pathumwan District Court, Judgment, Black Case No. Or. 363/2558, Red Case No. Or. 134/2559, 11 February 2559 [2016]. The Court of First instance argued that the case should have been investigated by the police in whose jurisdiction Apichat was arrested, not the CSD.

57. Thai Lawyers for Human Rights, "The Defense on Which the Court Did Not Rule."

58. Ibid.

59. Appeal Court, Judgment, Black Case No. 1097/3559, Red Case No. 9075/2559, 6 June 2559 [2016]. The Appeal Court argued that this matter was considered during the pretrial hearings and the defense did not object.

60. Pathumwan District Court, Judgment, Black Case No. Or. 363/2558, Red Case No. Or. 134/2559, 19 December 2559 [2016].

61. Prachatai, "'A Complex Case' Second Delay in the Appeal Court Decision of 'Apichat' Who Held Up Sign against the Coup in Front of the BACC," 16 November 2560 [2017], https://prachatai.com/journal/2017/11/74152.

62. Appeal Court, Judgment, Black Case No. 559/2560, Red Case No. 2247/2561, 20 February 2561 [2018].

63. "Head of the NCPO Order No. 22/2561," *Ratchakitchanubeksa*, Book 135, Special Part 314 Ngo, 11 December 2561 [2018], 44–46.

64. This included, for example, the case against Jatupat Boonpattararaksa and other student activists for a protest in Khon Kaen province on the first anniversary of the coup and the case against five academics and writers in Chiang Mai in the case of holding up the sign reading An Academic Conference Is Not a Military Camp at the International Conference on Thai Studies in July 2017.

65. The Appeal and Supreme Court decisions are read in the Court of First Instance. There is often a significant time lapse of many months between the date a decision is rendered and when it is read.

66. Supreme Court, Judgment, No. 3055/2562, 9 September 2562 [2019].

67. Pathumwan District Court, Judgment, Black Case No. Or. 363/2558, Red Case No. Or. 134/2559, 11 February 2559 [2016], 6.

68. Appeal Court, Judgment, Black Case No. 1097/3559, Red Case No. 9075/2559, 6 June 2559 [2016], 3.

69. Pathumwan District Court, Judgment, Black Case No. Or. 363/2558, Red Case No. Or. 134/2559, 19 December 2559 [2016], 10.

70. Appeal Court, Judgment, Black Case No. 559/2560, Red Case No. 2247/2561, 20 February 2561 [2018], 8.

71. Ibid., 8–9, emphasis added.

72. Ibid., 10.

73. Ibid.

74. See chapter 3 for analysis of Worachet's legal struggle against the NCPO.

75. Krisada Suphawanthanakul, "Worachet Pakeerut: On the Judiciary and Coupocracy," *Prachatai*, 10 July 2561 [2018], https://prachatai.com/journal/2018/07/77786.

76. Ibid.

77. Appeal Court, Judgment, Black Case No. 559/2560, Red Case No. 2247/2561, 20 February 2561 [2018], 17–18.

78. Ibid., 18.

79. Article 219 of the Criminal Procedure Code stipulates "In a case in which a Court of First Instance has sentenced the defendant for a term not exceeding two years or to a fine not exceeding forty thousand baht or to both, if they appeal court has also imposed the penalty on the defendant not exceeding those specified, the parties shall be prohibited from appealing on questions of fact to the Supreme Court."

80. Supreme Court, Judgment, No. 3055/2562, 9 September 2562 [2019].

81. Thai Lawyers for Human Rights, "The Defense on Which the Court Did Not Rule: Case File of 'Apichat Pongsawat.'"

82. Prachatai, "Decision in the Case of 'Apichat' Held Up a Sign against the Coup in Front of the BACC, 11 February," 9 February 2559 [2016].

83. Appeal Court, Judgment, Black Case No. 559/2560, Red Case No. 2247/2561, 20 February 2561 [2018], 22.

84. Worachet Pakeerut commented, "If this court acts in such a way, we can say that actually, the court is the figure that says when the coup has been successful, through the dimension of punishment of people [who protest]"; Krisada Suphawanthanakul, "Worachet Pakeerut: On the Judiciary and Coupocracy."

85. For text of Article 47, please see note 32 in the introduction. Article 279 of the 2017 Constitution stipulates "All announcements, orders and acts of the National Council for Peace and Order or of the Head of the National Council for Peace and Order which are in force on the day prior to the date of promulgation of this Constitution or which will be issued under section 265 paragraph two, irrespective of their constitutional, legislative, executive or judicial force, as well as the performance of the acts in compliance therewith shall be considered constitutional, lawful and effective under this Constitution. Repeal of or amendment to such announcements or orders shall be made in the form of an Act, except in the case of announcements or orders that, in nature, are the exercise of executive power, a repeal or amendment shall be made in the form of an order of the Prime Minister or a resolution of the Council of Ministers, as the case may be."

86. Prachatai, "11 February 2016 Set for Decision"; Prachatai, "Decision in the Case of 'Apichat.'"

87. Thai Lawyers for Human Rights, "The Defense on Which the Court Did Not Rule."

88. Ibid.

89. Ibid.

90. Prachatai, "Decision in the Case of 'Apichat.'"

91. Appeal Court, Judgment, Black Case No. 559/2560, Red Case No. 2247/2561, 20 February 2561 [2018], 17.

92. See chapter 1 for the for the analysis and new decision in the rebellion case against the NCPO brought by Resistant Citizen.

93. Apichat commented: "I want my case to expiate the stain of those who are prosecuted for opposing the coup, for them to no longer be guilty. The decision will be a form of remedy for this group, because expression in opposition to a coup is not a crime in any way"; Prachatai, "Case Dismissed against 'Apichat.'"

CHAPTER 3

1. Article 15 *bis* of the Martial Law Act of 1914 stipulates "If there is a reasonable ground to suspect that any person is the enemy or violates the provisions of this Act or the order of the military authority, the military authority shall have the power to detain such person for inquiry or for other necessities of the military. Such detention shall be for no longer than seven days." This translation is from the Office of the Juridical Council, "Martial Law Order Buddhist Era 2457 (1914 AD)," https://www.icj.org/wp-content/uploads/2012/12/Thailand-Martial-Law-1914-eng.pdf.

2. For example, see NCPO Order No. 1/2557, issued by the NCPO on 22 May 2014, and published four days later; "NCPO Order No. 1/2557," *Ratchakitchanubeksa*, Book 131, Special Part 85 Ngo, 26 May 2557 [2014], pp. 1–2.

3. Prachatai, "Court Dismisses Case against 'Worachet' for Not Reporting to the NCPO, Points Out That the Law Has Been Used as a Tool of the Junta's Power for 7 Years," 8 June 2564 [2021], https://prachatai.com/journal/2021/06/93411. Hundreds more people were summoned during the five years of NCPO rule through phone calls, social media messages, and the unannounced arrival of soldiers at one's home or workplace.

4. One person who reported being tortured was Kritsuda Khunasen, a Red Shirt activist who was detained for twenty-nine days from 27 May until 24 June 2014. She was kept blindfolded, and her hands were bound while detained. She was interrogated daily, beaten, suffocated, and repeatedly threatened with further violence. See Amnesty International, *Thailand, Attitude Adjustment: 100 Days under Martial Law* (London: Amnesty International, 2014), ASA Doc. 39/011/2014, 29–31.

5. For a range of accounts of experiences of detention, see iLaw, *When I Was Summoned for Attitude Adjustment: Memories of Individuals Summoned to Bases by the NCPO* (Bangkok: iLaw, 2563 [2020]).

6. Thanapol was summoned by NCPO Order No. 5/2557 on 24 May 2014;

"NCPO Order No. 5/2557," *Ratchakitchanubeksa*, Book 131, Special Part 85 Ngo, 26 May 2557 [2014], 11–12.

7. Thanapol Eawsakul, "An Account of Reporting Oneself," *Prachatai*, 3 June 2014, https://prachatai.com/english/node/4080.

8. "NCPO Announcement No. 41/2557," *Ratchakitchanubeksa*, Book 131, Special Part 92 Ngo, 30 May 2557 [2014], 7.

9. "NCPO Announcement No. 37/2557," *Ratchakitchanubeksa*, Book 131, Special Part 92 Ngo, 30 May 2557 [2014], 3.

10. For an excellent introduction to the military court under the NCPO, see Nalini Thitawan, ed., *842+* (Bangkok: iLaw, 2560 [2017]).

11. For text of Article 47, please see note 32 in the introduction. For text of Article 48, please see the introduction.

12. In addition to the three cases discussed here, the other eleven individuals who were prosecuted for not responding to the NCPO's summons were Chaturon Chaisaeng, Yeamyod, Tom Dundee, Samran, Jittra Kotchadet, Sanguan, Nut, Narongsak, Pongsak, Pruetnarin, and Noi. This does not mean that the remainder of the 172 reported themselves. Many fled the country and went into exile. The NCPO chose not to prosecute others. The arbitrary selection of who was prosecuted and who was not was another technique of repression employed by the junta.

13. The NCPO formally ceased to exist when a new cabinet was formed on 10 July 2019 following the 24 March 2019 general election. However, the NCPO remained influential through both the continued power of key figures such as General Prayuth Chan-ocha as prime minister and many others. The junta-authored 2017 Constitution, discussed in chapter 4, further shaped politics and constrained people's participation in politics.

14. Siraphop had already been imprisoned in excess of the eight-month sentence he received due to being detained without bail while awaiting and undergoing trial in another case.

15. Sombat was summoned by NCPO Order No. 3/2557, which was announced on 23 May 2014 and published in the *Ratchakitchanubeksa* on 26 May 2014; "NCPO Order No. 3/2557," *Ratchakitchanubeksa*, Book 131 Special Part 85 Ngo, 26 May 2557 [2014], 5–9.

16. Thai Lawyers for Human Rights, "Rereading the Witness Testimony in the Case of the Polka Dot Editor Not Reporting to the NCPO," 21 September 2558 [2015], https://tlhr2014.wordpress.com/2015/09/21/sombat-2/; Thai Lawyers for Human Rights, "Tomorrow Morning at 9 am, Dusit District Court Will Hear the Supreme Court Verdict on Nuring's Case of Not Reporting Himself," 8 August 2560 [2017], https://tlhr2014.com/archives/4842.

17. Thai Lawyers for Human Rights, "A Conversation with 'Polka Dot Editor' on a Day on Which He Has No Doubts about Why the Country Is Not a Democracy," 30 July 2563 [2020], https://tlhr2014.com/archives/20010.

18. Quoted in Mutita Chuachang, "Sombat Boonngamanong: Unconventional NGO Worker and the 'Sovereign State' Acknowledged by the Court," in *The People Rebel: Nine Cases of Opposition to the Coup during the NCPO Period,* ed. Noppon Archamas (Bangkok: Thai Lawyers for Human Rights, 2562 [2019]), 81–82.

19. Thai Lawyers for Human Rights, "A Conversation with 'Polka Dot Editor'; iLaw, "Sombat Boonngamanong: Violation of the Order Summoning to Report to the NCPO," *Freedom of Expression Documentation Center,* https://freedom.ilaw.or.th/case/613.

20. Thai Lawyers for Human Rights, "As If the NCPO Never Left: Six Years After the Coup and the Persistence of Human Rights Violations," 22 May 2020, https://tlhr2014.com/en/archives/17808.

21. Sombat is also known by the nicknames "Polka Dot Editor" and "Mouse." For his activist biography, particularly during the April-May 2010 red shirt protests and their aftermath, see Benjamin Tausig, *Bangkok Is Ringing: Sound, Protest and Constraint* (New York: Oxford University Press, 2019), esp. pp. 33–59.

22. "'Sombat Boonngamanong' and Opposition to the 19 September 2006 Coup: Interview with Sombat Boonngamanong," in *People against Coups*, ed. Jessada Chotikitphiwat and Withayakorn Boonruang (Bangkok: Laizen, 2012 [2555]), 121.

23. See Article 212 of the 2007 Constitution, Article 5 of the 2014 Interim Constitution, and Article 213 of the 2017 Constitution.

24. Thai Lawyers for Human Rights, "6 Years on the Path of Fighting the Article 116 Case of 'Polka Dot Editor' before Hearing the Decision This 30 July," 29 July 2563 [2020], https://tlhr2014.com/archives/19944.

25. Quoted in Mutita, "Sombat Boonngamanong," 86.

26. Thai Lawyers for Human Rights, "NCPO Announcements Do Not Have Retroactive Punishments, Case of Polka Dot Editor Not Reporting to the NCPO," 21 September 2559 [2015], https://tlhr2014.wordpress.com/2015/09/21/sombat.

27. iLaw, "Sombat Boonngamanong."

28. Thai Lawyers for Human Rights, "Appeal Court Says That the NCPO Seized Power Successfully and Is Sovereign State, Sentenced Sombat Boonngamanong to Two Months Imprisonment in Not Reporting Case," 30 June 2559 [2016], https://tlhr2014.wordpress.com/2016/06/30/sombat_appealcourt.

29. iLaw, "Sombat Boonngamanong."

30. Ibid.

31. Ibid.

32. Thai Lawyers for Human Rights, "Tomorrow Morning at 9 am."

33. Ibid.

34. Supreme Court, Judgment, 3578/2560, 1 June 2560 [2017], 8–9.

35. Ibid., 9.

36. Ibid., 10.

37. Krisada Suphawanthanakul, "Worachet Pakeerut: On the Judiciary and Coupocracy," *Prachatai*, 10 July 2561 [2018], https://prachatai.com/journal/2018/07/77786.

38. Ibid.

39. Sasipa Pruksadachan, *The Law May Be the Law* (Bangkok: Illuminations Editions, 2564 [2021]), 209–10.

40. Piyabutr Saengkanokkul, *The Court of the Coup: The Judiciary, Dictatorship and the Rule of Coups* (Bangkok: Fa Diew Kan, 2560 [2017]), 187.

41. He was summoned by NCPO Order No. 44 on 1 June 2014 and was supposed to report himself by 3 June 2014; "NCPO Order No. 44," *Ratchakitchanubeksa*, Book 131, Special Part 101 Ngo, 5 June 2557 [2014], 5–6; and Thai Lawyers for Human Rights, "Conversation with 'Rungsila,' the Poet Who Exchanged Freedom for Nearly 5 Years to Fight a 112 Case on a Day When Society Is Still Afraid," 16 January 2564 [2021]. https://tlhr2014.com/archives/25137

42. iLaw, "Siraphop: The Hunted Poet," translated by Tyrell Haberkorn, 25 November 2015, https://freedom.ilaw.or.th/node/277.

43. Wiraphong Suntrachatrawat, "The Poetics of 'Rungsila' Who Will Not Bow His Head into the Darkness," in *The People Rebel: Nine Cases of Opposition to the Coup during the NCPO Period*, ed. Noppon Archamas (Bangkok: Thai Lawyers for Human Rights, 2562 [2019]), 119.

44. iLaw, "Siraphop: The Hunted Poet."

45. Ibid.

46. Ibid.

47. Prachatai, "'Summon to Report Again and Will Still Engage in Civil Disobedience' Testimony of 'Rungsila' Poet behind Bars," 24 May 2559 [2016], https://prachatai.com/journal/2016/05/65951.

48. Thai Lawyers for Human Rights, "Conversation with 'Rungsila'"; iLaw, "Siraphop: The Hunted Poet."

49. iLaw, "Siraphop: The Hunted Poet."

50. Ibid.

51. Wiraphong, "Poetics of 'Rungsila,'" 121.

52. Thai Lawyers for Human Rights, "Conversation with 'Rungsila.'"

53. iLaw, "Siraphop: The Hunted Poet."

54. Ibid.

55. Prachatai, "'Summon to Report Again and Will Still Engage in Civil Disobedience.'"

56. Thai Lawyers for Human Rights, "Conversation with 'Rungsila'"; Working Group on Arbitrary Detention, Human Rights Council, Opinion No. 4/2019 concerning Siraphop Kornarut (Thailand), Opinions adopted by the Working Group on Arbitrary Detention at its 84th session, 24 April–3 May 2019, 30 May 2019, A/HRC/WGAD/2019/4.

57. Thai Lawyers for Human Rights, "Conversation with 'Rungsila.'"

58. iLaw, "Siraphop: Violation of the Order to Report to the NCPO," *Freedom of Expression Documentation Center*, https://freedom.ilaw.or.th/case/583.

59. Ibid.

60. Prachatai, "'Summon to Report Again and Will Still Engage in Civil Disobedience.'"

61. iLaw, "Siraphop: Violation of the Order to Report to the NCPO."

62. Quoted in Wiraphong, "Poetics of 'Rungsila,'" 122.

63. Thai Lawyers for Human Rights, "Siraphop Testified That He Did Not Report According to the NCPO's Order Because the Junta are Rebels," 23 May 2559 [2016], https://tlhr2014.com/archives/.

64. Prachatai, "8 Months Imprisonment, Suspended for 2 Years, for Rungsila the Writer Who Refused the Sovereignty of the NCPO and Did Not Report," 25 November 2559 [2016], https://prachatai.com/journal/2016/11/69000.

65. Ibid.

66. iLaw, "Siraphop: Violation of the Order to Report to the NCPO."

67. Ibid.

68. Ibid.

69. Prachatai, "8 Months Imprisonment."

70. Quoted in Wiraphong, "Poetics of 'Rungsila,'" 116.

71. Quoted in ibid., 116.

72. Quoted in ibid., 133.

73. Duncan McCargo and Peeradej Tanruangporn, "Branding Dissent: Nitirat, Thailand's Enlightened Jurists," *Journal of Contemporary Asia* 45.3 (2015): 419–42.

74. Khana Nitirat, *People's Manual to Topple Coups* (Bangkok: Khana Nitirat, 2555 [2012]), 16.

75. Ibid., 5.

76. Elizabeth Fitzgerald, "A Catalogue of Threats against the Khana Nitirat," *New Mandala*, 24 January 2012, http://asiapacific.anu.edu.au/newmandala/2012/01/24/a-catalogue-of-threats-against-the-khana-nitirat/; Asian Human Rights Commission, "Thailand: Threats to Political Freedom Intensify with Assault on HRD and Law Professor," 4 March 2012, http://www.humanrights.asia/news/ahrc-news/AHRC-STM-040-2012.

77. Khana Nitirat, "Statement of the Nitirat (Enlightened Jurists): The Unconstitutionality and Illegality of the Promulgation of Martial Law," trans. Tyrell Haberkorn, *Prachatai*, 20 May 2014, https://prachatai.com/english/node/3973.

78. *Prachatai*, "Nitirat Academic Sawatree Released from Military Camp," 9 June 2014, https://prachatai.com/english/node/4108.

79. Khana Nitirat, "Declaration of the Khana Nitirat: The Draft Constitution and the Referendum," *Prachatai*, 10 June 2016, https://prachatai.com/english/node/6251.

80. Prachatai, "Military Court Grants Bail to 'Worachet' to Be Released from Prison This Evening," 18 June 2557 [2014], https://prachatai.com/journal/2014/06/54079.

81. iLaw, "Worachet: Violation of Order to Report to the NCPO," *Freedom of Expression Documentation Center*, https://freedom.ilaw.or.th/case/618.

82. Ibid.

83. Prachatai, "First Day of Civil Court Examination of Case of 'Worachet' Not Reporting to the NCPO," 29 July 2563 [2020], https://prachatai.com/journal/2020/07/.

84. iLaw, "Worachet."

85. Prachatai, "First Day of Civil Court Examination."

86. Constitutional Court Ruling No. 30/2563, 2 December 2563 [2020].

87. Ibid., 28.

88. Ibid., 32.

89. Prachatai, "Court Dismisses Case against 'Worachet.'"

90. Ibid.

91. Ibid.

92. Krisada, "Worachet Pakeerut."

CHAPTER 4

1. The People's Party, which carried out the transformation from absolute to constitutional monarchy on 24 June 1932, did not have a constitution to abrogate.

2. "NCPO Announcement No. 5/2557," *Ratchakitchanubeksa*, Book 131, Special Part 84 Ngo, 26 May 2557 [2014], 4. Articles 8–25 of the 2007 Constitution, the sections related to the position of the king, were exempted from abrogation.

3. Article 70 of the 2007 Constitution stipulated "Every person shall have a duty to uphold the nation, religions, the king and the democratic regime of government with the king as head of state under this constitution."

4. The 2014 Interim Constitution comprised forty-eight articles. For the Thai version, see *Ratchakitchanubeksa*, Book 131, Part 55 Ko, 22 July 2557 [2014], 1–17. An unofficial English translation was completed by the Office of the Juridical Council: http://web.krisdika.go.th/data/outsitedata/outsite21/file/Constitution_of_the_Kingdom_of_Thailand_Interim,B.E._2557_(2014).pdf.

5. Article 44 of the 2014 Interim Constitution stipulates "In the case where the Head of the National Council for Peace and Order deems necessary for the purpose of reforms in various fields, for the enhancement of unity and harmony among people in the country, or for the prevention, restraint, or suppression of any act which undermines public order or national security, the Monarchy, the national economy,

or State affairs, irrespective of whether such act occurred inside or outside of the Kingdom, the Head of the National Council for Peace and Order, with the approval of the National Council for Peace and Order, shall have power to order, restrain, or perform any act, whether such act has legislative, executive, or judicial force; the orders and the acts, including the performance in compliance with such orders, shall be deemed lawful and constitutional under this Constitution, and shall be final. When those have been carried out, a report shall be submitted to the President of the National Assembly and the Prime Minister for acknowledgement without delay." Like similar measures in earlier dictator-authored charters, such as Article 17 in Field Marshal Sarit Thanarat's 1959 Interim Constitution, Article 44 removed all restraints on and legalized extrajudicial actions. Article 17 of the 1959 Interim Constitution stipulated "During the enforcement of the present constitution, whenever the prime minister deems it appropriate for the purpose of impressing or suppressing actions, whether of internal or external origin, which jeopardize the national security or the throne or subvert or threaten law and order, the prime minister, by resolution of the council of ministers, is empowered to issue orders to take steps accordingly. Such orders or steps shall be considered legal." The 1959 Interim Constitution was in force from February 1959 until 20 June 1968. Among other repressive actions, eleven individuals were executed on Field Marshal Sarit's orders, and another sixty-five individuals were executed on those of Field Marshal Thanom Kittikachorn. General Prayuth and the NCPO used Article 44 not to carry out executions but to summarily seize land, order transfers of civil servants, and take many other actions. See iLaw, "Report on the Exercise of Power under Section 44 of the Interim Constitution of Thailand," 18 November 2015, https://ilaw.or.th/node/3938.

6. The Constitution Drafting Committee (CDC) was led by Mechai Ruchuphan. This was the second CDC and the second draft constitution prepared at the request of the NCPO. The first draft was prepared by a CDC led by Bwornsak Uwanno, a well-known monarchist jurist, but was vetoed in September 2015 by the NCPO's National Reform Council because, "with its emphasis on empowering the citizenry to monitor abuses by elected politicians, [it] was still not sufficiently authoritarian for the generals"; Duncan McCargo, Saowanee T. Alexander, and Petra Desatova, "Ordering Peace: Thailand's 2016 Constitutional Referendum," *Contemporary Southeast Asia* 39.1 (April 2017): 67.

7. For the original Thai text of the law, see *Ratchakitchanubeksa*, Book 133, Part 34 Kho, 22 April 2559 [2016], 1–21. For an unofficial English translation, which I cite from here, see Asian Network for Free Elections, "Organic Act on Referendum for the Draft Constitution B.E. 2559 (2016)," 24 June 2016, https://anfrel.org/organic-act-on-referendum-for-the-draft-constitution-2016/.

8. Wirawat Somnuk, "The Referendum, Cases, and Those Who Rose Up to Press for 'Justice,'" in *Dissident Citizen: Nine Cases of Opposition to the Coup during the*

NCPO Period, ed. Noppon Archamas (Bangkok: Thai Lawyers for Human Rights, 2562 [2019]), 38.

9. Withit Chandawong, *The Role of Life, Thinking and Politics of Teacher Khrong Chandawong: From His Mother's Womb to the Scaffold on the Execution Field* (Sakhon Nakhon: Faculty of Humanities and Social Sciences, Ratchaphat University, 2552 [2009]).

10. Asian Network for Free Elections, *Thailand Constitutional Referendum 2016: A Brief Assessment Report* (Bangkok: Asian Network for Free Elections, November 2016), 4.

11. Khana Nitirat, "Declaration of the Khana Nitirat: The Draft Constitution and the Referendum," *Prachatai*, 10 June 2016, https://prachatai.com/english/node/6251.

12. Article 265 of the draft stipulated "The National Council for Peace and Order holding office prior to the promulgation of this Constitution shall continue to perform duties until the Council of Ministers newly appointed following the first general election according to the Constitution takes office. During the performance of the duties pursuant to Paragraph One, the Head of the National Council for Peace and Order shall continue to have the duties and powers as provided in the Constitution of the Kingdom of Thailand Interim B.E. 2557, amended by the Constitution of the Kingdom of Thailand Interim B.E. 2557, Amendment (No. 1) B.E. 2558 and the Constitution of the Kingdom of Thailand Interim B.E. 2557, Amendment (No. 2) B.E. 2559. The provisions of the aforementioned Constitution specifically in respect of the powers of the Head of the National Council for Peace and Order and the National Council for Peace and Order shall remain in force." I cite from the unofficial English translation of the draft constitution coordinated by the International Commission on Jurists that was first disseminated on 24 June 2016 and can be downloaded at https://www.icj.org/thailand-english-translation-of-draft-constitution/.

13. Khana Nitirat, "Declaration of the Khana Nitirat."

14. Article 269 stipulated "At the initial period, the Senate shall consist of two hundred and fifty members appointed by the king upon the advice of the National Council for Peace and Order."

15. Melissa Crouch, *The Constitution of Myanmar: A Contextual Analysis* (London: Bloomsbury Publishing, 2019).

16. For the text of Article 279, please see note 85, chapter 2

17. Khana Nitirat, "Declaration of the Khana Nitirat."

18. Article 5 stipulated "The Constitution is the supreme law of the State. The provisions of any law, rule, or regulation, or any action which are contrary to or inconsistent with the Constitution shall be unenforceable. Whenever no provision under this Constitution is applicable to any case, it shall be acted or decided in accordance with the constitutional practice in the democratic regime of government

with the King as Head of the State. In the event where the circumstance under Paragraph Two arises, the President of the Constitutional Court shall convene a joint meeting of the President of the House of Representatives, the Opposition Leader in the House of Representatives, the President of the Senate, the Prime Minister, the President of the Supreme Court, the President of the Supreme Administrative Court, the President of the Constitutional Court, and the Presidents of Constitutional Organizations to make decision thereon. The joint meeting under Paragraph Three shall elect one among themselves to preside over each session. In case of the absence of any position holder, the joint meeting shall be composed of the existing holders of the positions. A decision of the joint meeting shall be made by the majority of votes. In case of an equality of votes, the presiding member shall have an additional vote as a casting vote. The decision of the joint meeting shall be deemed final and binding on the National Assembly, the Council of Ministers, the Courts, the Constitutional Organizations, and State organs."

19. Article 4 stipulates "The human dignity, right, liberty and equality of the people shall be protected. The Thai people shall enjoy equal protection under the Constitution," but Article 25 stipulates that, "Where provisions of the Constitution are specifically enacted to protect the rights and liberties of the Thai people and no act is prohibited or restricted by the Constitution or other laws, a person shall have right and liberty to commit such act and be protected under the Constitution in so far as the exercise of such right or liberty does not affect or harm to the security of the State, public order or good morals of people, and is not in violation of the rights and liberties of other persons."

20. iLaw, "iLaw Maintains That Article 61 of the Draft Constitution Referendum Act Is Unconstitutional, Asks for Every Side to Allow the People to Campaign," 30 June 2559 [2016], https://ilaw.or.th/node/4176.

21. Ibid.

22. Thai Lawyers for Human Rights, "The New Constitution Has Been Promulgated, But There Are More Than 104 'Referendum Defendants' Still Being Prosecuted," 7 April 2560 [2017], https://tlhr2014.com/archives/3924.

23. Human Rights Watch, "Thailand: Junta Bans Referendum Monitoring," 21 June 2016, https://www.hrw.org/news/2016/06/21/thailand-junta-bans-referendum-monitoring

24. Thai Lawyers for Human Rights, "New Constitution Has Been Promulgated."

25. Thai Lawyers for Human Rights, "Not Free and Fair, a Campaign with Which One Must Pay with One's Freedom: Situation Update on the Violation of Rights before the Referendum," 12 July 2559 [2016], https://tlhr2014.com/archives/1089.

26. Prachatai, "Freedom of Expression Unnecessary for Thailand: Deputy Junta Head," 29 June 2016, https://prachatai.com/english/node/6308.

27. For an account of the May 1992 protests in Chiang Mai, see Rosalind Morris, "Surviving Pleasure at the Periphery: Chiang Mai and the Photographies of Political Trauma in Thailand, 1976–1992," *Public Culture* 10.2 (1999): 341–70.

28. iLaw, "'The Little Screw' Who Is 'Still Breathing and Not Yet Defeated' Who Holds Fact to Create a Standard in Draft Constitution Referendum Cases," 25 April 2560 [2017], https://freedom.ilaw.or.th/node/504.

29. On the range of ideological and politics views among the Octobrists, see Kanokrat Lertchoosakul, *The Rise of the Octobrists: Power and Conflict among Former Left-Wing Student Activists in Thai Politics* (New Haven, CT: Yale University Council on Southeast Asian Studies, 2016).

30. iLaw, "'The Little Screw' Who Is 'Still Breathing and Not Yet Defeated.'"

31. Ibid.

32. Ibid.

33. Ibid.

34. Ibid.

35. iLaw, "Samart: Distributed Flyers in Chiang Mai," *Freedom of Expression Documentation Center*, https://freedom.ilaw.or.th/case/736.

36. Ibid.

37. Ibid.

38. Thai Lawyers for Human Rights, "Chiang Mai Provincial Court Holds Witness Hearings in 'Uncle Vote No Flyer' Case on 22–23 February 2017," 18 October 2559 [2016], https://tlhr2014.com/archives/2424.

39. Trial observers noticed that the prosecutor was very intent. He conferred extensively with the police and soldier witnesses prior to testimony was given and during all lunch breaks. He phrased questions in a way that presumed only certain answers. Even the judges warned the prosecutor that he was a civil servant and should not act as though he was a plaintiff. The prosecutor responded that he had to fight as hard as possible so that the attorney general could not fault him for failing to perform his duty. iLaw, "Samart: Distributed Flyers in Chiang Mai."

40. The judges warned Lieutenant Colonel Phitsanuphong that the people were not the enemies of the soldiers and that he should not testify as if they were. They asked why tens of soldiers were needed to make an arrest of one citizen. Were the soldiers on trial, as they should be, these would be essential questions. iLaw, "'The Little Screw' Who Is 'Still Breathing and Not Yet Defeated.'"

41. Thai Lawyers for Human Rights, "The Constitution Has Been Promulgated but Draft Constitution Referendum Cases Continue: Testimony in the Case of 'Uncle Samart' Who Placed Vote No Flyers," 10 April 2560 [2017], https://tlhr2014.com/archives/3954.

42. Ibid.

43. Ibid.

44. iLaw, "Samart: Distributed Flyers in Chiang Mai."

45. TLHR, "Constitution Has Been Promulgated but Draft Constitution Referendum Cases Continue."

46. iLaw, "Samart: Distributed Flyers in Chiang Mai."

47. TLHR, "Constitution Has Been Promulgated but Draft Constitution Referendum Cases Continue."

48. iLaw, "Samart: Distributed Flyers in Chiang Mai."

49. TLHR, "Constitution Has Been Promulgated but Draft Constitution Referendum Cases Continue."

50. Ibid.

51. iLaw, "Samart: Distributed Flyers in Chiang Mai."

52. Ibid. On cross-examination, the prosecutor asked an inappropriate question that the judges asked not to record, which is if he had asked permission from the rector of the university to give testimony or not, because he was a civil servant, and it would potentially damage the state. Here, again, the prosecutor overstepped.

53. Ibid.

54. Ibid.

55. Thai Lawyers for Human Rights, "Closing Declaration in the Case of 'Uncle Samart' Who Placed Vote No Flyers, before Hearing the Decision at the Court Tomorrow," 23 April 2560 [2017], https://tlhr2014.com/archives/4057. The primary irregularity was that the soldiers did not have the authority to be part of the arrest operation in this case. Head of the NCPO Order 3/2558 gave military officials some police powers in certain kinds of cases against the crown and the state, but the Draft Constitution Referendum Act was not included.

56. TLHR, "Closing Declaration in the Case of 'Uncle Samart.'"

57. Ibid.

58. iLaw, "'The Little Screw' Who Is 'Still Breathing and Not Yet Defeated.'"

59. Ibid.

60. Thai Lawyers for Human Rights, "Court Dismisses Case against 'Uncle Samart' for Placing Vote No Flyers, Opine That the Message Does Not Fall Meet the Terms of a Crime under the Draft Constitution Referendum Act," 24 April 2560 [2017], https://tlhr2014.com/archives/4077.

61. Chiang Mai Provincial Court, Judgement, Black Case No. Or. 3542/2559, Red Case No. Or. 1531/2560, 24 April 2560 [2017], 7–8.

62. iLaw, "'The Little Screw' Who Is 'Still Breathing and Not Yet Defeated.'"

63. Thai Lawyers for Human Rights, "Case of Placing 'Down With Dictatorship, Long Live Democracy' Flyers Is Final after the Prosecutor Did Not Appeal," 4 November 2560 [2017], https://tlhr2014.com/archives/5406.

64. iLaw, "'The Little Screw' Who Is 'Still Breathing and Not Yet Defeated.'"

65. Ekachai Hongkangwan was convicted of violation of Article 112 for selling CDs that contained an ABC Australia documentary and copies of WikiLeaks documents. On 28 March 2013, he was sentenced to three years and four months in the

Bangkok Remand Prison but was released after nearly two years and eight months on 15 November 2015 following a reduction in his sentence by the Supreme Court.

66. iLaw, "Piyarat: Tore Referendum Ballot," *Freedom of Expression Documentation Center*, https://freedom.ilaw.or.th/case/732.

67. Ibid.

68. Ibid.

69. Piyarat Chongthep, "Down with Dictatorship! Long Live Democracy," trans. Tyrell Haberkorn, *Prachatai*, 7 August 2016, https://prachatai.com/english/node/6450.

70. Prachatai, "'Toto' Hopes for History to Record the Reduction of Legitimacy of the Referendum Like 'Chayan Chayaporn Who Tore His Ballot,'" 7 August 2559 [2016], https://prachatai.com/journal/2016/08/67323.

71. iLaw, "Piyarat: Tore Referendum Ballot."

72. Thai Lawyers for Human Rights, "Court Questions Defendants in Referendum Ballot Tearing Case, Toto Maintains He Tore Ballot Because He Disagreed with the Violation of Rights of Those Who Opposed the Draft Constitution," 15 July 2560 [2017], https://tlhr2014.com/archives/4676.

73. Dave and Jirawat followed Toto to the police station to make sure he was safe. There is a history of disappearances being carried out by the police and military during the process of arrest in Thailand. This is also why Thanapol Eawsakul went with Apichat Pongsawat when he was arrested for protesting in front of the Bangkok Art and Culture Center on the second day after the coup as discussed in chapter 2.

74. iLaw, "Piyarat: Tore Referendum Ballot."

75. Thai Lawyers for Human Rights, "Court Questions Defendants in Referendum Ballot Tearing Case."

76. Ibid.

77. iLaw, "Piyarat: Tore Referendum Ballot."

78. Ibid.

79. Thai Lawyers for Human Rights, "From 'Toto and Friends' to 'Chayan Chayaporn'": Looking Back at Ballot Tearing Cases before the Court Rules Tomorrow," 25 September 2560 [2017], https://tlhr2014.com/archives/5272.

80. iLaw, "Piyarat: Tore Referendum Ballot."

81. Ibid.

82. Ibid.

83. Ibid.

84. Ibid.

85. Ibid.

86. Ibid.

87. Thai Lawyers for Human Rights, "Court Questions Defendants in Referendum Ballot Tearing Case."

88. Ibid.

89. iLaw, "Piyarat: Tore Referendum Ballot."

90. Prakanong Provincial Court, Judgment, Black Case No. Or. 5952/2559, Red Case No. 3789/2560, 26 September 2560 [2017].

91. Prachatai, "Four Months Imprisonment for 'Toto' Tore Referendum Ballot and Confessed, Suspended for 1 Year," 26 September 2560 [2017], https://prachatai.com/journal/2017/09/73402.

92. Ibid.

93. Thai Lawyers for Human Rights, "Appeal Court Decision Punishes Defendants in Ballot Tearing Case for Creating Disorder," 15 August 2561 [2018], https://tlhr2014.com/archives/8486.

94. Thai Lawyers for Human Rights, "Referendum Ballot Tearing Case, Appeal Court Decision to be Read 15 August 2018", 14 August 2561 [2018], https://tlhr2014.com/archives/8471.

95. Appeal Court, Judgment, Black Case No. 523/2562, Red Case No. 6884/2561, 7 June 2561 [2018].

96. iLaw, "Piyarat: Tore Referendum Ballot."

97. Thai Lawyers for Human Rights, "Traces of 4 Years of Struggle in the 'Referendum Ballot Tearing Case' before the Supreme Court Decision Tomorrow," 20 July 2563 [2020], https://tlhr2014.com/archives/19656.

98. Ibid.

99. Ibid.

100. iLaw, "Piyarat: Tore Referendum Ballot."

101. Thai Lawyers for Human Rights, "Traces of 4 Years of Struggle in the 'Referendum Ballot Tearing Case.'"

102. iLaw.

103. iLaw.

CHAPTER 5

1. "Ministry of Justice Order No. 314/2558," *Ratchakitchanubeksa*, Book 132, Special Part 215 Ngo, 11 September 2558 [2015], 7.

2. Thai Lawyers for Human Rights, "Military Prison: Justice Forbidden Entry," 18 March 2559 [2016], https://tlhr2014.wordpress.com/2016/03/18/military_prison/.

3. Article 150 of the Criminal Procedure Code stipulates that a postmortem inquest must be carried out in each case of a death in custody.

4. Noura Erakat, *Justice for Some: Law and the Question of Palestine* (Palo Alto, CA: Stanford University Press, 2019), 7.

5. Peter Leyland, "Genealogy of the Administrative Courts and Consolidation

of Administrative Justice in Thailand," in *New Courts in Asia*, ed. Andrew Harding and Penelope Nicholson (London: Routledge, 2010), 231–50.

6. Davina Cooper, *Everyday Utopias: The Conceptual Life of Promising Spaces* (Durham, NC: Duke University Press, 2014), 25.

7. Ibid., 38.

8. NCPO Announcement No. 37/2557 placed all new cases against the crown and state from 30 May 2014 in the military court system. This continued until 12 September 2016. "NCPO Announcement 37/2557," *Ratchakitchanubeksa*, Book 131, Special Part 92 Ngo, 30 May 2557 [2014], 3.

9. TLHR, "Military Prison: Justice Forbidden Entry."

10. Adem Karadag and Yusuf Mieraili were arrested for allegedly being involved in the bombing of the Erawan Shrine in central Bangkok on 17 August 2015. Police Sergeant Major Prathin Chanket, Natthapol Nawanle, Wallop Boonchan, Pahiran Kongkham, Weerachai Chaboonmee, Thanakrit Thongngernperm, Chatchai Sri-wongsa, and Chatchanok Sriwongsa were arrested for allegedly planning to attack "Bike for Dad," a bicycle race organized by the then crown prince to celebrate the eighty-eighth birthday of then king Bhumipol Adulyadej in December 2015. Zheng Yang, Sun Junwei, Li Kunpeng, and Ma Geng were arrested for attempting to rob a gun shop in the Wang Burapha neighborhood in Bangkok on 8 March 2015. International Federation for Human Rights (FIDH), *Behind the Walls: A Look at Conditions in Thailand's Prisons after the Coup* (Geneva: FIDH, 2017), 31.

11. Thai Lawyers for Human Rights, "A Year of Civilian Detention in a Prison on Military Base: What Do We Know about the Detainees There?," 14 November 2016, https://tlhr2014.com/archives/2730.

12. Ibid.

13. Passed following the promulgation of the 1997 "People's Constitution," the OIA intended to both standardize the way in which members of the public could request access to government information that impacted them and created a unit based in the Prime Minister's Office, the Office of the Official Information Commission, to handle these requests.

14. TLHR sent the letter requesting information to the commander of the Bangkok Remand Prison on 8 March 2016. Thai Lawyers for Human Rights, Letter No. TLHR 3/2559, 8 March 2559 [2016], "Subject: Request for Statistics of Detainees in the Nakhon Chaisri Temporary Prison." On 15 March 2016, the acting commander of the Bangkok Remand Prison sent a letter of refusal; Bangkok Remand Prison, Letter No. Yo Tho 0718/2623, 15 March 2559 [2016], "Subject: Request for Statistics of Detainees in the Nakhon Chaisri Temporary Prison."

15. Thai Lawyers for Human Rights, Appeal to Chair of the Official Information Commission, "Subject: Appeal to the Order of Denial of Release of Information by the Bangkok Remand Prison, 25 March 2559 [2016].

16. The large, communal cells often lead to dangerous overcrowding in the regu-

lar prison system, with many prisons at 300–400 percent capacity. FIDH, *Behind the Walls*, 38–39.

17. Department of Corrections, "The Case of the Death of a Detainee" (press release), 24 October 2558 [2015].

18. Quoted in Thai Lawyers for Human Rights, "Military Prison: Justice Forbidden Entry."

19. Ibid.

20. Quoted in Ibid.

21. Supanut Boonsod, "The Military Judicial Process and the Concealed Legal System," Thai Lawyers for Human Rights, 13 April 2559 [2016], https://tlhr2014.wordpress.com/2016/04/13/military_justice/.

22. Quoted in Thai Lawyers for Human Rights, "Military Prison: Justice Forbidden Entry."

23. Ibid.

24. They were initially held at a prison on the grounds of Thaweewattana Palace, the palace of then crown prince Vajiralongkorn. In 2012, a quiet notice in the *Ratchakitchanubeksa* designated part of his palace as a prison with the purview of the Department of Corrections; Ministry of Justice Order No. 146/2555, "Designation of Area of Phutthamonthon Prison," *Ratchakitchanubeksa*, Book 129, Special Part 62 Ngo, 3 April 2555 [2012]. Despite this designation, the Department of Corrections has never provided any information to the public on the prison.

25. Department of Corrections, "The Case of the Death of a Detainee."

26. Thai Lawyers for Human Rights, Union for Civil Liberty, Human Rights Lawyers Association, Enlaw, and Cross Cultural Foundation, "Opinion of Human Rights Organizations On the Judicial Process in the Case of Suriyan Sujaritpol and Police Major Prakrom Warunprapa," 28 October 2558 [2015].

27. International Commission of Jurists and Human Rights Watch, "Joint Letter to Permanent Mission of Thailand to the UN, Re: Nakhon Chaisri Facility," 24 November 2015.

28. Quoted in Thai Lawyers for Human Rights, "Military Prison: Justice Forbidden Entry."

29. Prachatai, "Resurgent Truth with Pansak Srithep: 'I accuse . . . !'" 9 September 2557 [2014], https://prachatai.com/journal/2014/09/55454.

30. Ibid.

31. In December 2013, the Office of the Attorney General charged Abhisit Vejjajiva and Suthep Thaugsuban, prime minister and deputy prime minister at the time of the 2010 crackdown, with premeditated murder for giving the orders to use lethal force. This was the first time that individual state officials in Thailand were indicted in a case of mass violence against the people. For families of those killed, including Pansak Srithep, as well as human rights lawyers, the initiation of the case was a pathbreaking step toward ending impunity. The case caused panic for Abhisit and

Suthep, as well as many in the army who wondered if they would be the next to be charged. But in August 2014, four months after the coup and before witness hearings began, the case unexpectedly dismissed with the explanation that the Criminal Court did not have jurisdiction over the case because Abhisit and Suthep held political office at the time of the alleged crimes and so they should be investigated by the National Anti-Corruption Commission. Many criticized this decision, noting that premeditated murder is a violent crime and not a subtype of corruption. I write extensively about this case in Tyrell Haberkorn, *In Plain Sight: Impunity and Human Rights in Thailand*, 189–215.

32. Ibid.

33. Ibid.

34. Thai Lawyers for Human Rights, "The Court of Justice Agrees That My (Dear) Snatched Election Case Is in Jurisdiction of the Military Court," 10 June 2559 [2016], https://tlhr2014.wordpress.com/2016/06/10/newcitizencase/.

35. NCPO Announcement No. 7/2557 was revoked on 11 December 2018 so that political parties, including the junta's own, could campaign in advance of the March 2019 election. "Head of the NCPO Order No. 22/2561," *Ratchakitchanubeksa*, Book 135, Special Part 314 Ngo, 11 December 2561 [2018], 44–46. Although all cases of alleged violation of this announcement should have been immediately halted or dismissed once the announcement was revoked, this was not uniformly the case, as the Supreme Court decision in the case of Apichat Pongsawat examined in chapter 2 indicates.

36. Following the election and the appointment of a new cabinet, Head of the NCPO Order No. 9/2562, issued on 9 July 2019, transferred all civilian cases still being prosecuted in the military court system to the civilian criminal court system. "Head of the NCPO Order No. 9/2562," *Ratchakitchanubeksa*, Book 136, Special Part Ngo, 9 July 2562 [2019], 24–26.

37. Thai Lawyers for Human Rights, "A.112-Computer Crimes Act Case 'The People Walk' Says 'Nong Cher's Father' Exercised Freedom in Accordance with Constitution," 16 December 2563 [2020], https://tlhr2014.com/archives/24041.

38. Prachatai, "1 Year Anniversary of Mor Yong's Death, 'TLHR' Releases Statistics of Detainees and Wardens at MCB 11," 16 November 2559 [2016], https://prachatai.com/journal/2016/11/68844.

39. Administrative Court, Indictment No. 2132/2558, Pansak Srithep vs. Minister of Justice, 9 December 2558 [2015], 2 (available to read at TLHR office).

40. Ibid., 3.

41. The Computer Crimes Act was passed in 2007 and provided the authorities with "grants the authorities vast powers to investigate and gather evidence of an offence committed by or via computer." It has frequently been used in combination with Article 112 to criminalize alleged lèse-majesté online. Sinfah Tunsarawuth and Toby Mendel, "Analysis of Computer Crime Act of Thailand," May 2010, *Thai Netizen*

Network, https://thainetizen.org/wp-content/uploads/2010/07/Analysis-of-Computer-Crime-Act-of-Thailand-By-Sinfah-Tunsarawuth-and-Toby-Mendel.pdf, 10.

42. Administrative Court, Indictment, No. 2132/2558, 4.

43. Ibid.

44. Ibid., 4–5.

45. Ibid., 5.

46. Ibid., 6.

47. Ibid., 7.

48. Ibid.

49. Ibid., 8–9

50. Ibid., 7.

51. Thai Lawyers for Human Rights, "Military Prison: Justice Forbidden Entry."

52. Administrative Court, Indictment No. 2132/2558, 7.

53. Response by the Accused, Administrative Court, Black Case No. 2132/2558, 21 February 2560 [2017], 7 (available to read at TLHR office).

54. Ibid.

55. Ibid., 8–9.

56. Ibid., 9–10.

57. Ibid., 10.

58. Ibid., 11–12.

59. Counter-response by the Petitioner, Administrative Court, Black Case No. 2132/2558, 2 (available to read at TLHR office).

60. Ibid., 3.

61. Ibid., 4.

62. Ibid., 6–7.

63. Ibid., 9.

64. Ibid., 11.

65. Central Administrative Court, Judgment, Black Case No. 2132/2558, Red Case No. 453/2562, 26 April 2562 [2019], 12.

66. Ibid., 15.

67. Ibid., 17.

68. Ibid., 17.

69. Ibid., 19–20.

70. Quoted in Thai Lawyers for Human Rights, "Military Prison: Justice Forbidden Entry."

EPILOGUE

1. Arnon Nampha, *The Monarchy and Thai Society* (London: PEN International, 2021), 12.

2. Panusaya Sitthijirawattanakul, Parit Chiwarak, Panupong Jadnok, and Arnon Nampha, *The Day the Sky Trembled: A Call to Reform the Monarchy* (London: PEN International, 2021).

3. Thongchai Winichakul, "A Hypocritical Nation Is Not What the Youth Want," trans. Tyrell Haberkorn, *Prachatai*, 17 August 2020, https://prachatai.com/english/node/8728.

4. These numbers are updated regularly here: Thai Lawyers for Human Rights, "Statistics of Those Prosecuted in Article 112 Cases since 24 November 2020," https://tlhr2014.com/archives/23983.

5. Prachatai (@Prachatai), "7:30 pm, Demonstrators Bring Poster 'In the Name of the People, the Court of the People,' Demands to the Court to Release Political Detainees and Place it in Front of Image of Rama 10," Twitter, 6 March 2564 [2021], 7:42 pm, https://twitter.com/prachatai/status/1368180104531243010.

6. One example is the hunger strike for bail rights that Tawan (Tantawan) Tuatulanon and Bam (Orawan) Phuphong carried out from 18 January to 11 March 2023. See 112 Project, "The Hunger Diaries," Justice in Translation 2/2023, March 2023, https://seasia.wisc.edu/wp-content/uploads/sites/1794/2023/04/Justice-in-Translation-Hunger-Diaries.pdf.

7. David Engel and Jaruwan Engel, *Tort, Custom and Karma: Globalization and Legal Consciousness in Thailand* (Palo Alto, CA: Stanford University Press, 2010).

8. Daranee Charncheongsilpakul was initially sentenced to eighteen years, later reduced to fifteen years on appeal, for three counts of violation of Article 112 for speeches deemed to defame Bhumipol (Rama 9). She was pardoned in 2016. See Tyrell Haberkorn, "Engendering Sedition: Ethel Rosenberg, Daranee Charncheongsilpakul, and the Courage of Refusal," *positions: asia critique* 16.2 (August 2016): 621–65; and Daranee Charnchoengsilpakul, *Diary of Da Torpedo's Final Struggle* (Bangkok: In the Name of Peace and Order, 2563 [2020]).

9. Prawais Praphanukul. "Declaration No. 1," *Fa Diew Kan* 15.2 (2560 [2017]): 10.

BIBLIOGRAPHY

ENGLISH-LANGUAGE MATERIALS

Abrams, Philip. "Notes on the Difficulty of Studying the State (1977)." *Journal of Historical Sociology* 1.1 (March 1988): 58–89.

Amnesty International. *Thailand, Attitude Adjustment: 100 Days under Martial Law*. ASA Doc. 39/011/2014. London: Amnesty International, 2014.

Arnon Nampha. *The Monarchy and Thai Society*. London: PEN International, 2021.

Asian Human Rights Commission. "Thailand: Threats to Political Freedom Intensify with Assault on HRD and Law Professor." 4 March 2012. http://www.humanrights.asia/news/ahrc-news/AHRC-STM-040-2012.

Asian Network for Free Elections. "Organic Act on Referendum for the Draft Constitution B.E. 2559 (2016)." 24 June 2016. https://anfrel.org/organic-act-on-referendum-for-the-draft-constitution-2016/.

———. *Thailand Constitutional Referendum 2016: A Brief Assessment Report*. Bangkok: Asian Network for Free Elections, November 2016.

Baker, Chris, and Pasuk Phongpaichit. *A History of Thailand*. Cambridge: Cambridge University Press, 2014.

Brems, Eva. *Diversity and European Human Rights: Rewriting Judgments of the ECHR*. Cambridge: Cambridge University Press, 2015.

Brems, Eva, and Ellen Desmet, eds. *Integrated Human Rights in Practice: Rewriting Human Rights Decisions*. Cheltenham, UK: Edwin Elgar, 2017.

Cheesman, Nick. *Opposing the Rule of Law: How Myanmar's Courts Make Law and Order*. Cambridge: Cambridge University Press, 2015.

Cooper, Davina. *Everyday Utopias: The Conceptual Life of Promising Spaces*. Durham, NC: Duke University Press, 2013.

Cover, Robert. "Violence and the Word." *Yale Law Journal* 95 (1985): 1601–30.

Cowan, Sharon, Chloë Kennedy, and Vanessa Munro, eds. *Scottish Feminist Judgments: (Re)creating Law from the Outside In*. Oxford: Hart Publishing, 2019.

Crouch, Melissa. *The Constitution of Myanmar: A Contextual Analysis*. London: Bloomsbury Publishing, 2019.

Dalferro, Alexandra. "The 'People's Court' Supports and Celebrates Marriage

Equality in Thailand." *Fulcrum*, 31 May 2022. https://fulcrum.sg/the-peoples-court-supports-and-celebrates-marriage-equality-in-thailand/.

Douglas, Heather, Francesca Bartlett, Trish Luker, and Rosemary C. Hunter, *Australian Feminist Judgments: Righting and Rewriting Law*. Oxford: Hart Publishing, 2014.

Engel, David, and Jaruwan Engel. *Tort, Custom and Karma: Globalization and Legal Consciousness in Thailand*. Palo Alto, CA: Stanford University Press, 2010.

Enright, Máiréad, Julie McCandless, and Aoife O'Donoghue, eds. *Northern/Irish Feminist Judgments: Judges' Troubles and the Gendered Politics of Identity*. Oxford: Hart Publishing, 2017.

Erakat, Noura. *Justice for Some: Law and the Question of Palestine*. Palo Alto, CA: Stanford University Press, 2019.

Fitzgerald, Elizabeth. "A Catalogue of Threats against the Khana Nitirat." *New Mandala*, 24 January 2012. http://asiapacific.anu.edu.au/newmandala/2012/01/24/a-catalogue-of-threats-against-the-khana-nitirat/.

Ginsburg, Tom, and Tamir Moustafa. *Rule by Law: The Politics of Courts in Authoritarian Regimes*. Cambridge: Cambridge University Press, 2008.

Haberkorn, Tyrell. "Engendering Sedition: Ethel Rosenberg, Daranee Charnchoengsilpakul, and the Courage of Refusal." *positions: asia critique* 16.2 (August 2016): 621–51.

———. "The Hidden Transcript of Amnesty: The 6 October 1976 Massacre and Coup in Thailand." *Critical Asian Studies* 47.1 (2015): 44–68.

———. *In Plain Sight: Impunity and Human Rights in Thailand*. Madison: University of Wisconsin Press, 2018.

———. "Under and beyond the Law: Monarchy, Violence, and History in Thailand." *Politics & Society* 49.3 (September 2021): 311–36.

Hartman, Saidiya. "Venus in Two Acts." *Small Axe: A Journal of Criticism* 26 (2008): 1–16.

Human Rights Watch. "Thailand: Junta Bans Referendum Monitoring." 21 June 2016. https://www.hrw.org/news/2016/06/21/thailand-junta-bans-referendum-monitoring.

Hunter, Rosemary, Clare McGlynn, and Erika Rackley, eds. *Feminist Judgments: From Theory to Practice*. Oxford: Hart Publishing, 2010.

iLaw. "Report on the Exercise of Power under Section 44 of the Interim Constitution of Thailand." 18 November 2015. https://ilaw.or.th/node/3938.

———. "Siraphop: The Hunted Poet." Translated by Tyrell Haberkorn. 25 November 2015. https://freedom.ilaw.or.th/node/277.

International Commission of Jurists and Human Rights Watch. "Joint Letter to Permanent Mission of Thailand to the UN, Re: Nakhon Chaisri Facility." 24 November 2015. https://www.hrw.org/news/2015/11/24/joint-letter-permanent-mission-thailand-un.

International Federation for Human Rights (FIDH). *Behind the Walls: A Look at Conditions in Thailand's Prisons after the Coup*. Geneva: FIDH, 2017.

Kanokrat Lertchoosakul. *The Rise of the Octobrists: Power and Conflict among Former Left-Wing Student Activists in Thai Politics*. New Haven, CT: Yale University Council on Southeast Asian Studies, 2016.

Kasian Tejapira. *Commodifying Marxism: The Formation of Modern Thai Radical Culture, 1927–1958*. Kyoto: Kyoto University Press, 2001.

Khana Nitirat. "Declaration of the Khana Nitirat: The Draft Constitution and the Referendum." *Prachatai*. 10 June 2016. https://prachatai.com/english/node/6251.

———. "Statement of the Nitirat (Enlightened Jurists): The Unconstitutionality and Illegality of the Promulgation of Martial Law." Translated by Tyrell Haberkorn. *Prachatai*. 20 May 2014. https://prachatai.com/english/node/3973.

Kuhonta, Erik Martinez. "The Paradox of Thailand's 1997 'People's Constitution': Be Careful What You Wish For." *Asian Survey* 48.3 (2008): 373–92.

Lavers, Troy, and Loveday Hodson, eds. *Feminist Judgments in International Law*. Oxford: Hart Publishing, 2019.

Leyland, Peter. "Genealogy of the Administrative Courts and Consolidation of Administrative Justice in Thailand." In *New Courts in Asia*, edited by Andrew Harding and Penelope Nicholson, 231–50. London: Routledge, 2010.

Lobel, Jules. *Success without Victory: Lost Legal Battles and the Long Road to Justice in America*. New York: New York University Press, 2003.

Lorde, Audre. *Sister Outsider*. Trumansburg, NY: Crossing Press, 1984.

Mahmud, Tayyub. "Jurisprudence of Successful Treason: Coup d'État and Common Law." *Cornell International Law Journal* 27.1 (1994): 49–140.

Majury, Diana. "Introducing the Women's Court of Canada." *Canadian Journal of Women and the Law* 18.2 (2006): 1–12.

McCargo, Duncan. *Fighting for Virtue: Justice and Politics in Thailand*. Ithaca, NY: Cornell University Press, 2020.

———. "Network Monarchy and Legitimacy Crises in Thailand." *Pacific Review* 18.4 (2005): 499–519.

McCargo, Duncan, Saowanee T. Alexander, and Petra Desatova. "Ordering Peace: Thailand's 2016 Constitutional Referendum." *Contemporary Southeast Asia* 39.1 (April 2017): 65–95.

McCargo, Duncan, and Peeradej Tanruangporn. "Branding Dissent: Nitirat, Thailand's Enlightened Jurists." *Journal of Contemporary Asia* 45.3 (2015): 419–42.

Mérieau, Eugénie. *Constitutional Bricolage: Thailand's Sacred Monarchy vs. the Rule of Law*. Oxford: Hart, 2022.

———. "Thailand's Deep State, Royal Power, and the Constitutional Court (1997–2015)." *Journal of Contemporary Asia* 46.3 (2016): 445–66.

Morell, David, and Chai-anan Samudavanija. *Political Conflict in Thailand: Re-*

form, Reaction, Revolution. Cambridge, MA: Oelgeschlager, Gunn and Hain, 1981.

Morris, Rosalind. "Surviving Pleasure at the Periphery: Chiang Mai and the Photographies of Political Trauma in Thailand, 1976–1992." *Public Culture* 10.2 (1999): 341–70.

Munger, Frank. "Constructing Law from Development: Cause Lawyers, Generational Narratives, and the Rule of Law in Thailand." In *Law and Development and the Global Discourses of Legal Transfers*, edited by John Gillespie and Penelope Nicholson, 237–76. Cambridge: Cambridge University Press, 2012.

———. "Revolution Imagined: Cause Advocacy, Consumer Rights, and the Evolving Role of NGOs in Thailand." *Asian Journal of Comparative Law* 9 (2014): 29–64.

———. "Thailand's Cause Lawyers and Twenty-First-Century Military Coups: Nation, Identity, and Conflicting Visions of the Rule of Law." *Asian Journal of Law and Society* 2.2 (2015): 301–22.

———. "Trafficking in Law: Cause Lawyer, Bureaucratic State and Rights of Human Trafficking Victims in Thailand." *Asian Studies Review* 39.1 (2014): 69–87.

112 Project. "The Hunger Diaries." Justice in Translation 2/2023, March 2023. https://seasia.wisc.edu/wp-content/uploads/sites/1794/2023/04/Justice-in-Translation-Hunger-Diaries.pdf.

Panusaya Sitthijirawattana, Parit Chiwarak, Panupong Jadnok, and Arnon Nampha. *The Day the Sky Trembled: A Call to Reform the Monarchy*. London: PEN International, 2021.

Pasuk Phongpaichit and Chris Baker. *Thaksin: The Business of Politics in Thailand*. Chiang Mai: Silkworm Books, 2004.

Pavin Chachavalpongpun, ed. *Coup, King, Crisis: A Critical Interregnum in Thailand*. New Haven, CT: Yale University Center for Southeast Asian Studies, 2020.

People's Information Center (PIC). *Truth for Justice: A Fact-Finding Report on the April–May 2010 Crackdowns*. Bangkok: PIC, 2017.

Physicians for Human Rights and Asia Watch. *"Bloody May": Excessive Use of Lethal Force in Bangkok, the Events of May 17–20, 1992*. New York: Physicians for Human Rights, 1992.

Piyarat Chongthep, "Down with Dictatorship! Long Live Democracy." Translated by Tyrell Haberkorn. *Prachatai*, 7 August 2016. https://prachatai.com/english/node/6450.

Prachatai. "Freedom of Expression Unnecessary for Thailand: Deputy Junta Head." 29 June 2016. https://prachatai.com/english/node/6308.

———. "Nitirat Academic Sawatree Released from Military Camp." 9 June 2014. https://prachatai.com/english/node/4108.

Prajak Kongkirati. "Overview: Political Earthquakes." *Contemporary Southeast Asia* 41.2 (2019): 163–69.

Pridi Banomyong. *Pridi By Pridi: Selected Writings on Life, Politics, and Economy.* Translated by Chris Baker and Pasuk Phongpaichit. Chiang Mai: Silkworm Books, 2000.

Puey Ungpakorn. "Violence and the Military Coup in Thailand." *Bulletin of Concerned Asian Scholars* 9.3 (1977): 4–12.

Rajah, Jothie. *Authoritarian Rule of Law: Legislation, Discourse and Legitimacy in Singapore.* Cambridge: Cambridge University Press, 2012.

Reporters without Borders. "With the Military Junta Monitoring Facebook, a Political Message There Can Put a Journalist behind Bars." 9 July 2014. https://rsf.org/en/news/military-junta-monitoring-facebook-political-message-there-can-put-journalist-behind-bars.

Reynolds, Craig. *Thai Radical Discourse: The Real Face of Thai Feudalism.* Ithaca, NY: Southeast Asia Program Publications, 1994.

Sinfah Tunsarawuth and Toby Mendel. "Analysis of Computer Crime Act of Thailand." *Thai Netizen Network*, May 2010. https://thainetizen.org/wp-content/uploads/2010/07/Analysis-of-Computer-Crime-Act-of-Thailand-By-Sinfah-Tunsarawuth-and-Toby-Mendel.pdf.

Sinpeng, Aim. *Opposing Democracy in the Digital Age: The Yellow Shirts in Thailand.* Ann Arbor: University of Michigan Press, 2021.

Stanchi, Kathryn, Linda Berger, and Bridget Crawford, eds. *Feminist Judgments: Rewritten Opinions of the United States Supreme Court.* Cambridge: Cambridge University Press, 2016.

Streckfuss, David. *Truth on Trial in Thailand.* London: Routledge, 2010.

Subrahmanyan, Arjun. *Amnesia: A History of Democratic Idealism in Modern Thailand.* Albany: State University of New York Press, 2021.

Tausig, Benjamin. *Bangkok Is Ringing: Sound, Space, and Media at Thailand's Red Shirt Protests.* Oxford: Oxford University Press, 2019.

Thai Lawyers for Human Rights. "As If the NCPO Never Left: Six Years after the Coup and the Persistence of Human Rights Violations." 22 May 2020. https://tlhr2014.com/en/archives/17808.

———. "The Owners of Sovereignty: Resistant Citizen, the Supreme Court, and the 2014 Coup." 12 March 2019. https://tlhr2014.com/en/archives/11291.

———. "Public Statement on the Fifth Anniversary of the Seizure of Power by the NCPO." 17 July 2019. https://www.tlhr2014.com/?p=13027&lang=en.

———. "A Year of Civilian Detention in a Prison on Military Base: What Do We Know about the Detainees There?" 14 November 2016. https://tlhr2014.com/archives/2730.

Thak Chaloemtiarana. *Thailand: The Politics of Despotic Paternalism.* Bangkok: Social Science Association of Thailand, 1979.

Thanapol Eawsakul. "An Account of Reporting Oneself." *Prachatai*, 3 June 2014. https://prachatai.com/english/node/4080.

Thongchai Winichakul. "A Hypocritical Nation Is Not What The Youth Want." Translated by Tyrell Haberkorn. *Prachatai*, 17 August 2020. https://prachatai.com/english/node/8728.

———. *Moments of Silence: The Unforgetting of the October 6, 1976, Massacre in Bangkok.* Honolulu: University of Hawai'i Press, 2020.

———. *Thailand's Hyper-Royalism: Its Past Success and Present Predicament*, IS-EAS Trends in Southeast Asia 7. Singapore: Institute of Southeast Asian Studies, 2016.

Working Group on Arbitrary Detention, Human Rights Council. Opinion No. 4/2019 concerning Siraphop Kornarut (Thailand). Opinions adopted by the Working Group on Arbitrary Detention at its 84th session, 24 April–3 May 2019, 30 May 2019. A/HRC/WGAD/2019/4.

THAI-LANGUAGE MATERIALS

Anon Chawalawan. "'[I] Do Not Accept Illegitimate Power': The Struggle of Apichat Pongsawat and the Court That Constructed 'Coupocracy.'" In *The People Rebel: Nine Cases of Opposition to the Coup during the NCPO Period*, edited by Noppon Archamas, 35–78. Bangkok: Thai Lawyers for Human Rights, 2562 [2019]. [อานนท์ ชวาลาวัณย์. "'ไม่ยอมรับอำนาจเถื่อน': การต่อสู้ ของอภิชาต กับศาล สถาปนา 'ระบอบแห่งการรัฐประหาร.'" ใน *ราษฎรกำแหง: บันทึก 9 คดี ต้านรัฐประหารในยุค คสช.* กรุงเทพฯ: ศูนย์ทนายความเพื่อสิ ทธิมนุษยชน, 2562. 35–78.]

Apichat Pongsawat. "From the Heart of 'Bond Apichat' before the Court Decision, Defendant in Case of Holding Up a Poster against the Coup." *Prachatai*, 10 February 2016. https://prachatai.com/journal/2016/02/63990. [อภิชาต พงษ์สวัสดิ์. "ความในใจก่อนฟังคำพิพากษา 'ปอนด์ อภิชาต' จำเลยคดีชู ป้ายประท้วงรัฐประหาร." ประชาไท, 10 กุมภาพันธ์ 2559. https://prachatai.com/journal/2016/02/63990.]

Daranee Charnchoengsilpakul. *Diary of Da Torpedo's Final Struggle.* Bangkok: In the Name of Peace and Order, 2563 [2020]. [ดารณี ชาญเชิงศิลปะกุล. *บานทึกการต่อสู้ ครั้งสุดท้ายของ ดา ตอร์ปิโด.* กรุงเทพฯ:ในนามของความสงบเรียบร้อย, 2563.]

Department of Corrections. "The Case of the Death of a Detainee" (Press release), 24 October 2558 [2015]. [กรมราชทัณฑ์. แถลงข่าว, "กรณี ผู้ต้องขังเสียชี วิต." 24 ตุลาคม 2558.]

iLaw. "Apichat: Protest against the Coup." *Freedom of Expression Documentation Center.* https://freedom.ilaw.or.th/case/679. [iLaw. "อภิชาต: ชุมนุมต้านรัฐประหาร." ฐานข้อมูลคดี. https://freedom.ilaw.or.th/case/679.]

———. "iLaw Maintains That Article 61 of the Draft Constitution Referendum Act Is Unconstitutional, Asks for Every Side to Allow the People to Campaign."

30 June 2559 [2016], https://ilaw.or.th/node/4176. [iLaw. "ไอลอว์ ยืนยัน พ.ร.บ.
ประชามติฯ มาตรา 61 ขัดหลักเสรีภาพ ขอทุกฝ่ายเปิดให้ประชาชนรณรงค์ได้." 30 มิถุนายน
2559. https://ilaw.or.th/node/4176.]

———. "'The Little Screw' Who Is 'Still Breathing and Not Yet Defeated' Who
Holds Fact to Create a Standard in Draft Constitution Referendum Cases."
25 April 2560 [2017]. https://freedom.ilaw.or.th/node/504/. [iLaw. "'ลมหายใจยัง
ไม่แพ้' ของ 'น็อตตัวเล็กๆ' ที่ยึดสู้ สร้างบรรทัดฐานคดีพ.ร.บ.ประชามติฯ." 25 เมษายน 2560,
https://freedom.ilaw.or.th/node/504.]

———. "Piyarat: Tore Referendum Ballot." *Freedom of Expression Documentation
Center.* https://freedom.ilaw.or.th/case/732. [iLaw. "ปิยรัฐ: ฉีกบัตรประชามติ." ฐาน
ข้อมูลคดี. https://freedom.ilaw.or.th/case/732.]

———. "Samart: Distributed Flyers in Chiang Mai." *Freedom of Expression Documentation Center.* https://freedom.ilaw.or.th/case/736. [iLaw. "สามารถ: แจกใบปลิว
โหวตโนที่ เชียงใหม่." ฐานข้อมูลคดี. https://freedom.ilaw.or.th/case/736.]

———. "Siraphop: Violation of the Order to Report to the NCPO." *Freedom of
Expression Documentation Center.* https://freedom.ilaw.or.th/case/583. [iLaw.
"สิรภพ: ฝ่าฝืนคำสั่งรายงานตัว คสช.," ฐานข้อมูลคดี. https://freedom.ilaw.or.th/case/583.]

———. "Sombat Boonngamanong: Violation of the Order Summoning to Report
to the NCPO." *Freedom of Expression Documentation Center.* https://freedom.
ilaw.or.th/case/613 [iLaw. "สมบัติ บุญงามอนงค์: ฝ่าฝืนคำสั่งรายงานตัว คสช." ฐานข้อมูล
คดี. https://freedom.ilaw.or.th/case/613.]

———. *When I Was Summoned for Attitude Adjustment: Memories of Individuals Summoned to Bases by the NCPO.* Bangkok: iLaw, 2563 [2020]. [iLaw. เมื่อฉัน
ถูกเรียกปรับทัศนคติ: บันทึกความทรงจำของบุคคลที่ถูก คสช. เรียกเข้าค่าย. กรุงเทพฯ: iLaw,
2563.]

———. "Worachet: Violation of Order to Report to the NCPO." Freedom of Expression Documentation Center. https://freedom.ilaw.or.th/case/618. [iLaw. "วร
เจตน์: ฝ่าฝืนคำสั่งรายงานตัว คสช." ฐานข้อมูลคดี. https://freedom.ilaw.or.th/case/618.]

Jaran Kosanan. *Law, Rights, and Liberties in Thai Society: Parallel Lines from 1932
until the Present.* Bangkok: Coordinating Group on Religion and Society, 2528
[1985]. [จรัญ โฆษณานันท์. กฎหมายกับสิทธิเสรีภาพในสังคมไทย: เส้นขนานจาก 2475 ถึง
ปัจจุบัน. กรุงเทพฯ: กลุ่ม ประสานงานศาสนาเพื่อสังคม, 2528.]

Jessada Chotikitphiwat and Withayakorn Boonruang, eds. *People against Coups.*
Bangkok: Laizen, 2012 [2555]. [เจษฎา โชติกิจภิวาทย์ และ วิทยากร บุญเรือง, บรรณาธิการ.
ประชาชนต้านรัฐประหาร. กรุงเทพฯ: ลายเส้น, 2555.]

Khana Nitirat. *People's Manual to Topple Coups.* Bangkok: Khana Nitirat, 2555
[2012]. [คณะนิติราษฎร์. คู่มือประชาชนล้มรัฐประหาร. กรุงเทพฯ: คณะนิติราษฎร์, 2555.]

Krisada Suphawanthanakul. "Worachet Pakeerut: On the Judiciary and
Coupocracy." *Prachatai*, 10 July 2561 [2018]. https://prachatai.com/jour-
nal/2018/07/77786. [กฤษฎา ศุภวรรธนะกุล. "วรเจตน์ ภาคีรัตน์: ว่าด้วยตุลาการและ

ระบอบแห่งการรัฐประหาร.” 10 กรกฎคม 2561. *ประชาไท*. https://prachatai.com/journal/2018/07/77786.]

Mutita Chuachang. “Sombat Boonngamanong: Unconventional NGO Worker and the ‘Sovereign State’ Acknowledged by the Court.” In *The People Rebel: Nine Cases of Opposition to the Coup during the NCPO Period*, edited by Noppon Archamas, 79–114. Bangkok: Thai Lawyers for Human Rights, 2562 [2019]. [มุทิตา เชื้อช่ง. “สมบัติ บุญงามอนงค์: เอ็นจีโอแหกคอกกับ ‘รัฐธาธิปัตย์’ ที่ถูกรับรองโดยศาล.” ใน *ราษฎรกำแหง: บันทึก 9 คดี ต้านรัฐประหารในยุค คสช*, นพพล อาชามาส, บรรณาธิการ. กรุงเทพฯ: ศูนย์ทนายความเพื่ อสิ ทธิมนุษยชน, 2562. 79–114.]

———. “When ‘Citizens’ Resist the NCPO: The Rebellion Lawsuit and the Court’s Ruling in 2014.” In *The People Rebel: Nine Cases of Opposition to the Coup during the NCPO Period*, edited by Noppon Archamas, 231–60. Bangkok: Thai Lawyers for Human Rights, 2562 [2019]. [มุทิตา เชื้อช่ง. “เมื่ อ ‘พลเมือง’ โต้กลับ คสช.: การฟ้องข้อหากบฏและคำวินิจฉัยของศาลในปี 2557.” ใน *ราษฎรกำ แหง: บันทึก 9 คดี ต้านรัฐประหารในยุค คสช*., นพพล อาชามาส, บรรณาธิการ. กรุงเทพฯ: ศูนย์ทนายความเพื่ อสิ ทธิมนุษยชน, 2562. 231–60.]

Nai Winai Khun Udom, ed. *Case File*. N.p.: Charity Science Press, n.d. [นายวินัย คุณอุดม, ผู้ รวบรวม. *สำนวนคดี*. กรุงเทพฯ: สำนักพิมพ์วิทยาสาสน์สงเคราะห์.]

Nalini Thitawan, ed. *842+*. Bangkok: iLaw, 2560 [2017]. [นลินี ฐิตะวรรณ, บก. *842+*. กรุงเทพฯ: iLaw, 2560.]

Nattapoll Chaiching. *Dream the Impossible Dream: Counter-revolutionary Movements in Siam (1932–1957)*. Bangkok: Fa Diew Kan Press, 2556 [2013]. [ณัฐพล ใจจริง. ขอฝันใฝ่ในฝันอันเหลือเชื่ อ: ความเคลื่ อนไหวของ ขบวนการปฏิปักษ์ปฏิวัติสยาม (พ.ศ. 2475–2500). กรุงเทพฯ: ฟ้าเดียวกัน, 2556.]

Nattapoll Chaiching. *The Military Chief, the Feudal Lord, and the Eagle*. Bangkok: Fa Diew Kan, 2563 [2020]. [ณัฐพล ใจจริง. ขุนศึก ศักดินา และ พญาอินทรี. กรุงเทพฯ: สำนักพิมพ์ฟ้าเดียวกัน, 2563.]

Noppon Archamas, ed. *The People Rebel: Nine Cases of Opposition to the Coup during the NCPO Period*. Bangkok: Thai Lawyers for Human Rights, 2562 [2019]. [นพพล อาชามาส, บรรณาธิการ. *ราษฎรกำแหง: บันทึก 9 คดี ต้านรัฐประหารในยุค คสช*. กรุงเทพฯ: ศูนย์ทนายความเพื่ อสิ ทธิมนุษยชน, 2562.]

Noppon Archamas. “Consider Military Junta’s Order to Ban of Political Gatherings as State Repression in Thailand.” *Nithisangkhomsat* 12.2 (July–December 2562 [2019]). [นพพล อาชามาส. “พินิจคำสั่ง “ห้ามมั่วสุมชุมนุมทางการเมือง” ของคณะรัฐประหารไทยในฐานะเครื่ องมือการ ปราบปรามโดยรัฐ.” *นิติสังคมศาสตร์* 12.2 (ก.ค.-ธ.ค. 2562).]

Phairoj Chaiyanam. *Constitutions: Laws and Important Documents in the Politics of Thailand*. Bangkok: Thammasat University Press, 2519 [1976]. [ไพโรจน์ ชัยนาม. *รัฐธรรมนญ: บทกฎหมายและเอกสารสำคัญในทางการเมืองของประเทศไทย*. กรุงเทพฯ: สำนักพิมพ์มหาวิทยาลัยธรรมศาสตร์, 2519.]

Phairoj Wayuphap. *Judgment Writing and the Language of Writing*. Bangkok:

Banaratch, 2564 [2021]. [ไพโรจน์ วายุภาพ. *การเขียนคำพิพากษากับภาษาเขียน*. กรุงเทพฯ: ปณรัชซ, 2564.]

Piyabutr Saengkanokkul. *The Court of the Coup: The Judiciary, Dictatorship and the Rule of Coups*. Bangkok: Fa Diew Kan, 2560 [2017]. [ปิยบุตร แสงกนกกุล. *ศาล รัฐประหาร: ตุลาการ ระบอบเผด็จการ และนิติรัฐประหาร*. กรุงเทพฯ: สำนักพิมพ์ ฟ้าเดียวกัน, 2560.]

Prachatai. "'Apichat' Fights Case of Violation of NCPO Order for Assembly in Front of BACC, Evidence Hearings on 10 June." 20 May 2558 [2015].https://prachatai.com/journal/2015/05/59353 [ประชาไท. "'อภิชาต' สู้คดีฝ่าฝืนคำสั่งคสช. ชุมนุมหน้าหอศิลป์ นัดตรวจพยานหลักฐาน 10 มิ.ย." 20 พฤษภาคม 2558. https://prachatai.com/journal/2015/05/59353.]

———. "Apichat-Pansak-Rangsiman-Piyabutr: Debate on 'The Judiciary in a Special Situation.'" 22 February 2559 [2016]. https://prachatai.com/journal/2016/02/64214. [ประชาไท. "อภิชาต-พันธ์ศักดิ์-รังสิมันต์-ปิยบุตร: อภิปราย 'องค์กรตุลาการในสถานการณ์พิเศษ.'" 22 กุมภาพันธ์ 2559. https://prachatai.com/journal/2016/02/64214.]

———. "Appeal Court Dismisses Resistant Citizen Case against 'Prayuth and Co.' for Overthrow, Explains That the Constitution Has Already Provided Amnesty." 18 February 2559 [2016]. https://prachatai.com/journal/2016/02/64149. [ประชาไท. "อุทธรณ์ยกฟ้องคดีพลเมืองโต้กลับฟ้อง 'ประยุทธ์และพวก' ล้มการปกครอง ชี้ มีรธน.นิรโทษฯไว้แล้ว." 18 กุมภาพันธ์ 2559. https://prachatai.com/journal/2016/02/64149.]

———. "Case Dismissed against 'Apichat' for Holding Up Sign against the NCPO, Court Notes That CSD Did Not Have Authority to Bring Case." 11 February 2559 [2016]. https://prachatai.com/journal/2016/02/63996 [ประชาไท."ยกฟ้องคดี 'อภิชาต' ชูป้ายต้าน คสช.-ศาลระบุกองปราบไม่มีอำนาจทำคดี." 11 กุมภาพันธ์ 2559. https://prachatai.com/journal/2016/02/63996.]

———. "'Chalad Worachak' Opens Up about His Hunger Strike Opposing a Coup (Once Again) at Age 71." 8 June 2557 [2014]. https://prachatai.com/journal/2014/06/53872 [ประชาไท. "เปิดใจ 'ฉลาด วรนัตร' กับการอดอาหารต้านรัฐประหาร(อีกครั้ง)ในวัย 71." 8 มิถุนายน 2557. https://prachatai.com/journal/2014/06/53872.]

———. "'A Complex Case' Second Delay in the Appeal Court Decision of 'Apichat' Who Held Up Sign against the Coup in Front of the BACC." 16 November 2560 [2017]. https://prachatai.com/journal/2017/11/74152. [ประชาไท. "'คดีซับซ้อน' เลื่อนพิพากษาศาลอุทธรณ์ครั้งที่ 2 คดี 'อภิชาต' ชูป้ายค้านรัฐประหารหน้าหอศิลป์ฯ." 16 พฤศจิกายน 2560. https://prachatai.com/journal/2017/11/74152.]

———. "Court Dismisses Case against 'Worachet' for Not Reporting to the NCPO, Points Out That the Law Has Been Used as a Tool of the Junta's Power for 7 Years." 8 June 2564 [2021]. https://prachatai.com/journal/2021/06/93411. [ประชาไท. "ศาลยกฟ้องคดีไม่รายงานตัวต่อ คสช.ของ 'วรเจตน์' ชี้ 7 ปีกฎหมายเป็นเครื่องมืออำนาจรัฐประหาร." 8 มิถุนายน 2564. https://prachatai.com/journal/2021/06/93411.]

———. "Decision in the Case of 'Apichat' Held Up a Sign against the Coup in Front of the BACC, 11 February." 9 February 2559 [2016]. https://prachatai.com/journal/2016/02/63966. [ประชาไท. "พิพากษาคดี 'อภิชาต' ชูป้ายต้านรัฐประหารหน้าหอศิลป์ฯ 11 ก.พ.นี้." 9 กุมภาพันธ์ 2559. https://prachatai.com/journal/2016/02/63966.]

———. "8 Months Imprisonment, Suspended for 2 Years, for Rungsila the Writer Who Refused the Sovereignty of the NCPO and Did Not Report." 25 November 2559 [2016]. https://prachatai.com/journal/2016/11/69000. [ประชาไท. "จำคุก 8 เดือนรอลงโทษ 2 ปี รุ่งศิลานักเขียนผู้ปฏิเสธรัฐธาธิปัตย์ คสช. ไม่รายงานตัว." 25 พฤศจิกายน 2559. https://prachatai.com/journal/2016/11/69000.]

———. "11 February 2016 Set for Decision in Case of 'Apichat' Who Held Up a Sign Opposing the Coup, He Fights to Create a Norm." 5 November 2558 [2015]. https://prachatai.com/journal/2015/11/62300 [ประชาไท. "11 ก.พ.59 พิพากษาคดี 'อภิชาต' ชูป้ายต้านรัฐประหาร เจ้าตัวยันสู้คดีสร้างบรรทัดฐาน." 5 พฤศจิกายน 2558. https://prachatai.com/journal/2015/11/62300.]

———. "Feelings of 'Bond Apichat,' Defendant in the Case of Holding Up a Sign to Protest the Coup." 10 February 2559 [2016]. https://prachatai.com/journal/2016/02/63990. [ประชาไท. "ความในใจก่อนฟังคำพิพากษา 'ปอนด์ อภิชาต' จำเลยคดีชูป้ายประท้วงรัฐประหาร." 10 กุมภาพันธ์ 2559. https://prachatai.com/journal/2016/02/63990.]

———. "First Day of Civil Court Examination of Case of 'Worachet' Not Reporting to the NCPO." 29 July 2563 [2020]. https://prachatai.com/journal/2020/07/88817. [ประชาไท. "สืบพยานคดี 'วรเจตน์' ไม่ไปรายงานตัวต่อ คสช. ในศาลพลเรือนนัดแรก." 29 กรกฎาคม 2563. https://prachatai.com/journal/2020/07/88817.]

———. "Four Months Imprisonment for 'Toto' Tore Referendum Ballot and Confessed, Suspended for 1 Year." 26 September 2560 [2017], https://prachatai.com/journal/2017/09/73402. [ประชาไท. "คุก 4 เดือน 'โตโต้' ฉีกบัตรประชามติ รับสารภาพเหลือรอลงอาญา 1 ปี." 26 กันยายน 2560. https://prachatai.com/journal/2017/09/73402.]

———. "Military Court Grants Bail to 'Worachet' to Be Released from Prison This Evening." 18 June 2557 [2014]. https://prachatai.com/journal/2014/06/54079 [ประชาไท. "ศาลทหารให้ประกัน 'วรเจตน์' ปล่อยตัวจากเรือนจำค่ำนี้." 18 มิถุนายน 2557. https://prachatai.com/journal/2014/06/54079.]

———. "1 Year Anniversary of Mor Yong's Death, 'TLHR' Releases Statistics of Detainees and Wardens at MCB 11." 16 November 2559 [2016]. https://prachatai.com/journal/2016/11/68844. [ประชาไท. "1 ปี ความตายหมอหยอง 'ศูนย์ทนายสิทธิ' เปิดสถิติผู้ต้องขัง-ผู้คุมเรือนจำมทบ.11." 16 พฤศจิกายน 2559. https://prachatai.com/journal/2016/11/68844.]

———. "Resurgent Truth with Pansak Srithep: 'I accuse . . . !'" 9 September 2557 [2014]. https://prachatai.com/journal/2014/09/55454. [ประชาไท. "คืนความจริงกับ พันธ์ศักดิ์ ศรีเทพ : "ข้าพเจ้าขอกล่าวหา" ("I accuse . . . !")], 9 กันยายน 2557. https://prachatai.com/journal/2014/09/55454.]

———. "7:30 pm, Demonstrators Bring Poster 'In the Name of the People, the Court of the People,' Demands to the Court to Release Political Detainees and Place It in Front of Image of Rama 10." Twitter (@Prachatai), 6 March 2564

[2021], 7:42 pm. https://twitter.com/prachatai/status/1368180104531243010. [ประชาไท (@Prachatai). "19.30 น. มีผู้ชุมนุมนำป้าย "ในปรมาภิไธยประชาชน ศาล ประชาชน" ซึ่งเป็นข้อเรียกร้องต่อ ศาลให้ปล่อยตัวผู้ต้องหาทางการเมือง ขึ้นไปวางพาดที่หน้า พระบรมฉายาลักษณ์ ร.10." Twitter. 6 มีนาคม 2564, 19.42 น. https://twitter.com/prachatai/status/1368180104531243010.]

———. "'Summon to Report Again and Will Still Engage in Civil Disobedience' Testimony of 'Rungsila' Poet Behind Bars." 24 May 2559 [2016]. https://prachatai.com/journal/2016/05/65951 [ประชาไท. "'เรียกรายงานตัวอีกครั้งก็ยังจะอารยะขัดขืน' คำเบิกความ 'รุ่งศิลา' กวีหลังกรงขัง." 24 พฤษภาคม 2559. https://prachatai.com/journal/2016/05/65951.]

———. "'Toto' Hopes for History to Record the Reduction of Legitimacy of the Referendum Like 'Chayan Chayaporn Who Tore His Ballot.'" 7 August 2559 [2016]. https://prachatai.com/journal/2016/08/67323. [ประชาไท. "'โตโต้' หวัง ประวัติศาสตร์จารึก ลดความชอบธรรมประชามติเหมือน 'ไชยยันต์ ฉีกบัตรเลือกตั้ง.'" 7 สิงหาคม 2559. https://prachatai.com/journal/2016/08/67323.]

Prawais Praphanukul. "Declaration No. 1." *Fa Diew Kan* 15.2 (2560 [2017]): 9–10. [ประเวศ ประภานุกูล. "คำแถลงการณ์ (ฉบับที่ 1)." ฟ้าเดียวกัน 15.2 (2560 [2017]): 9–10.]

Sasipa Pruksadachan. *The Law May Be the Law*. Bangkok: Illuminations Editions, 2564 [2021]. [ศศิภา พฤกษฎาจันทร์. กฎหมายย่อมเป็นกฎหมาย. กรุงเทพฯ: Illuminations Editions, 2564.]

Somchai Preechasinlapakun. "The Coup Rule of Law." In *The 19 September Coup: Coup for Democracy with the King as Head of State*, edited by Thanapol Eawsakul, 190–202. Bangkok: Fa Diew Kan, 2550 [2007]. [สมชาย ปรีชาศิลปกุล. "หลัก นิติรัฐประหาร." ใน รัฐประหาร 19 กันยา: รัฐประหารเพื่อระบอบประชาธิปไตยอันมี พระมหา กษัตริย์ทรงเป็นประมุข, ธนาพล อิ๋วสกุล, บรรณาธิการ. กทมฯ: ฟ้าเดียวกน, 2550.]

———. "Some Problems of Law Related to Coups." Master's thesis, Faculty of Law, Thammasat University, 2539 [1991]. [สมชาย ปรีชาศิลปะกุล. "ปัญหาทางกฎหมายบาง ประการเกี่ยวกับการปฏิวัติ." บัณฑิตวิทยาลัย, คณะนิติศาสตร์ มหาวิทยาลัยธรรมศาสตร์, 2539.]

Somyot Chuathai. *The Historical Case of 6 October: Who Are the Murderers?* Bangkok: People's Legal Assistance Fund, 2531 [1987]. [สมยศ เชื้อไทย. คดีประวัติศาสตร์ 6 ตุลา ใครคือฆาตกร. กรุงเทพฯ: กองทุนช่วยเหลือประชาชนทางกฎหมาย, 2531.]

Supanut Boonsod. "The Military Judicial Process and the Concealed Legal System." *Thai Lawyers for Human Rights*. 13 April 2559 [2016]. https://tlhr2014.wordpress.com/2016/04/13/military_justice/. [ศุภณัฐ บุญสด. "กระบวนการยุติธรรม ทางทหารและระบบกฎหมายที่ปิดตาย : เครื่องมือในทางการเมืองของคณะ รักษาความสงบแห่ง ชาติ." ศูนย์ทนายความเพื่อสิทธิมนุษยชน. 13 เมษายน 2559. https://tlhr2014.wordpress.com/2016/04/13/military_justice/.]

Suthachai Yimprasert. *The Plan to Plunder the Thai Nation: On the State and Opposition to the State during the Second Regime of Field Marshal Phibun Songkhram (2491–2500 BE)*. Bangkok: 6 October Commemorative Press, 2553 [2010], originally published in 2531 [1988]. [สุธาชัย ยิ้มประเสริฐ. แผนชิงชาติไทย: ว่าด้วยรัฐและการต่อ

ต้านรัฐ สมัยจอมพล ป.พิบูลสงคราม ครั้งที่สอง (พ.ศ. 2491–2500). กรุงเทพฯ: สำนักพิมพ์ 6 ตุลารำลึก, 2553 (2531).]

Thai Lawyers for Human Rights. "A.112-Computer Crimes Act Case 'The People Walk' Says 'Nong Cher's Father' Exercised Freedom in Accordance with Constitution." 16 December 2563 [2020]. https://tlhr2014.com/archives/24041. [ศูนย์ทนายความเพื่อสิทธิมนุษยชน. "ยกฟ้อง ม.116—พ.ร.บ.คอมฯ คดี "พลเมืองรุกเดิน" ชี้ "พ่อน้องเฌอ"ใช้เสรีภาพ ตาม รธน." 16 ธันวาคม 2563. https://tlhr2014.com/archives/24041.]

———. "Appeal Court Decision Punishes Defendants in Ballot Tearing Case for Creating Disorder." 15 August 2561 [2018]. https://tlhr2014.com/archives/8486. [ศูนย์ทนายความเพื่อสิทธิมนุษยชน. "เปิดคำพิพากษาศาลอุทธรณ์ลงโทษจำเลยคดีฉีกบัตรประชามติฐานก่อความวุ่นวาย." 15 สิงหาคม 2561. https://tlhr2014.com/archives/8486.]

———. "Appeal Court Says That The NCPO Seized Power Successfully and is Sovereign State, Sentenced Sombat Boonngamanong to Two Months Imprisonment in Not Reporting Case." 30 June 2559 [2016]. https://tlhr2014.wordpress.com/2016/06/30/sombat_appealcourt/ [ศูนย์ทนายความเพื่อสิทธิมนุษยชน. "ศาลอุทธรณ์ชี้ คสช.ยึดอำนาจสำเร็จเป็นรัฏฐาธิปัตย์ สั่งจำคุกสมบัติ บุญงามอนงค์ 2 เดือน คดีไม่ไปรายงานตัว. 30 มิถุนายน 2559. https://tlhr2014.wordpress.com/2016/06/30/sombat_appealcourt/.]

———. "Appeal Court Upholds the Ruling and Dismisses the Case of Resistant Citizen against Prayuth and Others for Overthrowing the Government." 18 February 2559 [2016]. https://tlhr2014.wordpress.com/2016/02/18/resistance-citizen-appeal-prayuth-dismiss/. [ศูนย์ทนายความเพื่อสิทธิมนุษยชน. "ศาลอุทธรณ์พิพากษายืน ยกฟ้องคดีพลเมืองโต้กลับฟ้องประยุทธ์และพวกข้อหา ล้มล้างการปกครอง." 18 กุมภาพันธ์ 2559. https://tlhr2014.wordpress.com/2016/02/18/resistancecitizen-appeal-prayuth-dismiss/.]

———. Appeal to Chair of the Official Information Commission. "Subject: Appeal to the Order of Denial of Release of Information by the Bangkok Remand Prison." 25 March 2559 [2016]. [ศูนย์ทนายความเพื่อสิทธิมนุษยชน.หนังสืออุทธรณ์. "อุทธรณ์คำสั่งไม่เปิดเผยข้อมูลข่าวสารของเรือนจำพิเศษ กรุงเทพมหานคร. 25 มีนาคม 2559.]

———. "Case of Placing 'Down with Dictatorship, Long Live Democracy' Flyers Is Final after the Prosecutor Did Not Appeal." 4 November 2560 [2017], https://tlhr2014.com/archives/5406. [ศูนย์ทนายความเพื่อสิทธิมนุษยชน. "คดีเสียบใบปลิว 'เผด็จการจงพินาศ ประชาธิปไตยจงเจริญ' ถึงที่สุดแล้ว หลังอัยการไม่อุทธรณ์อีก." 4 พฤศจิกายน 2560. https://tlhr2014.com/archives/5406.]

———. "Chiang Mai Provincial Court Holds Witness Hearings in 'Uncle Vote No Flyer' Case on 22–23 February 2017." 18 October 2559 [2016]. https://tlhr2014.com/archives/2424. [ศูนย์ทนายความเพื่อสิทธิมนุษยชน. "ศาลจังหวัดเชียงใหม่นัดสืบพยานคดี 'ลุงแปะใบปลิวโหวตโน' 22–23 ก.พ.60." 18 ตุลาคม 2559, https://tlhr2014.com/archives/2424.]

———. "Closing Declaration in the Case of 'Uncle Samart' Who Placed Vote No Flyers, before Hearing the Decision at the Court Tomorrow." 23 April 2560

[2017], https://tlhr2014.com/archives/4057. [ศูนย์ทนายความเพื่อสิทธิมนุษยชน. "เปิดคำแถลงปิดคดี "ลุงสามารถ" แปะใบปลิวโหวตโน ก่อนศาลนัดฟังคำพิพากษารุ่งนี้," 23 เมษายน April 2017. https://tlhr2014.com/archives/4057.]

———. "The Constitution Has Been Promulgated but Draft Constitution Referendum Cases Continue: Testimony in the Case of 'Uncle Samart' Who Placed Vote No Flyers." 10 April 2560 [2017]. https://tlhr2014.com/archives/3954. [ศูนย์ทนายความเพื่อสิทธิมนุษยชน. "รธน.ประกาศใช้ แต่คดีประชามติยังไม่จบ: ประมวลปากคำพยานคดี 'ลุง สามารถ' แปะใบปลิวโหวตโน." 10 เมษายน 2560 [2017]. https://tlhr2014.com/archives/3954.]

———. "A Conversation with 'Polka Dot Editor' on a Day on Which He Has No Doubts about Why the Country Is Not a Democracy." 30 July 2563 [2020]. https://tlhr2014.com/archives/20010. [ศูนย์ทนายความเพื่อสิทธิมนุษยชน. "คุยกับ 'บก.ลายจุด'ในวันที่ เขาไม่สงสัยเลยว่า ประเทศจะไม่เป็น ประชาธิปไตย." 30 กรกฎาคม 2563. https://tlhr2014.com/archives/20010.]

———. "Conversation with 'Rungsila,' the Poet Who Exchanged Freedom for Nearly 5 Years to Fight a 112 Case on a Day When Society Is Still Afraid." 16 January 2564 [2021]. https://tlhr2014.com/archives/25137. [ศูนย์ทนายความเพื่อสิทธิมนุษยชน. "สนทนากับ "รุ่งศิลา" กวีที่ แลกอิสรภาพเกือบ 5 ปี สู้คดี 112 ในวันที่ สังคมยังหวาดกลัว." 16 มกราคม 2564. https://tlhr2014.com/archives/25137.]

———. "Court Dismisses Case against 'Uncle Samart' for Placing Vote No Flyers, Opine that the Message Does Not Fall Meet the Terms of a Crime Under the Draft Constitution Referendum Act." 24 April 2560 [2017]. https://tlhr2014.com/archives/4077. [ศูนย์ทนายความเพื่อสิทธิมนุษยชน. "ศาลยกฟ้องคดี "ลุงสามารถ" แปะใบปลิวโหวตโน ชี้ ข้อความไม่เข้าองค์ประกอบ ความผิดพ.ร.บ.ประชามติฯ." 24 เมษายน 2560. https://tlhr2014.com/archives/4077.]

———. "The Court of Justice Agrees that My (Dear) Snatched Election Case is in Jurisdiction of the Military Court." 10 June 2559 [2016]. https://tlhr2014.wordpress.com/2016/06/10/newcitizencase/. [ศูนย์ทนายความเพื่อสิทธิมนุษยชน. "ศาลยุติธรรมเห็นพ้องคดีเลือกตั้งที่ (รัก)ลัก อยู่ในอำนาจพิจารณาของศาล ทหาร." 10 มิถุนายน 2559. https://tlhr2014.wordpress.com/2016/06/10/newcitizencase/.]

———. "Court Questions Defendants in Referendum Ballot Tearing Case, Toto Maintains He Tore Ballot Because He Disagreed with the Violation of Rights of Those Who Opposed the Draft Constitution." 15 July 2560 [2017]. https://tlhr2014.com/archives/4676. [ศูนย์ทนายความเพื่อสิทธิมนุษยชน. "ศาลสืบจำเลยคดีฉีกบัตรประชามติ โตโต้ยันฉีกเพราะไม่เห็นด้วยกับการละเมิด สิทธิคนค้านร่าง รธน." 15 กรกฎาคม 2560 [2017]. https://tlhr2014.com/archives/4676.]

———. "The Defense on Which the Court Did Not Rule: Case File of 'Apichat Pongsawat.'" 11 February 2559 [2016]. https://tlhr2014.wordpress.com/2016/02/11/aphichart_acquit/ [ศูนย์ทนายความเพื่อสิทธิมนุษยชน. "ข้อต่อสู้ที่ศาลไม่ได้วินิจฉัย เปิดสำนวนคดีชุมนุม 'อภิชาต พงษ์สวัสดิ์.' 11 กุมภาพันธ์ 2559. https://tlhr2014.wordpress.com/2016/02/11/aphichart_acquit/.]

———. "From 'Toto and Friends' to 'Chayan Chayaporn': Looking Back at Ballot Tearing Cases before the Court Rules Tomorrow." 25 September 2560 [2017], https://tlhr2014.com/archives/5272. [ศูนย์ทนายความเพื่อสิทธิมนุษยชน. "จาก 'โต โต๊ะกับเพื่อน' ถึง 'ไชยันต์ ไชยพร': ย้อนทบทวนกรณีฉีกบัตรก่อนศาลนัด พิพากษาพรุ่งนี้." 25 กันยายน 2560. https://tlhr2014.com/archives/5272.]

———. Letter No. TLHR 3/2559. "Subject: Request for Statistics of Detainees in the Nakhon Chaisri Temporary Prison." 8 March 2559 [2016]. [ศูนย์ทนายความเพื่อ สิทธิมนุษยชน. จดหมายที่ TLHR 3/2559. "เรื่อง ขอสถิติผู้ต้องขังในเรือนจำ ชั่วคราวแขวง นครไชยศรี." 8 มีนาคม 2559.]

———. "Military Prison: Justice Forbidden Entry." 18 March 2559 [2016]. https://tlhr2014.wordpress.com/2016/03/18/military_prison/. [ศูนย์ทนายความเพื่อสิทธิ มนุษยชน. "คุกทหาร: ความยุติธรรมห้ามเข้า." 18 March 2559. https://tlhr2014.wordpress.com/2016/03/18/military_prison/.]

———. "NCPO Announcements Do Not Have Retroactive Punishments, Case of Polka Dot Editor Not Reporting to the NCPO." 21 September 2559 [2015]. https://tlhr2014.wordpress.com/2015/09/21/sombat/ [ศูนย์ทนายความเพื่อสิทธิ มนุษยชน. "ประกาศ คสช. ไม่มีโทษย้อนหลัง คดี บก.ลายจุด ไม่ไปรายงานตัวต่อ คสช." 21 กันยายน 2559. https://tlhr2014.wordpress.com/2015/09/21/sombat/.]

———. "The New Constitution Has Been Promulgated, but There Are More Than 104 'Referendum Defendants' Still Being Prosecuted." 7 April 2560 [2017], https://tlhr2014.com/archives/3924. [ศูนย์ทนายความเพื่อสิทธิมนุษยชน. "รัฐธรรมนูญ ใหม่ประกาศใช้ แต่ 'ผู้ต้องหาประชามติ' กว่า 104 ราย ยังถูก ดำเนินคดี." 7 เมษายน 2560. https://tlhr2014.com/archives/3924.]

———. "Not Free and Fair, a Campaign with Which One Must Pay with One's Freedom: Situation Update on the Violation of Rights before the Referendum." 12 July 2559 [2016], https://tlhr2014.com/archives/1089. [ศูนย์ทนายความเพื่อ สิทธิมนุษยชน. "Not Free and Fair การรณรงค์ที่ต้องจ่ายด้วยเสรีภาพ: ประมวลสถานการณ์ การละเมิดสิทธิ ก่อนออกเสียงประชามติ." 12 กรกฎาคม 2559. https://tlhr2014.com/archives/1089.]

———. "Not Yet at the Beginning: Reviewing 3 Years of Resistant Citizen's Rebellion Lawsuit against the NCPO before the Supreme Court Rules." 12 June 2561 [2018]. https://tlhr2014.com/archives/7744. [ศูนย์ทนายความเพื่อสิทธิ มนุษยชน. "ไปยังไม่ถึงจุดเริ่มต้น: ทบทวน 3 ปี กลุ่มพลเมืองโต้กลับฟ้องคสช. ข้อหากบฏ ก่อน ศาลฎีกาพิพากษา." 12 มิถุนายน 2561. https://tlhr2014.com/archives/7744.]

———. "The People Have Never Been Able to Convict: Looking Back at Rebellion Lawsuits Against Juntas From the Time of Field Marshal Thanom to the NCPO." 19 June 2561 [2018]. https://tlhr2014.com/archives/7831 [ศูนย์ทนายความ เพื่อสิทธิมนุษยชน. "ประชาชนยังไม่เคยเอาผิดได้: ย้อนดูคดีฟ้องคณะรัฐประหารเป็นกบฏ จาก ยุค จอมพลถนอมถึงคสช. 19 มิถุนายน 2561. https://tlhr2014.com/archives/7831.]

———. "Prosecution Witness Hearings in Case of Apichat Violating Prohibition on Assembly, Court Dismisses Petition on Legal Matter—Suggests Defendant

Confess." 15 September 2558 [2015]. https://tlhr2014.wordpress.com/2015/09/15/apichart/. [ศูนย์ทนายความเพื่อสิทธิมนุษยชน. "สืบพยานโจทก์คดีอภิชาตฝ่าฝืนประกาศห้ามชุมนุม ศาลยกคำร้องขอตีความ กม.– แนะจำเลยรับสารภาพ." 15 กันยายน 2558. https://tlhr2014.wordpress.com/2015/09/15/apichart/.]

———. "Referendum Ballot Tearing Case, Appeal Court Decision to Be Read 15 August 2018." 14 August 2561 [2018]. https://tlhr2014.com/archives/8471. [ศูนย์ทนายความเพื่อสิทธิมนุษยชน. "คดีฉีกบัตรประชามติ นัดฟังคำพิพากษาศาลอุทธรณ์ 15 ส.ค. 61." 14 สิงหาคม 2561. https://tlhr2014.com/archives/8471.]

———. "Rereading the Witness Testimony in the Case of the Polka Dot Editor Not Reporting to the NCPO." 21 September 2558 [2015]. https://tlhr2014.wordpress.com/2015/09/21/sombat-2/. [ศูนย์ทนายความเพื่อสิทธิมนุษยชน. "ย้อนอ่านคำเบิกความพยาน คดี บก.ลายจุด ไม่ไปรายงานตัวต่อ คสช." 21 กันยายน 2558. https://tlhr2014.wordpress.com/2015/09/21/sombat-2/.]

———. "Siraphop Testified That He Did Not Report according to the NCPO's Order Because the Junta Are Rebels." 23 May 2559 [2016]. https://tlhr2014.com/archives/2095. [ศูนย์ทนายความเพื่อสิทธิมนุษยชน. "สิรภพให้การ ไม่ไปรายงานตัวตามคำสั่งคสช. เพราะคณะรัฐประหารเป็นกบฏ." 23 พฤษภาคม 2559. https://tlhr2014.com/archives/2095.]

———. "6 Years on the Path of Fighting the Article 116 Case of 'Polka Dot Editor' before Hearing the Decision This 30 July." 29 July 2563 [2020]. https://tlhr2014.com/archives/19944. [ศูนย์ทนายความเพื่อสิทธิมนุษยชน. "6 ปี เส้นทางการต่อสู้คดี ม.116 ของ 'บก.ลายจุด' ก่อนฟังคำพิพากษา 30 ก.ค. นี้." 29 กรกฎาคม 2563. https://tlhr2014.com/archives/19944.]

———. "Tomorrow Morning at 9 am, Dusit District Court Will Hear the Supreme Court Verdict on Nuring's Case of Not Reporting Himself." 8 August 2560 [2017]. https://tlhr2014.com/archives/4842 [ศูนย์ทนายความเพื่อสิทธิมนุษยชน. "พรุ่งนี้ 9 โมงเช้า ศาลแขวงดุสิตนัดฟังคำพิพากษาศาลฎีกาคดีหนุ่ริ่ง ไม่เข้า รายงานตัว." 8 สิงหาคม 2560. https://tlhr2014.com/archives/4842.]

———. "Traces of 4 Years of Struggle in the 'Referendum Ballot Tearing Case' Before the Supreme Court Decision Tomorrow." 20 July 2563 [2020]. https://tlhr2014.com/archives/19656. [ศูนย์ทนายความเพื่อสิทธิมนุษยชน. "อ่านร่องรอย 4 ปี การต่อสู้ คดี "ฉีกบัตรประชามติ" ก่อนฟังคำพิพากษาศาลฎีกา พรุ่งนี้." 20 กรกฎาคม 2563. https://tlhr2014.com/archives/19656.]

Thai Lawyers for Human Rights, Union for Civil Liberty, Human Rights Lawyers Association, Enlaw, and Cross Cultural Foundation. "Opinion of Human Rights Organizations On the Judicial Process in the Case of Suriyan Sujaritpol and Police Major Prakrom Warunprapa." 28 October 2558 [2015]. [ศูนย์ทนายความเพื่อสิทธิมนุษยชน, สมาคมสิทธิเสรีภาพของประชาชน, สมาคมนักกฎหมายสิทธิมนุษยชน, และมูลนิธิผสานวัฒนธรรม. "ความเห็นองค์กรด้านสิทธิมนุษยชนต่อกระบวนการยุติธรรม กรณีนายสุริยัน สุจริตพลวงศ์และพ.ต.ต. ปรากรม วารุณประภา." 28 ตุลาคม 2559.]

Thanapol Eawsakul. "Approximately 20 Hours with Apichat Pongsawat: From the BACC to the Military Camp to the CSD." *Prachatai*. 23 May 2558 [2015].

https://prachatai.com/journal/2015/05/59441. [ธนาพล อิ๋วสกุล. "ประมาณ 20 ชั่วโมง ที่อยู่กับอภิชาต พงษ์สวัสดิ์: จากหอศิลป์ กทม. ค่ายทหาร ถึงกองปราบ." *ประชาไท.* 23 พฤษภาคม 2558. https://prachatai.com/journal/2015/05/59441.]

———, ed. *The 19 September Coup: coup for democracy with the king as head of state.* Bangkok: Fa Diew Kan Press, 2550 [2007]. [ธนาพล อิ๋วสกุล, บรรณาธิการ. *รัฐประหาร 19 กันยา: รัฐประหารเพื่อระบอบประชาธิปไตยอันมี พระมหากษัตริย์ทรงเป็นประมุข.* กทมฯ: ฟ้า เดียวกน, 2550.]

Thannapat Jarernpanit. "The Rule of Authoritarianism and the Justice Problem Through the Life of Anan Phakprapai." *Political Science and Public Administration Journal* 11 (July–December 2020 [2563]). [ธัญณ์ณภัทร์ เจริญพานิช. "อำนาจ รัฐออสิทธิ์ กับปัญหาความยุติธรรมผ่านชีวิต ของนายอนันต์ ภักดิ์ ประไพ." *วารสาร รัฐศาสตร์และ รัฐประศาสนศาสตร์ ปีที่* 11 ฉบับเพิ่มเติม (กรกฎาคม–ธันวาคม 2563).]

Thongchai Winichakul. "The Legal Privileged State and Royalist Rule of Law: History of the Genealogy of Thai-Style Rule by Law," 17th Puey Ungpakorn Special Lecture, 9 March 2020. Bangkok: Way Magazine, 2563 [2020]. [ธงชัย วินิจจะกูล. "นิติรัฐอภิสิทธิ์ และราชนิติธรรม: ประวัติศาสตร์ภูมิปัญญาของ Rule by Law แบบไทย," ปาฐกถา พิเศษป๋วย อึ๊งภากรณ์ ครั้งที่ 17, 9 มีนาคม 2563. กรุงเทพฯ: Way Magazine, 2563.]

Wiraphong Suntrachatrawat. "The Poetics of 'Rungsila' Who Will Not Bow His Head into the Darkness." In *The People Rebel: Nine Cases of Opposition to the Coup during the NCPO Period*, edited by Noppon Archamas, 115–42. Bangkok: Thai Lawyers for Human Rights, 2562 [2019]. [วีรพงษ์ สุนทรฉัตราวัฒน์. "ฉันทลักษณ์ของ 'รุง ศิลา' มิอาจน้อมศีรษะให้ดำคล้องจอง." ใน *ราษฎรกำแหง: บันทึก 9 คดี ต้านรัฐประหารในยุค คสช.* นพพล อาชามาส, บรรณาธิการ. กรุงเทพฯ: ศูนย์ทนายความเพื่อสิทธิมนุษยชน, 2562. 115–142.]

Wirat Toariyamitr, ed. *Imprinted on the Heart: Perspectives, Ideas and the Political Life of "Uthai Pimchaichon."* Bangkok: B-Yes Press, 2002 [2545]. [วิรัตน์ โตอารีย์ มิตร, เรียบเรียง. พิมพ์ไว้ในใจชน: *มุมมอง ความคิด และชีวิตการเมืองของ 'อุทัย พิมพ์ใจชน.'* กรุงเทพฯ: สำนักพิมพ์บีเยศ, 2545.]

Wirawat Somnuk. "The Referendum, Cases, and Those Who Rose Up to Press for 'Justice.'" In *Dissident Citizen: Nine Cases of Opposition to the Coup during the NCPO Period*, edited by Noppon Archamas, 261–88. Bangkok: Thai Lawyers for Human Rights, 2562 [2019]. [วีรวรรธน์ สมนึก. "เหตุประชามติ คดีความ กับเหล่า ผู้ลุกขึ้นทวงถามถึง 'ความยุติธรรม.'" ใน *ราษฎรกำแหง: บันทึก 9 คดี ต้านรัฐประหารในยุค คสช.* นพพล อาชามาส, บรรณาธิการ. กรุงเทพฯ: ศูนย์ทนายความเพื่อสิทธิมนุษยชน, 2562).]

Withit Chandawong. *The Role of Life, Thinking and Politics of Teacher Khrong Chandawong: From His Mother's Womb to the Scaffold on the Execution Field.* Sakhon Nakhon: Faculty of Humanities and Social Sciences, Ratchaphat University, 2552 [2009]. [วิทิต จันดาวงศ์. *บทบาทชีวิต แนวคิด การเมือง ครูครอง จันดาวงศ์: จาก ครรภ์มารดรสู่หลักประหารปลายทาง จิตกาธาน.* สกลนคร: คณะมนุษยศาสตร์และสังคมศาสตร์ ม.ราชภัฏสกลนคร, 2552.]

INDEX

All dates are indexed as if spelled out. For example: 24 March is indexed as if spelled out "twenty-four March." Page numbers in italic indicate figures.

The authorized representative in the EU for product safety and compliance is:
Mare Nostrum Group
B.V Doelen 72
4831 GR Breda
The Netherlands

www.ingramcontent.com/pod-product-compliance
Lightning Source LLC
Chambersburg PA
CBHW030343270326
41926CB00009B/937